# TRADITION AND AVANT–GARDE

## LITERATURE AND ART IN SERBIAN CULTURE
## 1900–1918

### JELENA MILOJKOVIC–DJURIC

EAST EUROPEAN MONOGRAPHS, BOULDER
DISTRIBUTED BY COLUMBIA UNIVERSITY PRESS, NEW YORK

1988

EAST EUROPEAN MONOGRAPHS, NO. CCXXXIV

# Contents

## Preface

The present volume evolved as a continuation of my doctoral dissertation at the University of Belgrade. My intention at that time was to explore the literary and artistic postulates, as well as ideologies that permeated Serbian culture between the World Wars. As I proceeded with my research I realized that the dialectical interdependence of continuity and innovation, tradition, and avant-garde was inherent in the creative thought of this period of Serbian cultural history.

This underlying polarity of order and experimentation, nationalism and internationalism, art as form of ideology and art as emanation of l'art pour l'art doctrine, was subsequently discussed in my book *Tradition and Avant-Garde: The Arts in Serbian Culture between World Wars,* published in 1984 in the East European Monograph Series. The book presented the revised form of my dissertation that I translated into English.

*Tradition and Avant-Garde: Literature and Arts in Serbian Culture 1900-1918,* explores further the cultural history of Serbia in a similar interdisciplinary fashion. As I research the fascinating works of writers, listened once again to the music composed at that time, and explored art galleries, I became increasingly aware of both intrinsic and extrinsic similarities that permeated these two periods. The exceptional economic and cultural growth in Serbia during the early years of the twentieth century introduced new outlooks and a wish for joining the mainstream of literary and artistic experimentation. However, the political upheavals leading to the annexation of Bosnia and Hercegovina and later to World War I changed the political and cultural scene. The premonition of an approaching apocalypse prior to World War I was comparable to the feeling of a possible annihilation at the eve of World War II. Both events prompted the writers and artists to abandon avant-garde experimentations. The ensuing respective national revivals influenced different stylistic and thematic choices ushering in the introduction of expressed patriotism and positive self reliance. There was a predilection for a revised form of realistic stylistic orientation that was already firmly entrenched in Serbian literary and artistic tradition. This repository eventually facilitated the introduction of socialist realism and its domination in the literatures and artistic and musical creations in Yugoslavia after

World War II.

I am indebted to Professor Sanojilo Rajičić, member of the Serbian Academy of Arts and Sciences and Secretary of its Department of Fine Arts and Music, who was always supportive of my research. His many recollections about the musical life in Belgrade and, in particular, about composer Milenko Paunović were very helpful. I owe gratitude to Professor Dejan Medaković, Vice–President of the Serbian Academy, also a member of my doctoral committee, who suggested that the period 1900–1918 should be the logical continuation of my research in cultural history. Dr. Dimitrije Stefanović always made me welcome at the Musicological Institute of the Serbian Academy and its Library. My colleagues, Dr. Nadežda Mosusova and Professor Vlastimir Peričić were very helpful in many ways concerning my research. Dr. Mira Petrić–Petković, Department of Language and Literature of the Serbian Academy, provided me with an extensive bibliography of Bogdan Popović's writings and helped with the acquisition of the photographs that added to the book. Professor Vlastimir Trajković loaned me valuable photographs from the archives of his grandfather, the composer Miloje Milojević. Dr. Dušan A. Radivojević gave me photographs from the archives of the First Singers' Society in Belgrade.

I also would like to express my gratitude to the librarians of the University Library Svetozar Marković in Belgrade, in particular to Milana Ilić–Djurdjulov for all her help and kindness. I spent many hours working in the pleasant atmosphere of the University Library that opened in 1926 with a generous grant from the Andrew Carnegie Endowment. I worked also in the reading room of the Serbian Academy of Arts and Sciences, and I would like to acknowledge the assistance of Ljubinka Vasić, Gordana Bojović, and their staff. Professor Clara Huggett, of the English Department at Texas A&M University, offered once again her valuable comments in stylistic matters.

This book is dedicated to my husband Dušan and daughter Mara who were, as always, my first readers.

## Chapter 1

## The National Revival in Serbian Cultural History
## 1900–1914

While some European nations accomplished their historical and national goals for self determination and unification during the 1860s and 1870s, in Serbia similar efforts spearheaded by the United Serbian Youth were brought to an abrupt halt. It was only after some three decades of delay that demands for national liberation and constitution were regenerated. Pursuing once again their national historical objectives, with a new program, the unfulfilled aspirations of the United Serbian Youth were carried on anew.[1]

This new regrouping was encouraged by the important political and social changes that took place after 1903 with the return of the constitutional parliamentary government. Prior to the dynastic succession, the unpopular and tyrannical regime of Aleksandar Obrenović brought the country to the verge of ruin. The people felt oppressed and their personal rights were threatened. The general displeasure was manifested during the demonstrations in March 1903. The demonstrators marched to the center of Belgrade voicing their dissatisfaction with King Aleksandar's domestic and foreign policies by shouting "Down with despotism!" The procession of some 5,000 students and workers was forcefully dispersed and their leaders, Dimitrije Tucović and Triša Kaclerović, both students, were obliged to go underground. These events hastened the opposition and the organized military leaders decided upon regicide. After the coup, parliament elected Petar Karadjordjević to the throne.[2]

King Petar and his government adhered more scrupulously to the Constitution. Soon a general uplifting was felt in all areas of social and political life. Jovan Skerlić, in his *History of New Serbian Literature*, pointed out that these changes influenced an awakening of the national spirit. In addition, Skerlić singled out the hoped for political rapproachement of Serbs and Croats in 1904 as a beginning to the solution of the most important national problem.[3]

Skerlić was actively engaged in the organization of the Southern

Slav Youth Congress and of the First Yugoslav Arts Exhibit in 1904 that marked the centennial of the First Serbian Uprising. Skerlić credited the fruition of these important events to the dedicated work of the Pobratimstvo student organization. It seemed to him that the youth were again in the forefront and that important issues were discussed with candor and determination. Real results were achieved as they had once before during the 1860s and 1870s.

The First Congress of Southern Slav Youth took place from 2–8 September 1904 in Belgrade, coinciding with the opening of the First Yugoslav Artistic Exhibit. More than 100 representatives from Bulgaria, Serbia, Croatia, and Slovenia were present at the Congress. According to Skerlić, the Southern Slav Youth Congress was one of the most important events of the recent past that took place in Serbia. Young forces had unselfishly moved forward like an avant–garde. The young organizers and participants had displayed a serious attitude towards social obligations and life in general. Skerlić pointed out that seldom had similar successful achievements occurred.[4]

The Youth Congress issued a resolution that stressed the need for rendering help to the Slavic population in occupied lands. The centuries–long Turkish occupation had reduced Serbia to a backward country. The importance of education was underlined as essential to the ultimate goal of liberation.[5]

The leaders of the Pobratimstvo youth organization appreciated Skerlić's participation and support. They felt a strong affinity with his political opinions and his moral and ethical views. Skerlić was by age close to the student leaders who accepted him as one of them. His presence was vividly felt and he was acknowledged as a splendid figure of national import.[6]

For the exceptional role that Skerlić played in the field of literature and in cultural and political development, Predrag Protić suggested that the period starting from 1900 until May 1914 should be named after Skerlić.[7]

In the field of music, I propose a similar recognition to the composer Stevan Stojanović Mokranjac, a leading musical figure of this period. Mokranjac's choral compositions, rooted in folk idiom, helped to establish a national style in Serbian music. He succeeded in preserving and fostering the spiritual and musical essence of folk music tradition. His compositions enjoyed great popularity and were often performed at various patriotic events during the years leading to national liberation. Most of all, Mokranjac was recognized by his contemporaries as a dedicated proponent of the Southern Slav movement.

In pictorial art, the monumental historical paintings of Paja Jovanović were understood, by his coevals, as an apotheosis of the Serbian past in awakening a national consciousness. Jovanović was acclaimed as the dean of Serbian pictorial art and held in high esteem by art critics from major European art centers.[8] In a still backward country where national goals for emancipation had not been resolved, visions of a former glory and prosperity strengthened a trust of a better tomorrow.

The exceptional contributions of Skerlić, Mokranjac, and Jovanović were not until now considered as mutually interdependent in the cultural climate of their time. As avid supporters of a revival of national unity, Skerlić, Mokranjac, and Jovanović were at the same time creators of this ideological consciousness. This period of intensified national struggle for liberation had exceptional support in literature, music, and the fine arts.

The Yugoslav idea and a desire for collaboration were the guiding forces that helped organize the First Yugoslav Artistic Exhibit in Belgrade in 1904. Professor of archeology, Miloje Vasić, addressed the students in the spring of 1904, proposing the arrangement of such an exhibit to commemorate the centennial celebration of the First Serbian Uprising.

Thanks to the generous help of many, and in particular of Jovan Skerlić, the exhibit was opened on 5 September 1904. Vasić stressed that the exhibit marked the first important success in the cultural unification of 4the Southern Slavs. The exhibit presented 96 artists from Slovenia, Croatia, Serbia, and Bulgaria, with an imposing total of 458 art works.

In the Serbian section, the paintings of Paja Jovanović were praised by several prominent art critics. Even the young generation of artists expressed admiration for Jovanović's artistic works. Thus, the young painter and art critic, Nadežda Petrović, declared that the canvases of Jovanović represented the crown of Serbian pictorial art. She singled out Jovanović's historical composition depicting Tsar Dušan.[9] Jovanović portrayed the most important event in Dušan's reign, *The Proclamation of Dušan's Law Codex,* in front of the church, accentuating the splendor of the military and political power of the emerging empire. The composition was depicted in an interplay of light and shadow, pointing to a careful plein–air exploration.

The exhibit presented a rich and varied panorama of artistic achievements. Most importantly it helped to establish personal ties and open prospects for possible collaboration. Already during the exhibit the young generation of artists joined in forming the First Yugoslav Colony. Nadežda Petrović was in the core of this group, together with her colleagues from student days in Munich, the Slovene

artists Rihard Jakopič and Ivan Grohar. The Croatian artists Ivan
Meštrović, Emanuel Vidović and Paško Vučetić, from Montenegro,
were also congenial members of this group. These artists wanted
to work together since they felt a strong kinship among themselves,
sharing a similar artistic credo and Yugoslav ideology. They hoped
to arrange exhibits together and present themselves united as Yugoslavs, without separation into national divisions. They wished to
create a new Yugoslav art that would be understood as a unique and
contemporary artistic style, its relevance intact even in comparison
with European art.

Nadežda Petrović, actively involved in the organization of the
First    Yugoslav    Exhibit, was always ready to support the many
projects in conjunction with it. She was soon nicknamed Nadinka
Dimitrievna by the writer Radoje Domanović, comparing her spirited participation in many cultural and political events with similar
attitudes of Russian revolutionary youths. While the exhibit lasted,
the young artists often met at the hospitable home, which was surrounded by a large garden, of Dimitrije Peas an esteemed historian
and outstanding member of the Petrović was was an esteemed historian and outstanding member of the Radical Party. Petrović diligently
collected historical documents and eventually published his research
that shed light on the financial and

In addition to the First Yugoslav Colony, the Lada Federation
of Arts Association was organized, followed later by the formation
of the Medulić association. The spirit of collaboration was apparent in several important visual manifestations that took place in the
first decade of the twentieth century. The artists exchanged visits in
order to become better acquainted with each other's work. They organized exhibits of their collective works and even arranged painting
sessions together in the country, in the open air. These coordinated
activities and the friendly collaboration among the artists remained
a hallmark of the first fighting years of the so–called Modern Yugoslav (Jugoslovenska Moderna). The artists were fighting against
academism in the artistic conceptions and favored French impression-
ism. They strove to create a Yugoslav artistic community by utilizing
the established cultural and political channels of collaboration.[11]

The gradual expansion of Serbian political goals to incorporate
the Southern Slav program transformed the Serbian Question into a
Central European Question. Austria–Hungary was opposed to the
emancipation of the Southern Slavs since this emancipation threatened the foundation of the dual monarchy. The overseeing of Serbian
plans became a matter of importance to Vienna. The beginning of
the twentieth century witnessed a series of inflammatory crises in-

volving Austria–Hungary and Serbia, concentrating on the Southern Slav movement.[12]

The growing political activities of the Southern Slav movement in Croatia and Serbia, the Serbo–Bulgarian entente, and unresolved export concessions were all factors leading to the Austro–Serbian customs war in 1906. The fact that Serbia won the customs war and even expanded her trade with new markets gave additional strength to the Southern Slav movement. However, these events hastened the annexation of Bosnia–Herzegovina in 1908.[13]

The announcement of the annexation of Bosnia–Herzegovina on 7 October 1908 caused great concern in Belgrade. Several large meetings and demonstrations held in the streets of Belgrade were directed against Austria–Hungary. The Serbian people were demanding decisive actions calling for a European Conference, the revision of the Berlin Treaty, and the political and economic independence of Serbia and Montenegro.[14]

One of the largest meetings protesting the annexation was organized on 12 October by Nadežda Petrović. Petrović took it upon herself, as her patriotic duty, to strengthen Slavic solidarity and ties between women living in Serbia and Montenegro and with women under Austro–Hungarian or Turkish occupation. She also strove to influence public opinion abroad by publicizing information about the unjust annexation. To this end Petrović first organized Odbor Srpkinja (The Council of Serbian Women) from the ranks of the members of the women's organization, Kolo srpskih sestara (The Circle of Serbian Sisters). The Council, together with Petrović, announced the public meeting in Kolarac hall protesting the annexation. At the appointed time, a large group of people gathered there, surpassing the capacity of the hall. The meeting was moved to the adjacent square in front of the National Theater. Petrović delivered her speech from the front balcony of the theater. According to an eyewitness, Petrović's appearance appealed to the public: ". . . an unusual woman, young and stately, blonde, who made an impression with her appearance as well as with her speech."

Petrović started her deliberation by recalling that the Berlin Congress of 1878, in truth, only exchanged the overlords and continued the slavery of Bosnia and Herzegovina. Instead of gaining self determination, the people were exploited by Austria–Hungary, the new foreign rulers, for another 30 years. The time had come to offer to the unfortunate population the needed support. This speech was often interrupted by exclamations, such as: "Let's declare war on Austria–Hungary! Boycott of Austro–Hungarian and German goods! Long live Serbian women!" Petrović ended her speech with a *Memo-*

*randum on Serbian Women.*

Afterwards a procession formed and marched through the main avenue of the city stopping in front of several foreign embassies, at the entrance to the court–palace of Petar I, and appeared before the Ministry of Foreign Affairs.[15]

Petrović's efforts did not end with this magnificent manifestation of solidarity with the population of Bosnia and Herzegovina. She wanted to inform women abroad about the efforts of Serbian Women. She wrote to the Federation of Women's Clubs of America asking for their support. Helen Taft, wife of the American President, William Howard Taft, was herself the honorary president of this organization. She answered Petrović's letter stating, "I express a deeply felt interest and sympathy for the needs of Serbian women in their just battle for national ideals. The love and sympathy of American women are on your side." Petrović also addressed her plea for support to the Association of Russian Women. President Shabanova answered by expressing her "solidarity with the stand taken by the patriotic Serbian women."[16]

The general political situation after the annexation of Bosnia and Herzegovina enhanced national aspirations in the country. This spirit was soon expressed in new literary publications. The young poets soon included in their poems an individual poetic introspection of a rediscovered national awareness. In the period leading to the eve of World War I, the young generation accepted the necessity of defending the continuance of living on native land.[17]

The literary critic, Borivoje Jevtić, noticed that this new spirit prevailed among the Serbian youth. He wrote in the journal, *Bosanska Vila*, about this changed attitude:

> It is known that the Serbian youth of today lead a different life as compared to a few years ago. The youth of today have clearer concepts and wishes and more realistic ideals. The youth that once liked the poems of destruction, castrophe, and nihilism, today love life not only for the sake of living, but equally because of the ideas and works that fill it . . . .
> The youth are preparing, building, and educating themselves for the future. And if there are among them deviations, standstills, and discords, all that cannot stop them on their path or destroy them, although it can cause a weakening.[18]

Jovan Skerlić stated that there was a revival of a strong belief in national unity and a renewed national energy. However, Skerlić was aware that next to patriotic poetry there existed among some writers an appreciation for other art doctrines such as *l'art pour l'art*, and also the cultivation of "poetry of convulsion," directed at the exploration of a so–called emotional abysses.

Skerlić favored patriotic poetry and declared that the newly written poems, due to their ideas, feelings, and literary expressions, excelled the patriotic poetry of the romantic era.[19] Among those poets who wrote with a new patriotic spirit, Skerlić singled out the young poet Veljko Petrović. His poems expressed a fresh and revolutionary feeling of devotion to his native country. Such was Petrović's poem Verujte prvo (Believe First):[20]

Prvo je: svaki neka zna šta hoće!
O maglu koplja nikad se ne lome.
Slobode? Dobro! Al' to nije voće
Što zrelo pada u šešir ma kome.
Verujte prvo! i stisnite pesti,
Pa onda tresti, tresti!
Gospodin, seljak, bogat i siroma',
U uspeh borbe verujte – i dosta,
I vaša snaga biće snaga groma,
I zamršena pitanja sva prosta,
Verujte prvo, i stisnite pesti,
Pa onda tresti, tresti!
—Mi svi sad znamo: hoćemo slobode,
I da smo svoji u rodjenoj kući–
I pre no što nam mač srca probode
O volju našu on će krto pući!
Mi verujemo! i stisnutih pesti,
Sa ruku naših lance ćemo stresti!

Believe First
First: let everybody know what he wants!
Spears are never broken against the fog.
Freedom? All right! But that is not the fruit
That falls ripe into anybody's hat.
Believe first! and clench the fists,
Then only shake, shake!
Lord, peasant, rich and poor
Believe in the success of the fight—and enough.
Your strength shall be the strength of thunder
And all confused questions simple.
Believe first, and clench the fists
Then only shake, shake!...
—We all know now: we want freedom,
And to be alone in our own house;–

Before the sword pierces our heart
Our will shall crack the sword!
We believe! and with clenched fists,
We shall shake the chains from our hands!

The poet Milan Ćurčin wrote in an unconventional and novel poetic mode. He was highly original and was among the first to introduce free verse into Serbian poetry. His irony and often bizarre outlook presented a marked contrast to the lyrical poems or patriotic verses as cultivated by other poets of the time. He was chastised for such an attitude since poetry, as well as musical and artistic works, often carried a patriotic connotation. Apparently the public and critic alike expected that the new works would follow a similar pattern. Such a view was presented in a review of Ćurčin's poetry by Milan Popović in the periodical *Delo*. Popović commented that Ćurčin's poetry was limited in its scope and most importantly did not encompass patriotic or universal and ethical themes:

> In his poetry you will not find patriotic themes, since he does not write about mankind, or about his Serbian feelings, his spiritual beliefs, his Serbian or humanistic ideals, or about the tender and lovely Serbian girl . . . he does not sing about justice and freedom, about the equality of men or about life.[21]

However, Ćurčin changed his poetic credo and started writing about his devotion to his ancestral lands and its people. Yet he did not idealize his fellow Serbians and even voiced his criticism of certain undesirable attitudes. He was aware that his compatriots were inhabitants of a small land. Therefore, their spiritual horizons were equally reflective of geographical, political, and cultural limitations. According to Ćurčin, the Serbs did not understand well enough the importance of closer ties with brotherly neighboring South Slavs. Surely, this statement pointed to Ćurčin's own appreciation of national goals of unification.

In addition, Ćurčin thought that his people were far from perfect, their human nature blemished with inherited sins. Although aware of all these shortcomings, he affirmed his ties to his homeland. These feelings were obviously strengthened by the premonition of another major war. In his poetic vision he anticipated the advances of an imaginary enemy and feared that his people were not numerous enough to fight a stronger intruder. The possible defeat and suffering of his people strengthened his decision to stand up and protect his homeland if necessary, sharing this determination with many others:[22]

Rodoljubiva pesma (Patriotic Poem)

O Rode! Pun si krupnih i sitnih ružnih strasti,
Primljenih od otaca, i rodjenih u tebi;
Od njih ta tudja pomoć ne može nikad spasti,
S njima ta k sebi svojski primio niko ne bi.
O Rode! Ti si malen, i sve je u tebi malo,–
Rasturen,–ni sam ne znaš dokle ti dopiru medje;
Ti brata svoga ne poznaš, i malo ti je stalo
Što su medj' vam staze sve bledje i bledje ...
Ja vidim rulju s brega, gda juri da te skrha,
I gledam tebe kako niz brdo i sam hrliš,
I nigde svetle tačke u viziji,—od vrha
Do dna grančice, nigde da rukom je obgrliš.
Pa ipak, Rode, mi smo tu—i na sve spemni—
Volja nam naša raste s brojem nevolja tvojih!
I takvi, mi smo jači neg nebo i šar zemni!
Veruj u snagu, Rode, dobrih sinova svojih!

Patriotic Poem
O nation mine! Charged with major and minor ugly
   passions.
Inherited from fathers and born with you anew;
Foreign help cannot save you from it all,
With all this no one can truly accept you.
O nation mine! You are small, and all in you is small,—
Scattered–you even do not know how far your boundaries
   extend;
You do not recognize your own brother, and you do not care
That the paths between you are few and vanishing...
I see a mob from the hill rushing to break you,
I see you precipitating hastily down the hill,
And nowhere a bright light in this vision,–from the top
To the bottom only twigs, nothing to embrace.
And yet, Nation, we are here–and ready for anything–
Our will is strengthened with your increased suffering!
Like this, we are stronger than the sky and the earth!
Believe in strength, Nation, in your good sons!

In 1910, a play written by Ivo Vojnović appeared called *Smrt majke Jugović (The Death of Jugović's Mother)*; a new version of the same play was published in 1911. Vojnović was attracted to the historical themes of Serbian history. This fact was even more noteworthy since Vojnović started his writing career in the ranks of Croatian writers.[23]

The next drama, written by Vojnović, *Lazarevo vaskrenje (The Resurrection of Lazar)*, had powerful national connotations as well. The drama premiered in the aftermath of the Balkan wars in Belgrade on 15 May 1913, and it was received with deeply felt appreciation. Miodrag Ibrovac wrote a review which appeared in *Srpski Književni Glasnik* stating that the past events would surely leave a deep imprint on Serbian literature since Serbian writers were always reflective of people and their aspirations. The numerous sacrifices and losses of human lives should inspire equally distinguished bards of Homeric stature to preserve the memories of these glorious achievements for generations to come.

Ibrovac quoted Vojnović's words explaining that his drama, *The Resurrection of Lazar,* had for its basis a real event and a real hero in the person of Lazar Kujundžic. However, Vojnović transposed the personality of Lazar to represent the whole Serbian people. Lazar's mother, Stana, represented all Serbian mothers and in addition personified the soul of the people. Vojnović commented that he chose the name Stana to allude to the stamina and permanence as her main characteristics that enabled her to revenge eventually the defeat on the field of Kosovo.[24] Vojnović himself wrote in the Prologue of the play that he dedicated this work "To the Serbian Mothers on the Altar of Their Martyrdom."

Jovan Skerlić wrote for the reputable journal *Srpski Književni Glasnik* from its inception in 1901. His reviews of newly published literary works established him as one of the leading critics. In time, Skerlić became the editor of *Srpski Književni Glasnik,* a position that further promoted his influence in cultural life. Skerlić's contributions to the Serbian social and political realm, as a representative in parliament, as well as an organizer and orator, sometimes overshadowed his literary role. Branko Lazarević, one of Skerlić's best students, described his former teacher primarily as a supporter of Yugoslav ideology and socialistic democracy.[25]

A parallel could be drawn between Skerlić's and Mokranjac's public role during this period. Mokranjac was also understood foremost as a supporter of Yugoslav unification. He even skillfully introduced his political beliefs in the programmatic concept of his choral composition. As an excellent connoisseur of folk music, Mokranjac used folk songs from ethnically different regions of present day Yugoslavia. In his 15 Rukoveti and Primorski napevi (Songs from the Littoral), Mokranjac introduced 90 songs from Serbia, Kosovo, Montenegro, Macedonia, Bosnia, and from the Croatian coast. Thus, he accomplished in his musical works a spiritual unification long before the political was achieved.[26]

Very often the choral concerts highlighted some of the patriotic and national celebrations with performances of Mokranjac's Rukoveti. Mokranjac also took the Belgrade Singers Society on tours abroad presenting the lesser known muokranjac, wrote about many guest tours conducted by the former student of Makranjac, wrote about many guest tours conducted by the Belgrade Singers Society. The Society was well received in many cities in Serbia as well as in the occupied South Slav regions under Austria–Hungary. These numerous recitals often accomplished national objectives and the Society was greeted with high honors.

On the occasion of a guest appearance in Sarajevo in 1910, the newspaper *Srpska Riječ* published an important editorial on its front page discussing the importance of this artistic mission. The Belgrade Singers Society toured Sarajevo, Mostar, Cetinje, and the Dalmatian coast in order to take part in the celebration following the accession to the throne of Nikola, King of Montenegro. In this editorial, the role of Stevan Mokranjac was compared to the role of Vuk Karadžić, who introduced Serbian folk language into Serbian literature. The editor declared that Mokranjac's musical genius succeeded in codifying the musical essence of Serbian folk songs in his famous choral compositions, Rukoveti. The prevailing characteristics of these songs reflected the melancholy and suffering of its people, but also expressed protest, rising above the miseries, like an eagle ready to soar:

Welcome Serbian Song!
The oldest Serbian Singers Society arrived today from the Serbian metropolis, headed by Mr. Stevan Mokranjac . .
. . We love Mokranjac's song because it is highly artistic, yet it is ours. The song strengthens us . . . and points to large and distant perspectives of a major battle, the revival and deliverance of the Serbian people. His art encompasses and unites all that is Serbian . . . and serves like an ideal and example showing that the Serbian people are one undivided entity . . . . We therefore are greeting him as Vuk of Serbian melody and Serbian singing artists . . . . To these apostles of an all Serbian culture, nonpolitical, we offer a wreath of love and respect.[27]

The reviewer added, very likely, the last sentence for the sake of censors, stating that the singers were "apostles of . . . culture . . . nonpolitical," although in the previous sentences he talked in political terms anticipating "a major battle, the revival and deliverance of all Serbian people."

During the same tour of 1910, Mokranjac and the members of the

Society were warmly greeted in Split. Although the singers arrived after midnight, mayor Jure Kapić, many dignitaries, and citizens were still waiting for their arrival. The welcoming speech was published in the *Pučki list* newspaper:

> Welcome dear brothers from the Serbian Beograd to the Croatian Split. I greet you in front of the municipality, and the town of Split that always thought that the Croats and Serbs are one people since the language that is heard in your beautiful Beograd, at the confluence of the Sava and the Danube, is also spoken in our coastal region . . . . Welcome dear brothers to this city that is equally yours and ours, where no difference exists between Croats and Serbs and where the flag of brotherhood is flying high.[28]

Milan Rakić wrote several patriotic poems while serving at the Serbian consulate at Kosovo. Skerlić pointed out the high artistic quality of these poems and concluded that patriotic poetry could achieve the same level of perfection as any other poetic genre.[29] Rakić's poem,   Na Gazi Mestanu (At Gazi Mestan),   with its prophetic vision, eventually became a program of the generation formerly identified with "western attitudes." It was published repeatedly and duly memorized by many.[30]

Interestingly enough, Skerlić's description of Rakić's patriotic attitude corresponded very much to the sentiments expressed by George Santayana. Santayana noted that the patriotism of the young Englishmen, on the eve of World War I, was courageous yet unpretentious. Many young men enlisted with quiet determination. The English poet, Rupert Brooke, was among the writers who expressed with eloquence a new devotion to his native country.[31]

In France, the national revival and the necessity of armament was supported by such prominent writers as Charles Peguy, Maurice Barres, and Paul Claudel. However, Romaine Rolland did not share the national enthusiasm and bellicose spirit expressed by many. He did not think that self–proclaimed national causes were universally justified. In Serbia, Isidora Sekulić, very much like Rolland, was deeply opposed to the war. Already in 1913, when many wounded and dead were brought from the battlefields of the Balkan Wars, she voiced her concern in her narration, *Pitanje (The Question)*.

Vladislav Petković Dis, a poet, shared a similar outlook. Disturbed by the numerous lives lost in the Balkan wars, he pondered possible justifications for these events. With the exceptional skill of a fine poet, he conjured in his poem, Cvetovi slave (The Blossoms of Glory), the haunting images of scattered war graves extending all over the Balkans. He described these shallow communal graves as hiding the young soldiers nestled together like innocent fledgling birds. His verses projected in an even rhythmical flow the sorrowful yet quiet acceptance of the losses, and an inability to forget the depth of human tragedies. The chosen images of young, beautiful bodies quietly decomposing, with "open wounds and dead eyes," spoke vehemently against annihilation. He chose for this poem the title "Cvetovi slave," in the style of the often used patriotic phraseology, thus providing a contrasting, even sarcastic tone to the poem itself. These verses show that Dis very likely thought that the victims were glorified only superficially and that nothing can truly replace the casualties of war and resulting misfortunes. Unselfish and heroic deeds were usually honored in the flowery words that became the accepted language of mourning, without real compassion. The nobility of these sacrifices, in a war for liberation, were inadequately and pretentiously described in vague and meaningless phrases. The poet thought that the victims were soon forgotten like "dead lilies and old noblemen." Petković's poem truly presents a powerful war requiem for all soldiers who have died thoughout the history of mankind:[32]

Cvetovi slave

Oni spavaju svi do jednog, redom,
u plitkom grobu, neskrštenih ruku
bez svoga pokrova i pod teškom bedom,
i trunu mirno, kao u sanduku.
Oni spavaju nesebični, blagi,
s ranama živim i mrtvim očima,
velike duše kao kamen dragi,
večita pesma koju im otima.
Oni spavaju ti naši sinovi,
u svojoj krvi, bezbrižni ko tići,
zaboravljeni ko mrtvi krinovi,
i ponositi ko stari plemići.
Oni spavaju po Balkanu celom
za dobro tudje, za spas svoga plemena:
nikad ne behu sa zastavom belom
ti mladi momci velikog vremena . . .

The Blossoms of Glory

They sleep all of them in a row,
in a shallow grave, hands uncrossed,
without a shroud and in great misfortune,
decomposing quietly like in a coffin.
They sleep unselfishly, mild,

with open wounds and dead eyes,
with a noble soul like a precious rock
eternal song escapes them.
They sleep, our sons,
in their own blood, worry free like young birds,
forgotten like dead lilies
and proud like old noblemen.
They sleep all over the Balkans
for the good of other, for the salvation of their people;
never gathered under a white flag
these young boys from a glorious time . . .

The war and the exodus from Serbia of the army and civilians brought a seeming standstill to creative thought. Yet, in exile or even in battlefields, reading and occasional writing did not stop completely. It was recorded that the *Anthology of Newer Serbian Lyrics* by Bogdan Popović was the most widely read book during the war.[33]

It is noteworthy that poetic language gradually became the preferred mode of expression: poets, in soldiers' uniforms, and their readers, soldiers themselves, found solace and strength in poetic incantations. Poetic verses, generally regarded as an esoteric art form, seemed powerful enough to transfigure the cruel everyday suffering of war and fear of death into bearable experiences. Miloš Crnjanski knew the depth of despair. He felt lost, "pale and alone," without God and friends. In his poem Prolog (The Prologue), he reassured his fellow soldiers that acceptance of grief would set them free:[34]

Ja pevam tužnima:
da tuga od svega oslobodjava.

I sing to the sad:
that grief liberates from all.

As the war years continued to drain the life sap of the Serbian nation and take a tremendous toll in human sacrifices, recurring testimonies of perseverance were witnessed. The ensuing literary, musical, and pictorial works stimulated a will to overcome suffering, disbelief, and annihilation. Most of all, these new literary and artistic creations strove to incorporate a novel reading of the national cultural tradition perpetuating and transmitting the legacy of their forebearers.

Chapter 2

# Fine Arts in Serbia at the Beginning of the Twentieth Century

## Historical Painting

The opening of the World Exhibit in Paris in 1900 was recorded in numerous reviews as a cultural event of exceptional magnitude as well as a manifestation of good will among different nations around the world. Preparations for this exhibit were taken very seriously since the chosen art works were supposed to represent the artistic and cultural achievements of participating countries. These aspirations led to the conclusion that the selected works should possess the highest artistic qualities. In Serbia, the following artists were chosen to present their works at the exhibit: Anastas Bocarić, Steva Todorović, Paja Jovanović, Marko Murat, Beta Vukanović, Djordje Krstić, Paško Vučetić, Leon Koen, Svetislav Jovanović, Živko Jugović, Antoaneta Vulić, Kirilo Kutlik, Nikola Milojević, Petar Ranosavić, all painters; and three sculptors: Petar Ubavkić, Simeon Roksandić, and Djordje Jovanović.[1]

Božidar S. Nikolajević wrote about the importance of the forthcoming World Exhibit in the journal, *Brankovo kolo*. His lengthy review is a valuable testimony of an informed contemporary, a young art historian, who at that time had submitted his dissertation at the University of Leipzig. While commenting on the art works of Serbian artists chosen for the exhibit, Nikolajević also explained his artistic concepts.[2]

Nikolajević stressed that the Exhibit was an event of great value that should be recorded as such, in order to serve future generations. It provided a magnificent meeting point for different cultures and acted as a mirror depicting the innermost qualities of people. Therefore, every nation endeavored to present its best. Nikolajević justly pointed out that the culture of a nation did not originate overnight, its growth presented a parallel process to the growth of a nation. That is why an artist is always attached to his native roots and the reason

that folk creations are as distinguished as the creations of single individuals. This statement pointed out Nikolajević's opinion about the
foremost quality of an art work as an inherent national consciousness.
The spirit of a people was contained equally well in the artifacts of
goldsmiths, woodcarvers, and weavers as artists. ns are as distinguished as the creations of single individuals. and weavers as well in
the pictorial and plastic creations of prominent artists.

In his review, Nikolajević discussed the historical genre composi-
tion by Marko Murat, The Entrance of Tsar Dušan to Dubrovnik, The
Fall of Stalać by Djordje Krstić, The Ambush of Hajduk Veljko on the
Turks by Petar Ranosavić and the sculpture, The Takovo Uprising by
Petar Ubavkić. All of these selected works presented a tribute to a
Serbian historical past depicted in a realistic and narrative manner.
In this group, it was only Murat that tried to consolidate old and new
attitudes, introducing a *plein air* technique. Thus, his composition,
with about 70 deftly placed human figures, radiated with sparkling
sunlit freshness.

It seemed to Nikolajević that some artists were hiding their works
from him unknown reasons, and it was doubtful that their work would
be finished in time for the exhibit in Paris. Artists had received financial help in the amount of about 3,000 dinars to defray the costs, but
Nikolajević thought that this sum was "miserable." The honorarium
of Paja Jovanović in the amount of 30,000 dinars was the exception. Jovanović received this remuneration for his composition, The
Proclamation of Dušan's Law Codex. All other artists, painters and
sculptors were employed as art teachers in high schools and burdened
with an excessive teaching load. The artists lived under difficult circumstances, trying to find some spare moments to create works that
would present Serbian culture and civilization to the world abroad.
Nikolajević summed up his presentation with a plea for help, quoting
Lessing's words, "The arts need bread."[3]

At the turn of the nineteenth century Serbian historical painting
received a strong impetus thanks to the monumental compositions
of Paja Jovanović. At the same time, these paintings represented
a new phase in Jovanović's artistic path. Jovanović's first creation,
belonging to an historical genre, was painted in 1896 upon the request
of the Archbishop and Church Council at Karlovac. The painting
was commissioned for the Millennium Exhibit commemorating 1,000
years of the Hungarian state and culture. The painting was entitled,
Serbian Emigration during Arsenije III Crnojević. The aim of the
composition was to point to the exceptional position that was granted
to the Serbian population in the Austro–Hungarian realm, since the
Serbs provided needed military aid. Archbishop Georgije Branković

and the Church Committee thought that Paja Jovanović should fulfill all expectations in depicting the emigration that took place in 1690. This commission, which was entrusted to Paja Jovanović, was spurred by a previous similar request by the Hungarian committee in Budapest for an historic painting depicting the foundation of the Hungarian empire. Mihaly Munkacsy was chosen as the artist, and he produced the much lauded composition of Arpad's Founding of the Hungarian Country.

Having all this in mind and wishing to counterbalance the achievement of Munkacsy, the Serbian Church Council nominated the well known historian, Ilarion Ruvarac, to serve as a consultant to Jovanović during his inspection of monasteries in Fruška Gora where he examined the written sources and various objects preserved from the time of the emigration. After this thorough initial preparation, Jovanović was ready to present the historical moment depicting it in one well chosen scene that summed up the essential concept of the Serbian migration. For this purpose the artist chose a large canvas extending six meters in length.[4]

Approaching his work on this composition, as well as a series of monumental renditions, Jovanović thoroughly researched historical and literary sources. He also produced drawings of human figures, isolated and in groups, their costumes, and different artifacts. Thus, he displayed his adherence to a method already adopted during his studies in Vienna at the Fine Arts Academy under Leopold Karl Müller. At the time of Jovanović's studies in Vienna, Müller was considered the best painter of historical compositions and genre scenes. Müller advised his students on the importance of researching the premises associated with the theme of the prospective painting. Jovanović followed his advice. Even as a student, during school holidays, he roamed the countryside around his native Vršac noting down his impressions of nature, people, and their customs. Later, he expanded his studies to Serbia, Montenegro and the Adriatic Coast. After the completion of his studies, Jovanović traveled through many European countries. Later he explored regions of North America, Asia Minor, and Africa. He preserved impressions in the form of sketches of human figures and pastoral scenes reflecting his experiences during his travels.[5]

After completion of the painting, The Emigration of Serbs, Archbishop Branković and several members of the Church Council voiced some serious concern about the concept of the composition. Jovanović portrayed the military and church dignitaries along with the exodus of people while the Archbishop envisaged a presentation stressing the arrival of an organized military force corresponding to historical data. Jovanović accepted the criticism and changed the right side of the painting. He omitted the young wife of Monasterlija riding with her infant on a horse as well as a group of people herding their sheep. Thus, the military force remained with their leaders and church dignitaries crossing the northern boundaries of their lands in order to protect the Austro–Hungarian empire from further Turkish invasion. Although these changes were incorporated relatively quickly, the painting was not finished in time for the Millennium Exhibit. The composition was therefore exhibited upon its completion in 1896 at the Archbishop's palace in Sremski Karlovci. The exhibit quickly became a remarkable cultural event stirring up a controversy of opinions. There were laudatory remarks as well as sharp criticism. Reproductions of the first variation of the painting appeared later in almost all Serbian periodicals, followed by lithographs in color.[6]

The immense popularity of Jovanović's, Emigration of Serbs, as well as the temporary disappearance of this painting during World War I, prompted the artist to produce a considerably smaller replica.[7]

Respecting the essential message that the painting had to convey stressing a unity of the Serbian people within the boundaries of the Austro–Hungarian Empire, Jovanović strove for accuracy in portraying the historical scene and personalities. Jovanović was restricted from creating a composition from the artistic point of view. The pictorial solution was dominated by the the frontal presentation of historical personalities with special attention to details and decorative elements. This painting represented the first work of large proportions, with a great number of imposing human figures. A diffused and uniform light emanating from a grey–blue sky prevailed, while an interplay of light and shade was almost nonexistent. Although this painting had not reached a high artistic expression, its historical theme is nevertheless presented convincingly with decorative highlights. The Emigration of Serbs depicted a well chosen and important historical moment stressing the significance of national unity at the moment when this idea was becoming prominent.

Further proof of growing interest in the past events of national history led to a new commission from the Ministry for Education granted to Paja Jovanović in 1898. The suggested theme was the uprising in Takovo that led to the partial liberation of Serbia. In order to present the painting as truthfully as possible, Jovanović had at his disposal the authentic garments and armaments of Prince Miloš and his warriors. Jovanović also went to Takovo where he sketched the large tree under which Miloš raised a flag and led the people to fight against the Turks.[8]

The Serbian royal court chose the same artist to paint the composition Proclamation of Dušan's Legal Codex in 1899. It was decided that this painting would officially represent Serbia at the World Exhibit in 1900. According to his established method, Jovanović first concentrated on researching the archives for historical material. He also visited the former stations of Dušan's life in the monasteries of Gračanica and Lesnovo, the field of Kosovo, and the cities of Prizren and Skoplje.

Jovanović also consulted Stojan Novaković, an historian, with whom he discussed the historical role of Emperor Dušan. With Novaković's agreement, Jovanović decided to depict the most important deed of this ruler—the proclamation of the Legal Code. Jovanović decided to present this historical event on an open space in front of the church, depicting the military and political power of the young empire.[9]

Jovanović started the composition in 1900 and managed to realize an impressive work of art. Due to a well studied placement of groups and figures, it was mentioned that the painting suggested a well staged theatrical scene. This impression was corroborated by a minute rendering of all of the details on the exceptionally rich garments of the main personalities, lending a rich and decorative tone to the composition. The painting showed a clear disposition of plans and distribution of masses and did not project a sense of crowding as in The Emigration of Serbs. The tightly executed drawing presented the basis of the composition, although its pictorial treatment showed greater coloristic freedom and even attempts of *plein air* techniques.[10]

The Proclamation of Dušan's Legal Code was awarded the highest honors at the World Exhibit and Jovanović was presented with the honorary degree of *Officier d'Academie*.[11] The same painting was exhibited four years later at the First Yugoslav Artistic Exhibit in Belgrade.[12] Three years later, the Proclamation of Dušan's Legal Code was exhibited in London.[13]

Appreciation of the historical genre in painting was not limited only to Serbian or South–Slavic countries. A lively interest existed in other European countries. Paja Jovanović executed several historical paintings illuminating the past of the German people. Duke Ferdinand commissioned him for the composition The Marriage of Feri IV to Elisabeth Habsburg. In this painting, Jovanović used a pointilistic technique using pure colors of the spectrum. He displayed yellow, blue, and red hues on a complementary principle, which is used in some impressionistic canvases. The composition was presented at the World Exhibit in Vienna in 1901, where it was awarded a gold medal.

Jovanović painted a composition based on the German historical event, Furor Teutonikus. After his initial research on the historical background, he implemented a somewhat freer approach. The painting was shown at the World Exhibit in Saint Louis in 1904, and it was awarded a silver medal. The same composition was exhibited in Salzburg in 1909, and it received a gold medal on this occasion.[14] Among historical compositions that followed, special mention is due the painting The Marriage of Emperor Dušan with Aleksandra, the Sister of the Bulgarian King. Jovanović achieved a fine artistic realization of the content in this work. The theme of this composition recounted a mutual past as well as a renewed interest among neighboring nations. The painting was displayed at the First Yugoslav Artistic Exhibit in Belgrade thereby furthering the idea of unification of South Slavs.

Jovanović created several other paintings with historical themes inspired by heroes of Serbian epic poetry, such as Boško Jugović and the Battle on Kosovo. There exist preserved studies of compositions of Kraljević Marko Delivering Justice, Karadjordje among the Rebels and Rade the Builder Presenting the Model of Manasija.[15]

Jovanović continued the spirit and method of this painting in the Cathedral in Novi Sad where he portrayed themes from Serbian ecclesiastical history, Saint Sava Crowns Stephen and Saint Sava Appeasing Brothers.

The ever growing popularity of historical paintings created by Jovanović or other painters and sculptors, such as Djordje Krstić, Marko Murat and Djordje Jovanović, resulted in repeated exhibitions of their works. The renowned literary and art critic Bogdan Popović wrote about these pictorial works in the newly founded journal *Srpski Knijiževni Glasnik* in 1901. In his first review published in this journal, Popović wrote about the composition, The Fall of Stalać, by Djordje Krstić. The painting was exhibited in the newly opened pictorial gallery of the Public Museum and elicited strong emotions among the viewers. Popović pointed out that this remarkable composition was executed with great diligence. Krstić was at that time at the height of his artistic career, well known as a fine artist, and enjoying popular esteem. Yet Popović also voiced his criticism by declaring that the composition did not adequately project the despair and passionate emotions of the uneven and bitter struggle against the Turkish intruders. The figures and groups were presented in a static manner, without enough cohesion, while the perspective was to a certain degree neglected.[16]

In the course of the same year, another exhibition was arranged with paintings of Paja Jovanović and Marko Murat which were previously shown at the World Exhibit in Paris. Both paintings were commissioned especially for the Paris exhibit. Popović wrote a laudatory review about both compositions depicting scenes from the life of Emperor Dušan, The Proclamation of Dušan's Legal Code by Jovanović and The Arrival of Emperor Dušan in Dubrovnik by Murat. Popović stressed the contemporaneity of the pictorial method and the *plein air* approach on the sunlit canvases, which is noticeable in the compositions of both painters. The exhibit was arranged in the Festive Hall of Velika Škola (Academy) in Belgrade.[17] In the same review, Popović announced that the exhibit of the sculpture, Kosovo Monument, by Djordje Jovanović was likely to open soon. Popović concluded that although circumstances under which it was possible to write about art were not as frequent as one could wish, there were still opportunities to discuss development in the arts. However, these opportunities were not used enough, especially by the people whose official capacity was to act on behalf of the artists and their works.[18]

The exhibits of historical compositions in Belgrade, which were previously presented at the World Exhibit in 1901, received favorable comments as well as widespread appreciation. The Serbian public, as well as a number of artists, shared the renewed national consciousness. In a country where many national questions had not yet been solved, the visions of a former glory and of an honorable past projected a sense of continuity, identity, and cultural tradition.

### Centennial Celebration of the Uprising

The centennial celebration of the uprising against the Turkish domination in Serbia in 1904 served as an occasion for the renewal of cultural ties the with other Slavic nations of the Balkans. In the framework of this celebration, Miloje Vasić originated the idea of an artistic exhibition of South Slavic artists. Vasić was a noted art historian, professor, and director of the National Museum, and his interpretation of the necessity of collaboration among the South Slavs was at the time understandable to many. The people on the Balkan peninsula would be able to reach the mainstream of European development only if they were united. The response of the artists and the ensuing collaboration reaffirmed the wish for unification of the South Slavic people. There was a genuine feeling of national consciousness perceived in a broader South Slavic context. Due to the circumstances, the artists were standing in the forefront as proponents of impending unification.[19]

The goal of this collaboration was summarized in an invitation of the Pobratimstvo youth organization, which was addressed to potential participants:

> College youth, convinced that not many Balkan people and especially Yugoslavs, can face competition with the larger

and more cultured Western nations except by uniting, directed its efforts to promoting and possibly achieving the idea of a close association in all fields of the cultural life of all Balkan peoples, and Yugoslavs initially. For this purpose, the college youth have decided to organize an exhibit of works this year, initially only by Yugoslav artists and artisans which should be opened in the month of September. The college youth have decided that the idea of unification of Yugoslavs can only be accomplished if they are closely acquainted with each other. In order to promote the mutual acquaintance of Yugoslavs, it would be very useful to arrange artistic exhibits by periodically alternating the main Yugoslav centers of Sofia, Belgrade, Zagreb, and Ljubljana. That is why the college youth are ready to commence the fruition of this idea by organizing a Yugoslav artistic exhibit in Belgrade.[20]

In the course of the preliminary preparations for the celebration of the centennial, the idea for a youth conference was repeatedly introduced. According to V. Carićević, who was close to the youth movement at that time, two tendencies were dominant:

. . . one part of the youth forces was directed towards the education of Serbian youth as honorable people's intelligensia . . . while the other part of the force was spent progagating the admirable thought of concord, agreement, and even more about the community of South Slav brotherhood.[21]

In this spirit, the Serbian youth society, Pobratimstvo, directed an invitation for cooperation among students in Bulgaria, Crotia, and Slovenia. There were many propositions for possible avenues of cooperation that would foster a strengethening of unity among South Slavs. During this period, a periodical, *Slovenski Jug (The Slavic South)*, was started as well as a host of similar publications. The centennial celebration became understood as a unique opportunity to foster further aspirations for the union of South Slavs.[22]

It was in this atmosphere that a well written article appeared, addressed to the student body of the College of Philosophy in Belgrade suggesting an opportunity for leadership in organizing the First Yugoslav Artistic Exhibit. This article appeared in *Štampa (The Press)* with a signature of "Artium Amicus," and it had a decisive impact. It was in fact written by a professor in the history of fine arts, Miloje Vasić. Vasić believed that the young students were eminently suited to take over the organizational tasks of such unique manifestations of cultural and political importance. In truth, Vasić had revived the idea of an older colleague, Professor Mihailo Valterović, about the necessity of collaboration between Yugoslav artists. Valterović had expressed this thought on the occasion of an exhibit opening in 1898.[23]

The students at the College of Philosophy in Belgrade accepted the challenge to organize an art exhibit. It was decided that the exhibit should take place during the sessions of the First Congress of the Academic South Slavic Youth. Jovan Skerlić expressed his enthusiasm concerning the participation of the youth organization when he wrote, "It seems that since the time of the sixties and seventies until the present, the youth movement was never more lively and showing more results."[24]

Following a proposal of the student youth, the exhibit was soon acknowledged by official circles. The exhibit was deemed suitable to honor not only the centennial of the uprising but the coronation of King Petar Karadjordjević as well. In addition, the ensuing collaboration would point out possibilities of unification of all South Slavs. Therefore, this effort to achieve cooperation and cultural unity among the still divided South Slav people soon gained political importance.

Thanks to the support of many people, the student youth managed to organize the largest Balkan exhibit in a relatively short time span of only five months. The exhibit committee, comprising 17 members, included mostly professors at the College of Philosphy and other professional people. Among the distinguished names, mention should be made of Marko Leko, rector of the Velika Škola (College of Philosophy); Mihailo Valterović, curator of the National Museum; Miloje Vasić, assistant to the curator; Professors Jovan Cvijić and Andra Stefanović; Simo Matavulj, writer; Steva Todorović, painter; Djordje Jovanović, sculptstvo.[25] Nedić, president of the student association, Pobratimostov.[25]

Special attention was directed towards the sale of the exhibited works. The invitation to participating artists contained the following information: "The student youth has decided to sponsor the sale and distribution of artistic works among all the people in order to perpetuate not only the great importance of art for the culture of the Yugoslav people but also as a most reliable aid in the realization of the idea of Yugoslav collaboration. . . . "[26]

King Petar I officially opened the First Yugoslav Exhibit in Belgrade on 5 September 1904. The exhibit displayed art works by 96 artists. The number of art works was impressive, totaling 458. The exhibit took place in the Velika škola (Academy), arranged in 15 sections. Due to an overwhelming response from the artists and the magnitude of exhibited paintings, woodcuts and sculptures, the exhibit showed a varied and opulent review of achievements in the visual arts. Attendance was favorable with 10,362 visitors recorded. A number of eminent art critics visited the exhibit and their reviews present a valuable account. Such reviews were written by Bogdan Popović, Miloje Vasić, Božidar Nikolajević, Vladimir Petković, Vladislav Petković Dis, Milan Šević, Anton Gustav Matoš, and Nadežda Petrović.[27]

The most comprehensive review was written by Bogdan Popović, editor of the periodical *Srpki Književni Glasnik (Serbian Literary Herald)*. Following the division of the exhibit into separate national sections, Popović kept this division in his account:

> In our art (Serbian art, J.M.Dj.), there does not exist a particular art movement. Among the Croats, however, we can follow a certain tradition, which is the influence of one artist upon another, and a more systematic support from the government. While our artists were working by themselves, there was no particular school, and the government assisted without overall plans . . . One further characteristic of our art is the custom to borrow objects for artistic execution from our historic past. . . . Our art is patriotic.[28]

Popović noted that one could single out the older and the younger group in Serbian art. The first group was not informed about modern art, while the other, comprised of Beta Vukanović, Marko Murat, Rista Vukanović, and Paško Vučetić, "follows the most modern movement today, exploring light, recording its changes, nuances, reflections, and values."[29] Popović singled out Paja Jovanović who dominated the Serbian section. According to Popović, Jovanović "stands out by himself." Jovanović had appropriated some aspirations of modern art, besides keeping some habits from the old school. Similar to the Croatian painter, Vlaho Bukovac, Jovanović was moving along with art movements and remained consistently modern. Especially noticeable were the lightness and precision of his design and the skillful composition and quiet harmony of his color schemes. For the Bulgarian section, Popović had little to praise, although he tried to justify this situation since the Bulgarian artistic development had a late beginning. The arts in Bulgaria were on the threshold between artistic aspirations and dilettantism.[30]

Nadežda Petrović also discerned the differences in artistic expressions among the South Slavic artists in her lengthy review:

> The Croats and Slovenes cultivate modern painting with its individual higher poetry and refined and original techniques. The Bulgarians illustrate folklife with their genre–paintings. Our Serbian art presents to us monumental folk epics, folk

poetry in pictures and depicts a splendid past of folk history . . . Croatian art, with longer experience, excells in the field of culture with the sculptures of Frangeš Mihanović and Meštrović. The Slovenians excel with their fairy tales of Vesel and landscapes of Jakopič and Jama and with a poetic feeling and individuality in technique. The Serbs excel with their genre paintings of Montenegro life and the monumental, decorative and historical modern art of Paja Jovanović.[31]

Petrović thought that the moral success of the exhibit was unexpectedly great. Every section had created for itself an independent entity, although varied Western influences were notable from the older or newer art schools. The crown of Serbian art was represented by Dušan's Coronation, due to the perfection of its composition, design, and pictorial technique. There were some malicious comments that Petrović heard from an unknown visitor who claimed that the church in Skoplje never looked as magnificent and that the attire could not have been as rich at that time. Petrović maintained that during the five centuries under Turkish domination many cultural monuments were not spared from fire and annihilation. The small, poor church in Skoplje, built in a dugout, does not bear any resemblance to the old glory, except perhaps in the wood carving of the iconostasis and some other preciocity. However, a multitude of historical monuments and old manuscripts from Byzantium, Venice, and Dubrovnik, as well as splendiforous monasteries, testified to the wealth and power of the Serbian rulers. This eloquent soliloquy of the young artist testified to her belief in the historical accuracy of the Serbian past as presented on the canvases of Jovanović as well as to her devotion to her native land.

Young artists had their own section at the exhibit, and Petrović thought that excellent new talents were presented. Most importantly the First Yugoslav Artistic Exhibit had laid the groundwork for further cooperation. United Yugoslavs would continue their collaboration and establish mutual exhibits. Petrović hoped that the artist would succeed in creating a distinguished school of Yugoslav art that would eventually take its place in the general history of fine arts as a whole.[32]

The First Congress of Yugoslav Youth took place from 2–8 September in Belgrade, coinciding with the opening of the First Yugoslav Artistic Exhibit. Jovan Skerlić credited these two exceptional events to the dedicated work of the Pobratimstvo student organization. The Congress of Yugoslav Youth was one of the most important events of the recent past that took place in Serbia. It was not easy to free oneself from various prejudices passed on to the young by the older generations. Congress proved that the young forces had unselfishly moved forward like an avant-garde. The youngest generation had a serious understanding of life and social obligations believing "that passive people do not have a place in history." Skerlić concluded his review with expressions of contentment since similar successes occurred seldom enough.[33]

The Youth Congress issued a resolution that underlined the feeling of national pride and devotion as well as the wish for rendering help to the population in occupied Serbian lands. The resolution stressed the importance of education in order to advance the cultural level of Serbian people. The centuries of long Turkish occupation resulted in reducing Serbia to a backward country. While advocating the importance of education in all fields of human endeavors, the ultimate goal of liberation was further stressed:

> The goal of this organization: in order to be able to alleviate and help its people in competition with other cultural nations, in education, economics, and other areas of public life, prepare its people for very high ideals; liberation of all Serbian nonliberated lands . . .[34]

## The Founding of the Association of Yugoslav Artists—Lada

The successful commencement of collaboration among South Slavs, started on the occasion of the centennial celebration, was continued. The artists proceeded to remain on the forefront of these endeavors. One of the questions raised at the First Yugoslav Artistic Exhibit entertained the idea of establishing a central Yugoslav Association, with separate sections for different national entities. Thus, at the conclusion of the exhibit, a delegation of artists was selected to repay the visit of Bulgarian artists. The delegation was led by the Bulgarian artist, Ivan Angelov, who was returning from Belgrade to Sofia. A group of reporters from various newspapers and periodicals joined the group. Nadežda Petrović also decided to visit Bulgarian colleagues, since she was keenly interested in new developments in art, and especially in nuturing further friendly ties with this neighboring country. At the meeting in Sofia, it was decided that the Yugoslav exhibit should become a permanent biannual event. Sofia was chosen as the site of the next exhibit. It was suggested that a conference should be arranged in Sofia in December of 1904 in order to negotiate the foundation of an association of Yugoslav artists. The conference took place as planned and a resolution of the newly established federation of national associations was signed on 29 December 1904. The resolution read:

Bulgarian, Serbian, Croatian and Slovenian artists founded the Association of Yugoslav Artists—Lada, and after mutual agreement accepted the proposed regulations . . . . The goal of the Association is to unite all Yugoslav artists in order to strengthen the national spirit and love for the fine arts. This goal will be achieved by arranging general exhibits in Bulgaria, Serbia, Croatia, and Slovenia as well as abroad.[35]

The resolution was signed by Robert Frangeš–Mihanović, Ferdo Vesel, Djordje Jovanović, Rista Vukanović, Oton Iveković, Rudolf Valdec, Anton Mitov, Ivan Mrkvička, and Vesin. National committees were formed and the initial bylaws were written in January 1905. Members of the Serbian committee were Marko Murat, Djordje Jovanović, and Steva Todorović. Robert Frangeš Mihanović, Rudolf Valdec, and Oton Iveković formed the Croatian counterpart, while the Slovenes chose Ferdo Vesel, Matija Jama, and Ante Gaber.[36]

On the occasion of the 25th anniversary of the Croatian Artistic Society on 20 April 1905, a joint conference took place with the participation of the Association of Yugoslav Artists Lada and the Association of Yugoslav Writers and Journalists. The conference was held at the Yugoslav Academy of Sciences and Arts in Zagreb, and Bogdan Popović was invited to preside. The delegation from Belgrade included Jelena Dimitrijević, Nadežda Petrović, Aleksandar Belić, Borislav Popović, Djordje Jovanović, Jovan Skerlić, Marko Murat, Rista Vukanović, and Rista Odavić. During the conference the rules and regulations of the Association of Writers and Journalists were approved. It was agreed that the Association had been founded in order to enhance mutual understanding and sponsor solidarity of the South Slavs in cultural fields of endeavor.[37]

Those artists, who were members of the Yugoslav Artists Association Lada and who attended the conference in Zagreb, were invited as guests of the Croatian Artists Association. The artists discussed in great length the preparation of the final version of the constitution. The Association was comprised of four national sections: Croatian, Serbian, Slovenian, and Bulgarian. The goal of the Association was to support artists in order to foster an indigenous development in the fine arts. It was approved that in presenting their works abroad the artists would appear as members of the Lada Association.[38]

The first exhibit by members of Lada was opened on Easter Day 1906. King Petar I opened the exhibit that presented not only a cultural but an equally political event. The artists were demonstrating their support for unification of South Slavs, stressing the collaboration achieved in the cultural field.

Bogdan Popović reviewed the exhibit and declared that this event presented "a joyous occasion." Popović noted that this exhibit was the first one by an organized group. Previously, the artists had individually arranged their own exhibitions. The exhibit showed a favorable development since the First Yugoslav Exhibit in 1904. Beta Vukanović brought 20 of her canvases which alone filled the fifth section of the exhibit. Among her paintings, Popović singled out After Bath as particularly successful. Nadežda Petrović and Petar Ranosavić presented their works in the sixth section. Popović noted that the public laughed at the paintings of these young artists, especially the paintings of Petrović. Popović himself thought that Petrović's paintings gave the impression of being executed in a hurry, without enough preparation and study. In spite of that, Petrović's intentions were "always artistic," and her technique had daring yet correct strokes. Djordje Jovanović was the only sculptor at the exhibit. Jovanović managed to present excellent characteristics of figures and forms with his reliable knowledge of anatomy and skillful modeling. In conclusion, Popović wished all artists the support of generous patrons: "Our people are not misers. If they could only know how much they would serve the cause of their nation as well as their own pleasure, I am convinced that they would be acquiring more art works."[39]

## The Role of Nadežda Petrović in the Development of Fine Arts in the Beginning of the Twentieth Century

Returning to Belgrade from studies in Munich in 1903, Nadežda Petrović engaged in many activities on the cultural as well as national and social levels. Belgrade was in the midst of a political crisis, when people felt threatened and everybody spoke in subdued voices as if fearing to be overheard since it seemed "that every third man in the streets was either a paid policeman or an informer."[40]

The administration, under the rule of Alexandar Obrenvić, was burdened by party conflicts, political crises and finally by the abolition of the party conflicts, political crises and finally by the abolition of the constitution. Shortly after Petrović's return on 23 March 1903, an organized demonstration took place with the participation of 5,000 students and workers. Demonstrators walked to the city square shouting "Down with despotism." Petrović witnessed this encounter. The student organizers of the demonstration, Dimitrije Tucović and Triša Kaclerović, were forced to go underground. The situation in Serbia deteriorated even further and, according to Petrović, became "heavy with an oppression of personal rights."[41]

After the coup, Parliament elected Petar Kardjordjević to the throne. Serbia became a constitutional and parliamentary monarchy. Petrović noted that: "The memorable year 1903 laid ground for free thinking while nuturing a wish for the realization of national ideals and goals . . . . The people were awakened as if after a difficult dream."[42]

In the course of the same year, Nadežda Petrović and Delfina Ivanić, deeply concerned with the Turkish prosecution in the occupied regions, decided to offer relief to the innocent victims. Delfina Ivanić described in retrospect her memories about the conversations with Nadežda Petrović concerning the organization of relief:

> The conversation dealt with the pitiful conditions which our people were subjected to by Turkey, about the aborted uprising in Madedonia, tortures, jailings, hangings, and banishment into exile of our people to Asia Minor. Talking about these misfortunes, the conversation ended with the conclusion that it is necessary for Serbia to offer a helping hand and solace in order to show that we are with them in these moments of most difficult times and suffering.[43]

These noble intentions found full support among eminent personalities of the time, such as Branislav Nušic, Jaša Prodanović, and Andra Nikolić. Mita Petrović, Nadežda Petrović's father, proved to be especially helpful. Nadežda Petrović recorded how this humanitarian action was shaped:

> My first counselling session with my father and noted politicians convinced me to call upon a few intelligent women and present to them a plan that would enable a decisive action . . . trusting that swift help is the best help . . . . Some responded right away, ready for any work and sacrifice, but there were many whose husbands and fathers thought that it was yet too early for women to appear as national fighters and workers.[44]

The largest women's meeting in Kolarac Hall on 15 August 1903 soon followed. The meeting was attended by several thousand women. Nadežda Petrović opened with her speech:

> One has to wonder why the furor of a decaying Turkey is being imposed upon us . . . . We cannot hope that any help will be provided by the rest of educated Europe. . . . They do not care about several million Serbs and other Slavs. . . . Forty villages from Kičevo and 36 from Debar were destroyed, men were murdered, and women, daughters, and children were disgraced by Turks. Shame for the twentieth century, a century of civilization, a century of emancipated womanhood. . . . Let us start to work jointly and embrace this cause as our own.

The speech delivered by Petrović lasted one hour and fifteen minutes. According to Delfina Ivanić, who attended the meeting, the speech was often interrupted by the public voicing strong support. Contemporaries thought that Petrović delivered the best and most successful speech by a Serbian woman so far.[45]

The founding of the women's organization, Kolo srpskih sestara (The Round of Serbian Sisterhood), soon followed. This organization became an important patriotic and humanitarian association. Pebrović became the first secretary and in this capacity she soon started collecting aid for the victims in ravaged villages.

The first fundraising occasion was a concert in the National Theater that took place on 7 November 1903. Petrović prepared the program herself. According to her concept, the program included "tableau vivant from Macedonia and Serbia," with the participation of the well known actors Milka Grgurova and Milka Stojković. The enacted scenes presented explicit patriotic and national content: The Apotheosis of the First Uprising and Glorification of Duke Miloš, The Uprising in Macedonia and Serbia, The Hanging and Torturing of Serbs, Burned Huts and Leading Away of Women, Girls and Children, The Portrait of Turkish Military Officials–Dahias. After the director of the theater had a consultation with a higher government official, it was decided to omit the living pictures in order to eliminate possible diplomatic intervention. The stage design was conceived by the sculptor Djordje Jovanović.

The final program consisted of a presentation of the epic song Buna na dahije (The Uprising against Dahije), with the traditional accompaniment of gusle–a folk string instrument. In addition, the following poems were recited: Stražar (The Sentry) by Djura Jakšić and Macedonia by Rista Odavić. Dramatic scenes were presented from Gorski vijenac (The Mountain Laurel), Stanoje Glavaš, Knez Ivo od Semberije (Prince Ivo from Semberija), and Stana Ranković. Petrović stated in her report to the Kolo Association that "the concert took place, after surmounting great difficulties, to the delight of the public and His Majesty the King." The monetary gain presented a well rounded amount.[46]

Only a few days later, on 19 November 1903, Petrović and Dobri were ready to conduct a small expedition to Macedonia with the collected aid in the form of money and clothing. They were accompanied by Jakov Ćirković, Secretary of the diocese Debar–Veles and officer in charge of education. Nadežda left a detailed itinerary, "Travel to Macedonia," of 36 handwritten pages which described her daily travels:

As a member of the patriotic and propaganda society, I

commenced my travels to Old Serbia and Macedonia on 19 November 1903 with a goal of national agitation and to disburse aid to our suffering brothers in Kičevo, Bitolj, the region of Rabetinska and Tunska River, Vododelnica, the river Treska confluent to Vardar and the Poreč region.[47]

The trip proved to be extremely difficult. After crossing the border, the party went on foot, in a carriage, and most often on horseback since the bridges were destroyed. However, the population offered a cordial welcome:

> Within a few hours, the whole township of Kičevo and vicinity knew of our arrival, and from many villages priests and teachers with town leaders arrived, asking us to visit them in order to see their plight and to talk to their people.[48]

The trip lasted four weeks and Petrović returned exhausted and seriously ill.[49]

The humanitarian action of the association, Kolo srpskih sestara, was declared in the report of Cvet. S. Stanojević, the Serbian consul at Bitolj, as a mission that left the best impression on everyone concerned. Stanojević wrote his report in Bitolj on 22 December 1903.[50]

The following year, Petrović took an active part in preparations for the First Yugoslav Artistic Exhibit. Next to her devotion in developing her own artistic potential, Petrović had a strong commitment for enhancing a general development of the fine arts. Petrović, nicknamed Jugoslovenska Nada (Yuglosav Hope), was eminently aware and supportive of cultural and national goals, nurturing foremost the idea of Yugoslav unification.

The preparations for the forthcoming Yugoslav Exhibit served as reason for closer collaboration between the painters and sculptors from Slovenia and Crotia with Jakopič, Grohar, Vesel, as well as Meštrović, Krizman, Vidović, and Becić. Paško Vučetić soon joined this group of younger artists. During the exhibit in September of 1904, and consequently in later years, the young artists met at the hospitable home of the Petrović family. The architect and painter, Branko Popović, wrote, in retrospect, about these meetings in a special atmosphere of friendly support of Yugoslav ideas and collaboration: "Under Nadežda's influence, the house of her father, the esteemed Mita Petrović, became the utmost artistic and Yugoslav house in Belgrade from 1904 until 1914.[51]

These young artists felt united by a similar station in life and chosen profession. Some of them met during their studies in Munich at the Academy of Arts directed by the Slovenian painter Anton Ažbe. For others the Yugoslav exhibit provided a basis for new acquaintance and resulting friendly ties. In this atmosphere, Petrović proposed an idea to establish a Yugoslav Artistic Colony. The Colony would unite young artists that felt like Yugoslavs and wanted to present their work united as a group without subdivision into different national groups. Thus, even their artistic work would eventually aspire to a new artistic quality, Yugoslav in its essence, and achieve an equality with the mainstream of contemporary European art. Their mutual work planned to encompass paintings and sketches from nature and exhibits were planned in the country and abroad. The foundation of the Yugoslav Academy of Fine Arts was projected as a final goal.[52]

Petrović strove to arrange a suitable place in Serbia for the members of the newly founded Colony to start their painting sessions from nature. In order to secure material backing for this project, Nadežda persistently visited several offices of education and fine arts. Her tenacity finally bore fruit, and in May of 1905 she informed Vesel and Jakopič that she had arranged for a free train ticket for traveling through Serbia:

> The minister told me that you should come here in order to start our work, and later he will give us monetary help, maybe up to 3,000 dinars . . . Then we will try to start the Yugoslav Academy here later in autumn. . . We should start our work in the Colony not later than 5 July. In the village (Sićevo, St. Petka in the Gorge) life will be very inexpensive.[53]

Petrović continued her negotiations with the minister in order to provide further support to the Colony and the planned exhibit. Her petition, addressed to the minister, contained the basic aspirations of the group and a plan of their mutual endeavors. Before dispatching it to the authorities, she circulated the petition among the members in order to receive their signatures. In addition to Petrović, the petition was signed by Jakopič, Vesel, Vidović, and Meštrović:

> In referral to previous negotiations in the month of July . . . conducted by Nadežda Petrović, painter and member of our Yugoslav artistic Colony, we offered . . . our services that will pertain to dissemination and elevation of Yugoslav culture, considering Serbia the natural center and therefore helping her to propagate development of the fine arts in order for us to rely on support and remuneration for further work. With this goal in mind, Miss Petrović submitted the petition that found agreement . . . for all that refers to the strengthening of the Yugoslav idea and community, thus the minister agreed that, starting from 1 January 1907, there

will be allocated a permanent fund for the members of the Yugoslav Colony that will provide for the upkeep and protection of their work, . . . that will serve as moral and material help for exhibits in European centers, as well as for exhibits in Belgrade, in Yugoslav urban centers, as well as in the hinterland . . . . The aim of the Yugoslav Colony is to try to understand the population of different Yugoslav regions as well as their character, to try to educate the people and collect all that is beautiful, interesting, and original about the people in order to present it to the Western world. . . . While getting to know the people and bringing forth their culture, they will strive to elevate their folk art by providing direct contact with artists. . . . An opportunity will be given to enable them to meet other Yugoslav peoples as well as their enslaved brothers.[54]

Nadežda Petrović and Ferdo Vesel were the first members of the Colony to work in the Sićevo region during 1905 and 1906. Later, they were joined by Rihard Jakopič, Ivan Grohar, Paško Vučetić, and eventually by Ivan Meštrović and Emanuel Vidović. According to Petrović, Vidović came in autumn "when the green shades changed into attractive hues and lost the appearance of green vegetables."

Members of the Colony were congenial friends, some since their early studies at Ažbe's Academy in Munich. Their friendly ties were strengthened while working together in organizing the First Yugoslav Artistic Exhibit. While working at the Exhibit, their circle was enhanced by the inclusion of new members. They felt united in their Yugoslav aspirations being on the vanguard of political and national goals. They also felt united in their wish to introduce the values of contemporary art where colors and light were understood as two basic prerogatives. Work in nature was considered as essential. While in Sićevo, the painters lived together in a rented house whereas Petrović stayed with a friend, a lady teaching in the same place. In the morning they would gather together to go on location to Saint Petka or to the banks of the Nišava River. They painted landscapes with villagers, the gorge with the river, and an old mill.[55]

The Exhibit of the First Yugoslav Colony was held in 1907, and it was interpreted as an outstanding manifestation of a small group of progressive contemporary artists. The preparations took a great deal of time and effort since it was necessary to write to all members in Slovenia and Crotia as well as to arrange shipment of the paintings for the exhibit in the National Museum. Petrović and Vučetić suggested that Meštrović's drawing, Guslar slepi (The Blind Gusle Player), be accepted for the poster. The poster was manufactured in Belgrade. During January and February 1907, the exhibit was arranged by Grohar with Meštrović's help. The Exhibit projected a clear and well organized display of paintings and sculptures with a distinct feeling of a contemporary approach. A photograph from the exhibit is preserved by Petrović's family. There were 105 art objects, representing 11 painters and one sculptor—Nadežda Petrović, Paško Vučetić, Ivan Grohar, Matiji Jama, Rihard Jakopič, Emanuel Vidović, Tomislav Krizman, Mirko Rački, Ante Katunarić, Nikola Mihailov, Aleksandar Božinov and the sculptor, Ivan Meštrovic. The Exhibit of the Yugoslav Artistic Colony was opened in a festive fashion on 29 February 1907. Since the Society of Slovenski Jug (Slavic South) helped organize the exhibit, Professor Petar Janković opened the exhibit with an appropriate speech. Janković was president of the club and of the reading room.[56]

In the periodical *Slovenski Jug* the exhibit and members of the Colony were greeted as another success on the road towards a cultural union of South Slavs. Therefore, the validity of existence of both the Association of Yugoslav Artists, Lada, and of the First Yugoslav Artistic Colony was pointed out as necessary and useful. While Lada was orgnanized on a federalistic principle, the Colony was comprised of younger artists on a union basis. The paintings and sculptures on display were declared to belong "to the most modern genre." The critics were unanimous in their praise of Meštrović's work, as well as with the paintings of Slovenian artists. The critics acknowledged Nadežda Petrović's art works. The exhibit remained open until 14 March 1907.[57]

Božidar Nikolajević wrote about the exhibit of the Colony, noting that the exhibit gave the opportunity to compare new works of old acquaintances. The only sculptor at the exhibit, Ivan Meštrović, made an impression with his poetic qualities as shown in his sculpture Na izvoru života (On the source of life). This sculpture represented those whose suffering pressed against the spherical rim of the fountain in order to replenish themselves with life–giving fluid. Among the painters Nikolajević singled out were the canvases of Emanuel Vidović: Tristitia, Opusteli dvori (Abandoned Court) and Na počinak (Bedtime). Nikolajević declared the exhibited paintings of Rihard Jakopič as closer in form to the sketches. Jakopič presented Nocturno Šuma (The Woods), and Poslednji sneg (The Last Snow). Nadežda Petrović and Paško Vučetić were the only Serbian artists represented. In Nikolajević's opinion, Petrović's paintings presented an improvement. These paintings were better than the ones she exhibited with Lada. She displayed Polje u leto (The Meadow in Summer), Opelo (Requiem), and Ribari na Dunavu (The Fishermen on the Danube).[58]

The review of Anton Gustav Matoš was detailed in order to give his undivided support to the members of the Colony:

All the exhibitors are not always interesting as artists; however, they are interesting as people. They all have individuality, with the exception of Nikola Mihailov; that is to say, they are modern and they have courage. These are people conscious of the new, of new thoughts and feelings without which there cannot be any progress. Only new people have new sensations. Among the exhibitors there are four national groups that distinguish themselves as four schools. Petrović is similar in her technique to the Slovenian and Vučetić in his inspiration to the Croatian school. The Bulgarians are the least interesting at this exhibit. The Slovenians are only impressionists; they are only interested in colors and their relationship. For them, color is like a word. Slovenes are most successful as imagery painters at this exhibit. They do not rationalize or moralize like Rački, they do not long and sing like the melanchoilic Vidović and his blind imitator, Katunarić, they do not flatter like Mihailov and they do not reform like Nadežda Petrović. Yet all of them are more personal than Paško Vučetić. They are our true artists . . . . All these paintings and all these artists have common traits. They are followers of modern ways of thought and expression. . . . It is characteristic that there is not a single historic or religious painting present. These artists do not care for tradition and take into consideration only the tradition of epic poetry (Meštrović), classical poetry (Rački), and classical decoration (Vučetić). They are all young since they are still searching and studying, and they are not pleased with mannerism of style and concept of worn out formulas. Therefore, the majority of works have features of sketches, studies, experiments of something not definitive to the horror of the fillisters. . . . The Exhibit of the Colony is very entertaining, didactic, and consoling which is proof that there are high aspirations for expressions of contemporary culture in the midst of our beautiful South.[59]

In retrospect, some 70 year later, Katarina Ambrozić, the biographer of Nadežda Petrović, stressed the validity of Matoš's reasoning. The historic role of the Colony was expressed mostly in the introduction of progressive artistic ideas that were shared by a group of artists. Thus, the pictorial and plastic works of members of the Colony represented the genesis of a modern movement in Yugoslav art.[60]

Nadežda Petrović also helped with the restoration of the Yugoslav Fine Arts Gallery. The Gallery was founded shortly after the closing of the First Yugoslav Artistic Exhibit in 1904, in order to commemorate the first Yugoslav cultural manifestation. At first, the Gallery was located at the National Museum and contained 18 art works that were purchased from the Exhibit. In the Gallery's collection, the following artists were represented: Ivan Angelov from Bulgaria; Klement Crnčić, Emanuel Vidović, Tomislav Krizman, Ivan Meštrović, Rudolf Valdec, Bela Čikos, Oton Iveković, Celestin Medović, Gvajc, and Josif Zolja from Crotia; Rihard Jakopič, Ivan Grohar, Matija Jama, and Ferdo Vesel from Slovenia; and Josif Danilovac and Steva Todorović from Serbia.[61]

In gallery rules, established by Dr. Miloje Vasić, it was stipulated that the acquisition of new art works should be oriented primarily to works presented at Yugoslav exhibits. Thus, the gallery should provide support for further growth of Yugoslav art. Vasić even suggested that similar galleries be established in other Yugoslav urban centers. In the meantime, with the changes in personnel of the administration, the necessary interest and support disappeared. Petrović tried to rekindle the establishment of art galleries as important cultural institutions.[62]

## The Founding of Schools of Fine Arts

The founding of the First Serbian School for Design and Painting in Belgrade in 1895 was greeted as a much needed educational institution. The founder was Kiril Kutlik, an artist of Czech origin and a former student of the Prague and Vienna Academies. Kutlik invited four more teachers to the faculty and started the school with five teachers in charge. Instruction of students was based on conservative methods. The first course was devoted to the copying of ornaments from the textbook by Taubinger. The last classes were devoted to drawings models. There was a yearly exhibit of works by students. In the second report on the progress of the school in 1906, it was stated that a number of teachers taught theoretical subjects with great devotion and no pay " . . . having in mind only the moral importance of the school." Kutlik himself taught design and painting every day.

The school soon brought together a future generation of artists. Some of them, like  Bora Stevanović,  Milan Milovanović,  Kosta Milićević, Dragomir Glišić, and Nadežda Petrović, stayed in touch because of their professional careers. They participated in exhibitions, different cultural actions and foremost through their artistic work, as collaborators, or even as opponents on some occasions.

The methodological aspect of the curriculum in Kutlik's school soon drew opposition. Thus, Djordje Krstić, a well versed and educated artist, wrote an open letter published in the newspaper, *Dnevni list (The Daily Paper)*. The letter was addressed to Kiril Kutlik, headmaster of the Painting and Drawing School, and in a polemic manner refuted the old–fashioned methods used in Kutlik's school. Krstić himself taught privately in his studio. Among his former student, Nadežda Petrović became best known.[63]

Unfortunately, Kutlik did not have a chance to teach his Serbian students very long. Born in 1869, his life ended too soon in 1900. After Kutlik's death, Rista Vukanović took over the school. The school consistently showed good results in both pedagogical and artistic aspects. The number of students was constantly increasing. In order to respond better to the innovative methods of the times, the curriculum was expanded in 1905. Three courses of study were established: a general course, a special course, and a section for female students. Rista Vukanović taught drawing, Djordje Jovanović taught modeling, Steva Titelbah taught architectonic design, Dragutin Inkiostri taught folk ornaments, Gvozden Klajić taught graphic art, Dr. Voja Djordjević taught anatomy, Božidar Nikolajević and Mihailo Valterović taught art history, Dr. Brana Petronijević taught aesthetics, Jovan Stojanović taught geometry, Marko Murat taught aquarelle, Beta Vukanović taught drawing and aquarelle, and Vukanović also taught needlepoint to the female students. There were courses in drawing models. Some aspects of applied art were also taught, including drawing and painting of floral designs on different surfaces like paper, silk, porcelain, glass, cotton, and copper as well as painting on draperies.[64]

The school, under the new name of The Fine Arts and Crafts School, efficiently continued with the education of the young. The exhibits of paintings and artifacts from students showed promising results and they were often reviewed in the leading journal, *Srpski Književni Glasnik*. Yet the school did not receive sufficient support from the educational agency. In a review of the exhibit of 1908, the reviewer addressed the following plea to the public:

> At the time of the opening of the exhibit of the Serbian Artistic Association, the exhibit of students' works from the School of Fine Arts and Crafts took place. This school is engaged in a very important business without enough attention and support from public or government officials. This only institution where the arts are cultivated is left under the care of those fine artists who created and managed it. The insignificant monetary support is hardly sufficient for

immediate necessities and teachers' honorariums. The dilapidated building facing Sava can easily fall apart suddenly
and will be unsuitable for the purpose of teaching art. . . .
Yet this school progresses and therefore proves the right for
its existence and support.[65]

The review of the School of Fine Arts and Crafts exhibit of students' works in 1911 brought new praise to teachers and students.
The exhibit was arranged in the school building which was not very
suitable for this occasion. Yet the exhibit, as a whole, had a pleas-
ing effect. In view of the fact that the educational agency gave only
modest financial support, the efforts of the teachers deserved special
praise. The reviewer noted that the exhibited paintings and sculptures did not show a whimsical wish for adopting some of the fashionable techniques of the new schools, not having developed a true
understanding for such an innovation. Although the reviewer stated
that he was not in opposition per se to new developments, he stated
that it was commendable that the students were not striving to emulate the new. It would be especially pernicious for "young souls" to
receive such instruction "second hand" from an instructor who was
not sufficiently versed himself. There might be an opportunity later
to explore new tendencies in the fine arts and make a decision to
accept such innovation or abandon them.[66]

It seems obvious that the reviewer was in all probability Branko
Lazarević, since the review was signed only with the initials B.L. He
was in essence in discord with innovators in the fine arts in general.
It is possible to conclude that he considered the teachers that were
proponents of such tendencies only as "second hand" intermediaries
and not fully developed artists with a sense of destination in their
works and explorations. Furthermore, the reviewer reproached the
school for not cultivating enough training in the applied arts and
crafts in order to prepare versed "workers in many fields of the applied
arts." With the exception of the research in stylized folk motives
and the resulting works of students in Inkiostri's class, there was
little more in this area of instruction. The vast majority of exhibited
works belonged in the realm of pure art—charcoal drawings, portraits,
studies of nude models, oil paintings, and aquarelles.[67]

The next academic year brought a new exhibit of students' works.
Another review duly appeared signed again by the same initials, most
likely belonging to Branko Lazarević. The reviewer reminded the public that he evaluated the last exhibit in the same journal. At that time
he had a general remark concerning the apparent lack of instruction
of the different crafts and applied arts. The situation did not change
and the exhibit of 1911 bore the same characteristics. Most of the ex-

hibited works represented students' work from fine arts classes. The school was not teaching crafts. The reviewer thought that the majority of students exhibiting landscapes and portraits could have had better luck with works resulting from different aspects of the study of the applied arts.[68]

## Chapter 3

### Development of Serbian Literature in the First Decade of the Twentieth Century

#### Collaboration of Yugoslav Writers

The successful collaboration of Yugoslav artists in an effort to arrange a unique exhibit of works of visual arts by their colleagues in September of 1903 inspired similar aspirations among the writers. The writers strove to encourage cultural collaboration among South Slavs. Most of all they wished to promote a better understanding of literary contributions by Yugoslav authors. At the same time, they aimed to establish similar professional and friendly ties with artists and sculptors. These aspirations led to a conference of Yugoslav writers and artists that coincided with the First Yugoslav Art Exhibit. The conference opened on 6 September 1904. Pavle Popović, professor of literature and esteemed literary critic, attended the conference and wrote about his impressions:

> One thing leads to another, and it is easy to lean toward something already built in order to build further. That must have been the thought of Yugoslav writers while observing the united action of their compatriots the artists. In their area of literary endeavors, they wished to establish a community among themselves. [1]

Popović informed the public that the members of the conference had decided to publish an almanac or an album as a literary/artistic memento that would include reproductions of artistic works from the exhibit as well as of literary contributions of the best South Slavic writers. That is why the Croatian writer, Djalski, suggested the publication of a Yugoslav journal. However, in the discussion, it was pointed out that some journals already published literary works of Croatian, Slovenian, and Bulgarian writers.

The discussions about Bulgarian literature convinced Popović that Bulgarian literature shared many common traits with Serbian literature. Popović reminded the audience that when visualizing the expanded Yugoslav union one should not neglect the appreciation of splendiferous world literatures. The Serbs especially should feel indebted to Western culture which enabled the creation of better literary works as well as higher literary aspirations. These conclusions bore likeness to similar views advocated by Bogdan Popović about the importance of a thorough knowledge of western literature. Popović thought that the example set by great European writers would enable further growth of Serbian literary thought.

Attending the conference were, among others: Djordje Jovanović, Jelena Dimitrijević, Jovan Dučić, Jovan Skerlić, Jovan Tomić, Lujo Vojnović, Pavle Popović, Rista Vukanović, Rista Odavić, Rihard Jakopič, Stevan Todorović, and Petko Todorov. Members of the conference decided that the planned almanac should carry the title, *First Yougoslav Almanac in Commemoration of the Centennial Celebration of the Serbian Uprising.* The conference closed with a festive banquet arranged for the members of the editorial board of *Srpski Knijiževni Glasnik.* Bogdan Popović was the guest speaker at the banquet.[2]

Popović thought that the First Yugoslav Artistic Exhibit showed how much could be achieved even in a relatively short span of time. The exhibit brought better understanding of the literary work of neighboring people which was not sufficiently known until that time. Popović thought that the motto of Yugoslav people should be, "Sincerely and Persistently." The Yugoslav exhibit had great value in promoting an all embracing Yugoslav union.[3]

Many eminent societies and institutions joined in the celebration of the centennial of the Serbian uprising. The Royal Serbian Academy of Science celebrated the centennial on 15 October 1904. The texts of speeches given at that occasion were published with the welcoming address of President S. M. Lozanić and Ljubomir Jovanović's speech about the Serbian uprising. Likewise the Literary Society, Srpska književna zadruga, which was established in Novi Sad in 1892, organized a festive meeting commemorating the centennial on 10 September 1904.[4]

The Board of the Literary Academy, Matica Srpska, addressed a proposal in Novi Sad to the well known historian, Stojan Novaković, commissioning him to write a report about the uprising under Karadjordje. Novaković accepted the proposal and wrote a report that also included an analysis of foreign interference on the consequent development of the Serbian uprising. Novaković's report was reviewed on the pages of *Srpski Književni Glasnik.* The reviewer, J. N. Tomić, stated that Novaković's report presented a valuable contribution to Serbian historiography.[5]

Yugoslav writers and journalists decided to hold their third meeting in the autumn of 1905. The writer, Sima Matavulj, had the pleasure of greeting the guests in University Hall on 6 November 1905. Matavulj spoke on behalf of the Serbian Literary Association. The guests from Croatia included Djalski, Vilden, and Smodlaka; from Bulgaria, Andrejčev and Božinov; from Slovenia, Plut and Zbašnik. The meeting was also attended by a number of Serbian writers and journalists.[6]

Aleksandar Belić read the agenda of the conference. The Serbian Literary Association wrote the agenda with a goal of improving literary ties as well as disseminating books and journals among the South Slavs. The agenda contained the following items:

1. Founding of a library
2. Improvements in acquisition of books
3. Promotion of Yugoslav books
4. Publication of dictionaries, grammars, and anthologies
5. Association of South Slavic Writers and Journalists

Djalski submitted the proposal for the rules and regulations of the Association which was accepted. It was agreed that the name of the Association would read, Association of Yugoslav Writers and Journalists (Slavic South). It was decided that meetings would take place every three years. The cities of Belgrade and Sofia were declared as seats of the Association. Skerlić, Belić, Djalski, Matavulj, Plut, Jocov, and Glišić participated in the discussions. It is interesting that, in the discussions, Djalski suggested that the Association should become a central entity independent of other literary societies. While Belić, talking on behalf of the Serbian literary society, advanced the opinion of the federal character of the Association while taking into account the literary societies of different Yugoslav countries.[7]

During the meeting, Pavle Popović delivered a lecture about the state of Serbian literature. Popović stressed that he felt honored to be chosen to expound his thoughts before such an illustrious group. The lecture was later supplemented and published in *Srpski Književni Glasnik.*[8]

In his lecture, Popović singled out the story as the most cultivated literary work. As one of the writers in this field, Laza Lazarević was noted for strong characterization and plot structure portraying people and their entwined lives. Milovan Glišić was cited for writing interesting and clearly outlined stories in an old fashioned way. Matavulj showed the duality of his literary creations in his work, *Bakonja fra Brne* where he conjured an epic caricature, whereas *Primorski običaji (The Customs of the Coastal Region)* showed different traits. Stevan Sremac captured his audience by the token of his irresistible yet simple and healthy humor in spite of his modest invention. Sremac had a tendency to pursue his writing only for the sake of amusement and almost always catered to lower social classes. Ivo Ćipiko and Borisav Stanković showed excellent talents for observation. Svetozar Ćorović improved his craft in a positive fashion. His literary output seemed to continue the tradition of Lazarević. Petar Kočić, in his series of stories about the disciple Simeon, found the right tone in depicting humorous scenes and well wrought images. Radoje Domanović exhibited in his stories both allegory and satire.

Popović thought that the novel was not equally represented. In the past, the novel was favorably represented in the works of Jaša Ignjatović. Svetolik Ranković wrote novels that were to a certain extent reminiscent of Turgenev. Popović concluded: "I wish for a true novel, the way our stories are, taken from life itself, from our miseries and misfortunes."[9]

Comparing the situation in the field of dramatic art, Popović declared that the situation was better, since the fortuitous arrival of Ivo Vojnović to Belgrade. Popović noted that Vojnović was well received as a recognized dramatist. Sometimes even the storywriters turned to drama, as in the case of Matavulj who wrote *Zavjet (Vow)*, Sremac who wrote *Ivkova slava (Ivkov's Celebration)*, Stanković who wrote *Koštana*, and Kočić who wrote *Jazavac pred sudom (Badger in a Court of Law*. Popović commented that Branislav Nušić showed good traits as a playwright.

In his further discussion about Serbian literature, Popović stressed that poetry was especially cultivated among Serbian writers in a fashion similar to storywriting. In particular, Aleksa Šantić enriched Serbian poetry with his poems. In the first phase of his writing, he paid special attention to the music of the flow of words and rhymes, while later he wrote poems that were distinguished as pure lyrical confessions. Jovan Dučić brought freshness of poetic ideas with refinement of cultivated expression. Milan Rakić described strong and sincere feelings. Mileta Jakšić was a lyrical poet with a vivid imagination. The poems of Svetislav Stefanović depicted culture and literary eloquence. Among the younger writers, Popović mentioned Sima Pandurović, Kosorić, and Milan Ćurčin.

The literary criticism was well represented, although Popović bemoaned the death of Nedić. Popović thought that as soon as literary criticism had achieved an independent literary genre and attracted writers devoted only to criticism, its objective value should be elevated. Although Popović's analysis of literary development in Serbia was limited in length, appropriate for publication on the pages of

*Glasnik,* it represented a valuable study. As a contemporary witness of the literary evolution, Popović left an authorative and valuable testimony of the literary scene.[10]

### The Role of the Journal *Srpski Književni Glasnik*

The literary journal, *Srpski Književni Glasnik (The Serbian Literary Herald),* published its two–hundredth volume in February of 1909. Starting from its first issue in February of 1901, many important literary works or works of scientific scope were published in *Glasnik.* Yet *Glasnik* was often under sharp critical attack for different reasons and from different viewpoints. In particular, the ideological concept of the editorial board was criticized. Thus, the journal, *Letopis Matice Srpske (Annals of the Serbian Queen Bee),* noted that *Glasnik* resembled a journal of the French immigrants ". . . like a publication of the society of La France extérieur." Since it was edited according to French paragons, many thought that it had lost the national foundation and relevance.[11]

The editors were aware of the importance of their literary journal in spite of critical commentaries. They firmly believed that the journal presented a cultural document for eventual research of the period. The journal achieved remarkable success in helping the affirmation to Serbian literature by publishing almost all that merited special attention at the time. Thus, the major poetic works of Jovan Dučić and Milan Rakić appeared in *Glasnik* as well as *Stradija (The Calamity)* and *Kraljević Marko po drugi put medju Srbima (Kraljević Marko, the Second Time among the Serbs)* by Radoje Domanović, *Koštana* by Borislav Stanković, *Zona Zamfirova* by Stevan Sremac, *Majčina Sultanija (Mother's Sultana)* by Svetozar Ćorović, the stories of Ivo Ćipiko and Petar Kočić, *Misli (Thoughts)* by Božidar Knežević and some other important works of Serbian literature. From foreign essays and studies *Glasnik* published *Balzak* by H. Taine, *The Future of Arts and Poetry* by M. Guyau, *Milton* by T. Macaulay, *From Freedom to Slavery* by H. Spencer, among others. Special attention was given to translations of literary works such as, *Former People* by Maxim Gorky, *Madame Bovary* by Gustave Flaubert, *Eugénie Grandet* by Honoret de Balzak, *Tartarain on the Alps* by Alfonce Daudet, *Florentine Nights, Nordarnei, and Gods in Exile* by Heinrich Heine, *Adolf* by Benjamin Constant, *The Crime of Sylvestre Bonnard* by Anatole France, *My Life* by Anton Chekhov, *Lauretta* and *The Life and Death of Captain Renot* by Alfred de Vigny, among others.

The editors concluded that the pessimistic predictions of their journal's short duration and its failure were not justified. The response of the Serbian and Slavic press, as well as the steady number of subscribers, attested to the moral and material success of *Glasnik*. Therefore, the editors concluded: "Like a traveler who passed a considerable portion of his journey, leaving a visible and permanent path after him *Srpski Književni Glasnik* cannot refrain from an understandable contentment of its success."[12]

Further accomplishemnts of this journal were recorded only two years later in February of 1911, marking the tenth anniversary of the founding of the journal. The special volume published at that time was sent free to subscribers. Statistical data showed that the journal was favorably received by the public and even better than any journal before it. The number of subscribers reached 1828. The editors remained actively engaged in their effort to fulfill the goals that were set:

> *Srpski Književni Glasnik* is not only endeavoring to preserve tradition but also to continue further on . . . in order to reach the high level of the best modern Western journals, to become a spiritual link between different sections of Serbian people . . . and between the Serbian nation and Serbian literature and the Western world and great Western literature.[13]

Jovan Skerlić, in his evaluation of the cultural and spiritual development in Serbia at the beginning of the twentieth century, stated that progress in Serbian literature was especially connected to the founding of *Srpski Književni Glasnik*. The founder and first editor was Bogdan Popović. Skerlić wrote:

> This was the first Serbian modern literary journal, Western according to its paragons and concepts, but national in its direct goals and literary works. It carried a liberal attitude in literary matters and was open to all talents and all literary generations. The journal had definite ideas in cultivating the literary taste of the public, gave examples of modern literary styles and, always with active literary criticism, and influenced the development of contemporary Serbian literature.[14]

The journal helped to establish the poetic fame of Jovan Dučić, whose poems were published in *Glasnik* over a long period of time. The publications of Dučić's poems also spoke of the acceptance and appreciation of the works of the young poet by distinguished editors and literary critics.

Bogdan Popović pointed out the importance of Dučić's poems, once again, in the introduction of *Antologija Novije Srpske Lirike (Anthology of the Newer Serbian Lyrics)*. Popović declared the poetry of Dučić, Šantić, and Rakić as of the highest order, distinguished by its artistic form and refinement. The expressive and eloquent poetic language was matched with a stylistic virtuosity.[15]

Milan Rakić, who was a poet of great insight and nobility, shared with Dučić a ranking position and was held in great esteem. Rakić described in retrospect the effect of Dučić's novel poetic contribution to the generation of young poets at the beginning of this century when he wrote:

> For me, all of Dučić's poems were a great event. Imagine, to read in our language one poem brought to perfection. The phenomenon of Dučić was for our people a revelation . . . . . I do think that Dučić, more than I, left a mark on an entire generation, an entire period. One can observe what were the wishes and preferences of a whole generation just by examining him.[16]

Dučić started his poetic writing under the influence of Vojislav Ilić. The poetry of Ilić opened new vistas and introduced him to new poetic models and polished poetic forms. Ilić's attitude helped to eliminate the shallow rhetoric marked by the ideology of United Serbian Youth, as well as the notion that artistic poetry was less valuable than folk poetry. The fluidity and grace of Ilić's metrics revealed new possibilities for the Serbian language. Ilić's influence was not limited only to Dučić but encompassed young poets who started writing during the 1890s. Among these poets were Milorad Mitrović, Melita Jakšić and Aleksa Šantić. However, Dučić emulated the poetry of French writers in the subsequent course of his creative path. As a result, Serbian poetry experienced an influx of French poetic modes following Dučić's example.[17]

Dučić published his first collection of poems under the title *Pjesme (Poems)*, in Mostar in 1901. The poems in this collection described the emotions of an adolescent with love being the principal concern in his young consciousness. This collection showed the influence of Vojislav Ilić with the introduction of certain motives as well as in the poetic vocabulary.

It is worth mentioning that the great popularity of Ilić's poetry, among men of letters as well as a wider circle of readers, kindled the idea of presenting a recital of his poetry. The National Theater staged an evening performance of selected poems of Ilić as a novel idea. On this occasion, the dramatic poems Pesnik (Poet), Radoslav, and Periklova smrt (Pericles Death) were recited, accompanied by the specially composed music by Stanislav Binički.[18]

Dučić was influenced even more by the French school of poetry during his stay in France. The poems of Albert Samain and Henri de Regnier were his greatest inspiration there. The second volume of his collected poems, *Pesme (Poems)*, published in Belgrade in 1908, denoted a decisive change in his poetric credo. The form of a poem is in the center of his attention: "Everything depends on the manner in which something is expressed."[19]

Milan Rakić, who was somewhat younger than Dučić, published his first poems in 1902 in the *Srspski Književni Glasnik* journal. Rakić signed his poems with a pseudonym. Even his early poems showed perfection and maturity of expression. His first collection of poems, Pesme (Poems), was published in 1903, and the second collection, Nove pesme (New Poems), appeared in 1912. Rakić's poetry did not reflect the influence of his Serbian poetic predecessors, showing instead the influence of French paragons from the start. Although Rakić did not publish many poems, the outstanding few that he wrote provided an exceptional and lasting place for him in Serbian literature. His poems express his innermost thoughts that are simultaneously personal and are of general human import.[20]

Bogdan Popović, the first editor of the literary journal *Srpski Književni Glasnik,* was musically endowed. He was a competent violinist and played in chamber music ensembles. He even appeared as a soloist with orchestras in concert recitals. Popović had a keen interest in furthering musical development, and musical events were regularly discussed on the pages of *Glasnik.* Besides concert reviews, Popović published studies and essays about different musical topics. Thus, the question of the national musical repertory was often discussed, as well as further development of a national style in music.

Composer Petar Krstić argued about the possibility of introducing the national music idiom into popular plays with singing.[21] Composer and conductor Stevan Hristić wrote a lengthy essay evaluating the contribution of Stevan Mokranjac in the development of Serbian music.[22] Hristić introduced the question of the national musical language in his review of the concert featuring the compositions of Tchaikovsky.[23]

However, Hristić was not consistent in his request for the cultivation of a national musical language. In his musical reviews, he advocated the importance of the national musical idiom, while as composer he did not adhere to this art doctrine. Thus, Hristić composed the first oratorio in Serbian music, Vaskrsenje (Resurrection) in 1912, where his music did not contain folk music inflections. That was precisely the main point which the music critic Milojević addressed to Hristić after the first performance of the oratorio Vaskrsenje.[24]

Miloje Milojević received an invitaiton to serve as music critic in *Srpski Književni Glasnik* in 1908. Milojević wrote the chronicle of musical events for many years. He reviewed the concert appearances of foreign and Yugoslav artists. He also addressed his attention to the repertoire policies and duly informed the public about new musical works. Milojević's first contribution, written for *Glasnik,* was a review of a collections of songs for voice and piano, *Iz naših krajeva (From Our Environs).* The songs in this collection were composed by Petar Konjović–Božinski.

Milojević aimed to present this volume in a wider framework of the past and present state of musical development in Serbia. In evaluating the importance of the newly composed collection of Konjović, Milojević, he displayed his skill as a music critic as well as his considerable erudition. Consequently, Milojević continued to write for the journal and became a well respected authority in the musical field. His criticisms and essays were written with the wish to elucidate musical matters and therefore they had to a certain degree a didactic quality. However, with Bogdan Popović as editor, the journal established similar editorial requirements. Popović believed that a successful journal should serve as a "regulator," in the sense of educating and elevating public awareness of cultural matters. In the course of time, Milojević attained a position in musical circles similar to the one Popović held in the field of literary and fine arts criticism.

In order to place Konjović's collection in the proper context, Milojević concisely presented the development of choral music in Serbia. Until that time, mainly vocal solo repertory and choral compositions were cultivated. Milojević stressed, in particular, the presence of folklore in artistic music and he concluded that an interest in arrangement of folk songs was as old as Serbian musical art itself. Starting with the efforts of Kornelije Stanković, Serbian composers continued arranging folk melodies. What Stanković could not accomplish during his short life eventually was passed on to others to pursue. Josif Marinković and Stevan Mokranjac achieved great skill in pointing out the essential characteristics of folk music inflections in their respective compositions. Mokranjac's Rukoveti (Handfuls) contained essential eand stressed their musical language. Mokranjac harmonized folk melodies stressed their inherent modal qualities. He also unveiled the originality of melody and rhythm peculiar to certain Yugoslav ethnic regions.

Mokranjac's example was followed by composers Joksimović, Binički, Krstić, and Hristić. The efforts of these composers preceded the collection of Konjović. While Konjović's songs were also founded on folk music idiom, they were presented in a thoroughly "modern arrangement."[25]

The journal, *Srpski Književni Glasnik*, played a decisive role in the literary and cultural coalescence of the South Slavs. The men of letters gave due credit to the editors and to their editorial policies in achieving this noble goal. Thus, Marko Car pointed to the merits of *Glasnik* in bringing together the Serbs and Croats. In a spirited essay published in *Glasnik*, Car explored the avenues of possible future collaboration among these two peoples. Car suggested that a consolidation center should be established on the "classical ground of ancient Dubrovnik." Such an undertaking, in the splendid town of Dubrovnik, would provide him with great joy.[26]

Car further explored his visions about starting a new journal. The journal would undertake the cultivation of aesthetic ideals in literature and enhance literary collaboration between Serbs and Croats. With this new endeavor, Car did not want to take over the subscribers from the periodicals which were already established and worthy. Instead, he hoped to introduce more literary taste and clarity because it had become a custom to denote agreeable and clear writing as that of a *feuilleton*. Many thought that only complicated and dull writing was good. Therefore, there appeared in current reviews an amazing number of "wise" books, and cumbersome and exceedingly documented articles that nobody read. These writings were only read by the specialists, that is to say culprits in such crimes and even extolled by them.

Concerning the cultivation of the literary union of Serbs and Croats, Car pointed to greater progress in more recent times. *Srpski Književni Glasnik* and *Savremenik*, the two leading literary journals, strove to help cultural and literary fusion.[27]

Marko Car addressed himself to the question of national art on the pages of *Glasnik* in an essay published in 1914. Car stressed his conviction that the literary production of a people should not be the product of blind imitation of other more advanced nations. Literary production should be the result of one's own energy and expression of a specific national genius. Nationality was rooted not only in common heritage and language, but also in common history, in oral and written literature, and in beliefs and tradition: "The true and pure national culture should always cultivate in one's own fashion that which is commonly human."[28]

Car expressed his concern about the tendency of internationalism in literature. He reminded the readers that he discussed in greater detail this phenomenon in his article about folk literature. These aspirations were a threat to eradicating the national character and deadening to the national spirit. Fortunately, the latest development brought the reaffirmation of the national consciousness, and "a recent exhilaration of our people" brought new national strength. The former apostles of internationalism were becoming less vocal about the international goals in literature.

However, Car was aware that artists often expressed ideas of a certain historical period that in a miraculous way showed common views. This phenomenon united writers and artists alike in different artistic endeavors, even in geographically remote countries, as members of a generation. Car thought that this ability to identify with one sweeping spiritual wave, conditioned by the general material and intellectual development, was able to leave its mark in the creations of veritable and true contemporaries in a unique and peculiar way. Car expressed this thought in the following manner:

> Artistic ideas that revolve around the world do not have nationality. . . if the artist has expressed only himself, his sensitivity, and his personal character. He gave to this idea a new emphasis, and therefore his work should be considered as original, that is national.[29]

Car mentioned some of the arguments that were quoted against the national character in the arts. There were statements that art had no other goal than its own perfection, and therefore no obligation to support any social movement. In opposition to this opinion, Car believed that the arts were endowed with a social obligation that transcended mere appeal: the arts ought to perform an educational and ethnic role as well. Car explained that the proponents of *l'art pour l'art* principle did not exclude other components that an art work should contain, when he wrote:

> I admit the validity of *l'art pour l'art* principle to the peddlers of this axiom in one aspect; that is in the requirement that an art work should be beautiful, but not in the sense that it should only be beautiful, but rather in the first instance beautiful.[30]

In the conclusion of his essay, Car called upon the newly founded Fine Arts Council for organizational affairs of Serbia and Yugoslavia which was started through the initiative of a few artists. Car thought that the program of the Council was well conceived but it was spread out too far, encompassing all South Slavic artists. It could have been better if the Council limited its scope to the Serbian–Croatian–Slovenian community. This spiritual union of Serbs, Croats, and Slovanians achieved a momentum with the   appearance of   Ivan Meštrović. This artist seemed to have understood the validity and greatness of the ethnic and aesthetic peculiarities of the national tradition as well as of its latent energy. Car expressed his confidence that Meštrović would lead the young Yugoslav art to "a healthy and natural path," provided he was able to overcome some stylistic paradoxes.[31]

Car gave, in addition, some recommendations to the critics in order to provide incentive for creation of art works by a token of "honest criticism." The critics should stimulate interest in the arts and also help in establishing an intelligent public. Domestic architecture should be called upon to educate the taste of large numbers of people. Most of all, a concerted effort was needed in order to ensure an advancement of work projects. Therefore, it is not proper to divide the already too few artists into older and younger, into "progressive" and "regressive." By the same precedent, it should not be stated that in comparison to Ivan Grohar and Ivan Meštrović, Vlaho Bukovac and Paja Jovanović "are not more contemporaneous." Such statements are meaningless since valuable works remain notwithstanding the art direction to which they belong.[32]

### The Role of the Journal *Bosanska Vila*

Besides the deserving contribution of the journal, *Srpski Književni Glasnik,* a regional periodical deserves special mention, *Bosanska Vila, list za zabavu, pouku i književnost (Bosnian Fairy, paper for entertainment, instruction and literature,)* published in Sarajevo. *Bosanska Vila* was founded in 1855 as the journal of the Serbian Teachers' Society in Sarajevo. The journal preserved, as a chronicle of its time and place, the thoughts that prevailed. Thus, the journal often served as a political forum by upholding the importance of national unity and promoting the Yugoslav idea.

Vladimir Ćorović presented a comprehensive history of the journal in his address on the occasion of the 25th anniversary of its founding. This festive speech was held at the celebration that took place on 26 December 1911 at the headquarters of the Teachers' Society in Sarajevo. The writer, Petar Kočić, delivered a speech, also, emphasizing the special contribution of Nikola Kašiković as the journal's editor. After these two speeches, there was a performance of a selection of musical compositions.[33]

Ćorović'a speech was consequently published on the first page of the journal, *Bosanska vila* in the January 1912 issue. Ćorović described the development of the journal from its very beginning. At first, the editors paid special attention to the collection and cultivation of varied folklore material, orally transmitted poetry and short stories, and beliefs and customs. Later, when *Bosanska Vila* became a journal with literary tendencies, it served as a forum for young poets and writers. Thus, starting from 1888, the poet Aleksa Šantić published his first verses. In the course of time, Šantić became one of the ardent contributors to the journal, faithfully submitting his numerous poems. Jovan Dučić published his first literary work, a short story, in the same year. Later Dučić contributed a number of his poems to the journal. Svetozar Ćorović began his literary work with a publication that appeared in 1889 on the pages of *Bosanska Vila*. Around the turn of the century, in 1899, Petar Kočić started his literary career with his first published work in *Bosanska Vila*. One of the proponents of new literary ideas, Dimitrije Mitrinović, also published in this journal in 1905.

Nikola Kašiković served as editor of the journal starting in 1887. His contribution was especially noted for his collections of folklore. Ćorović stressed that it was not easy to preserve the existence of the journal. There were some difficult times, as in the instance of prosecution of Dr. Jovan Paču and Dr. Djordje Krasojević:

> The editorial office was considered at times a den of treason.
> . . . One poem or declaration could put in jeopardy its entire existence, as in the case of Dučić, and when adolescent high school students, like Petar Kočić, were considered dangerous rebels. . . . Accomplishing 25 years of useful activities, *Vila* became more powerful and started to develop further with greater decisiveness. . . . *Vila* should remain Bosnian, but also Serbian, always aware of the great communion to which we belong.[34]

Aleksa Šantić wrote a poem commemorating the celebration of the founding, under an appropriate title, Himna Bosanske vile (Hymn of the Bosnian Fairy). The composer, Fr. Maćejovski, used the hymn as the basis for his festive composition for soloist and male choir. The composition was performed by the members of the Serbian Choral Society, Sloga, with the participation of the soloist M. Kulačić. In addition, two compositions by Stevan Stojanović Mokranjac were featured, Zaigrajte srca živa (Dance Wholeheartedly) and Primorski napjevi (The Songs from the Coastal Region). Petar Perunić performed a selection of epic folk songs accompanying himself on the stringed instrument, gusle. The program came to an end with a composition for male choir, The Autumn Arrived, by Stanislav Binički.[35]

In the second part of the program, a dance took place. Among the public attending the concert were Muslim and Croatian guests who wished to affirm the importance of the celebration with their presence. During the celebration, over 200 telegrams arrived and there were many written congratulations. High dignitaries, like King Petar I of Serbia, King Nikola of Montenegro, and Victor Emanuel of

Italy, sent their congratulations, confirming the exceptional standing that the journal enjoyed. The editor of the journal, Nikola Kašiković, received a laurel wreath which was presented by the Philantropic Organization of Serbian Ladies, as a gesture of appreciation. [36]

The journal often served as a forum for discussion about not yet attained goals of education and literary and artistic collaboration. The poet, Sima Pandurović, wrote often about the different tasks awaiting men of letters. In his editorial under the characteristic title "Bez programa" (Without a Program), on the front page of the journal *Bosanska Vila,* Pandurović noted that literature in Serbia and Bosnia showed signs of disorder and regional separatism. In his deliberations about possible causes of this state, Padurović pointed out that historical national development and public life were conditioned by the lack of political unity. All these factors prevented the South Slavic cultural coalescence. Pandurović thought that there was a veritable need for literary manifestoes and programs so that further work could be planned with specific goals in mind. Comparing the more recent development of literary schools and movements, Pandurović concluded that, in a literary history, important dates are created by outstanding individuals or more often by schools with their manifestoes and organized work on new ideas and methods.[37]

Pandurović noted that present Serbian literature was qualitatively better and richer with numerous published works. There are men versed in education and artistic concepts equal to any in their erudition with European schooling:

> The writers of today stand far ahead as compared to the writers of previous times, if compared according to their literary erudition, artistic means, invention, aesthetic qualities of their poetry, richness of their emotion, and expression. Today's diletantes and high school students write better poetry than Branko Radičević and Zmaj.[38]

However, the writers were in a difficult position and faced new tasks, since they were expected to amend in a few decades all that European nations had achieved in several centuries. In their quest for progress, the position of writers became even more difficult. By covering great intellectual distances, writers were approaching the period of enlightened Europe, yet at the same time they removed themselves from their own cultural environment, a largely uneducated people in a backward country. Besides, the literary public was not large and it was not sufficiently educated. It was necessary to cultivate their taste as an indispensable step towards popularization of literature. Until recently, the writers left this task to the critics and to their opinions which were published in daily newspapers. Therefore, the public heard only one side. The writers were "lonely, not organized, confused, working every man for himself." Pandurović believed that it was necessary to organize and work out one or several literary programs of this generation. The founders of eminent literary schools were not critics but poets. However, literary schools, theories, and criticisms do not alone produce artists. On the other hand, the artists should have their own literary theories, schools, and critics. As much as literary education is indispensable, it is of importance that "the modern artist should know what he wants . . . (and) prepare his program."[39]

Another writer, Dr. Milutin Uskoković, also wrote on the pages of *Bosanska Vila* about the lack of literary tradition in an insufficiently developed social milieu. Uskoković noted that not sufficient attention has been given to encourage the development of an important literary form such as the novel. One should only remember that the Russian writers gave in the form of their novels the best contribution to the cultural treasury of their people. Scandinavian writers, such as Hamsun and Lagerlöf as well as some other modern writers, cultivated this literary genre to a great extent. The Polish people have writers like Sienkiewicz and Przybyczewski who produced splendid works and "confirmed that Poland had not yet perished."[40]

Uskoković thought that an undeveloped milieu did not represent an obstacle for the cultivation of novels. Social life abounded with material for social novels in such situations as the sudden rise of some individuals from debased social positions to higher ranks or the crises that appear with penetration of changes into the patriarchal style of the life of the people. In addition, the transformation from modest entrepreneur to capitalism could serve as a theme for a novel, as well as the question of the rise of the intelligentsia and of bureaucracy:

> All these are nice themes for analyses and veritable mines of excellent material for description of comical and tragical situations, great subjects for great works. In order to arrange this raw material, our writers lack a number of things available to the novelist of the cultured people—in the first place we lack tradition.[41]

In countries with a long literary tradition, as in France, the novel developed over a long period of time. There were times when one publisher produced a new novel every day. The writers who decided to write novels already found existing forms, dialogues, and landscapes. What was even more important was the presence of a public that was used to accepting graciously "the literary fictions out of their own life and immediate surroundings."

Uskoković stressed that there was only a modest number of writers who devoted attention to the Serbian novel. Some of them wrote only one novel and then stopped. Milovan Vidaković was the first to commence work on a novel. As a result, he was assaulted, hurt, and ridiculed, despite his endeavors. It is not hard to find mistakes in Vidaković's work, but it behooves one to remember the time when Vidaković wrote his novels. It was a society of largely illiterates—the ruling prince did not know how to read. Vidaković, with his innocent soul, lauded the raptures of *Ljubomir in Elysium* as well as the love of *Selimir and Milena*. In spite of his shortcomings, Vidaković opened the path for further development of the Serbian novel. At the time, Vidaković had a large reading public and he helped create an audience for this literary genre. The novel, *Dva idola (Two Idols)*, by Bogoboj Atanacković presented the next step in the development of the novel. Jakov Ignjatović created a number of realistic novels that preserved their place in Serbian literature.

Milutin Uskoković, the author of this essay on the Serbian novel, wrote a novel himself under the title *Došljaci (Newcomers)*, published in 1910. *Došljaci* appeared under the auspicies of the Srpska knjiknjiževna zadruga (Serbian Literary Society) and immediately attracted the attention of the critics and public alike. The novel was declared in the review published in *Srpski Književni Glasnik* as "the book that one can read" and also as "the evidence of the power of the whole younger generation of novelists."[42]

Uskoković started his literary career with short sketches, impressions, and poems in prose. His first two books, *Pod životom (Under the Life)* and *Fragmenta vitae (Fragments of Life)*, presented him as a talented writer with an acuity of perception and with considerable stylistic skill.

In his novel, *Došljaci,* Uskoković depicted people who came to Belgrade from the provinces, dragging their suitcases, worried and determined at the same time. These were the newcomers who presented, at that time, the majority of inhabitants of Belgrade, except for a minority of oldtimers mainly of Greek and Jewish origin. The popularity of Uskoković's novels derived also from the fact that the readers could recognize themselves, and their consciousness was stirred up by the complexity that life presented at the time.[43]

The literary contribution of Petar Kočić attracted the attention of the critics and the public, and he enjoyed growing popularity. Kočić started his literary career with a collection of short stories, *S planine i ispod planine (From the Mountain and Under the Mountain)*, published in 1902. Soon followed two more collections under the same title.  The second book was published in 1904, and third was published in 1905.  Kočić's storytelling became better and more independent with every new book as he discarded previous literary examples.  Great success marked Kočić's satire, *Jazavac pred sudom (The Badger in the Court of Law)*, published in Vienna in the old and esteemed journal of Serbian students, *Zora*.  In a few short years, from the first edition until 1913, it was published in Cyrillic and Latin alphabets in 11 consecutive editions.[44]

The literary works of Petar Kočić was especially honored with an editorial which appeared in *Bosanska vila* in 1911.  The fact that the editorial was written by the famous poet, Jovan Dučić, was a special tribute to Kočić.  Dučić stressed that before the literary ascent of Kočić and his generation, including Ivo Ćipiko and Veljko Milićević, the Serbian village novel resembled a national prejudice since it was likened to a legend or even to idle talk.  Milovan Glišić and Janko Veselinović became aware during their lifetime that they were losing the reading public.  Kočić introduced already in his first stories an exceptional freshness of language and description of nature.  His prose had acquired "a happy and strong pulsation."[45]

Kočić depicted the village and villagers in a new and different way, as opposed to the previous idealized manner of Veselinović.  The village in Veselinović's story is an ideal place where autumn brings picturesque weddings with beautifully attired young men and women.  Kočić talks about the adolescents who, due to circumstances, were sent overseas at an early age to seek better ways, or were drafted into military duty where they were badly treated, even beaten.  The mountainous villages were devasted with heavy taxation and whims of Turkish agas and armed officials.  Dučić concluded:

> Kočić's books are the most patriotic ones in our entire literature. . . .  These are rhapsodies about the wretched peasant who is a martyr as opposed to the poetized peasant in golden garments with his grandfather's silver guns to shoot at weddings and church celebrations, as presented by Vaselinović. [46]

However, Dučić noted that Kočić mostly painted the environs and people in his stories instead of recounting events.  Kočić did not pay enough attention to composition and to deep structure.  He should also have abandoned the habit of using the local dialect, but he followed the bad example of Sremac.  Dučić thought that it was especially wrong to deal with current topics.  The misfortune that plagued the villages was the consequence of a difficult regime.  These were not eternal human conflicts or dissentions with higher moral and social principles because these were largely problems of subjugated people:

> The immortal story about man, that is the story about the immortal in us, about the good fortunes and misfortunes of men that are unchangeable in time and space. That is how one reads the tragedies of Sophocles and how one reads novels like *Salambo*.[47]

Dučić did not realize that the suffering of the Bosnian enslaved population was the same as the suffering of any other occupied nation deprived of basic human rights. Kočić depicted the eternal confrontation of those seemingly stronger by their brutal power and of those who defended human dignity and spirituality while disguised by the rags of poverty. Kočić's stories perceived truth about human conditions that surpassed the ephemeral framework of their setting. In addition, Kočić's stories presented a faithfully preserved testimony transposed in an artistic manner, achieving universality.

Jovan Dučić wrote a lengthy review in 1911 about the recently published poetic collection, *Utopljene duše (Drowned Souls)*, by Vladislav Petković Dis. The review appeared under the characteristic title, "The False Modernism in Serbian Literature," and was published in the journal, *Srpski Književni Glasnik*. Skerlić expressed scorn since he believed that the poems in this collection presented decadence and a lowly desire for "the paradise of mud." *Utopljene duše* contained the program of the new art:

> *Utopljene duše* forces us to accept without any restrictions the words of Taine-poetry, that is healthy. They instruct us to truly love the sincerity, naturalness, purity, faith, enthusiasm of spirit and the soul, and idealism in poetry. These words bring reconciliation with the previous and older poets, Njegoš, Zmaj, Jakšić, and Vojislav Ilić, and teach us to love their true, alive, and lifegiving poetry, poetry of their life that is at the same time poetry of our life, always young and modern, all-human poetry, poetry in one word.[48]

The poetry of Petković Dis found another response among the collaborators of the literary chronicle of the journal *Bosanska vila*. Thus, M. Dimitrijević presented with words of praise the new collection of poems by Petković Dis. Dimitrijević noted the musical cascade of verses, lively presentations of the content, sometimes approaching hallucinations. Dimitrijević thought that Petković Dis' poetic philosophy was more sensual than contemplative and therefore close to the nature of a painter than a philosopher. Dimitrijević stressed that while Pandurović was a proven master of rhymes, Petković Dis was a connoisseur of versification. Pandurović, Uskoković, and Petković Dis were products of a social milieu and interpreters of pessimism, confusion, and incompleteness.[49]

Branko Lazarević also wrote about Petković Dis' collection of poems, *Utopljene duše*, in an article entitled "Poet of the verse and tension," which was published in *Bosanska vila*, during the same year, 1911. Lazarević noted that there are divided opinions about the verses of this poet:

> According to one side, he (Petković Dis, J.M.Dj.) is "deca-
> dent" and a "symbolist," and a very good poet (interpreting
> like this—he is a very good poet because he is decadent and
> a symbolist). According to others, he is "decadent" and a
> "symbolist" and a very bad poet because he is decadent and
> a symbolist (interpreting like this—he is a very bad poet
> because he is decadent and a symbolist.)[50]

Lazarević thought that these opinions were not adequate as a critical evaluation. Those who uphold decadence and symbolism as the best expressions of the innermost consider Petković Dis as a fine poet. Others who uphold nationalistic poetry as well as the philosophy of positivism, work, and a healthy attitude negate the value of Petković Dis' poetry. Lazarević stressed that critics should not be partisans of a particular faction or school of thought.

> We critics are people that enter countless homes of other
> people, but our own we do not have . . . if we do not
> have a home, we have many because we are good friends
> of all artists, and their home is our home . . . . All big
> supporters of a "school" are already on a wrong path by the
> very fact that they are such (supporters—J.M.Dj.).[51]

Lazafević, in his capacity as critic, endeavored to determine whether symbolism or decadence was a direct expression of the intimate beliefs of poets or a superficial quality modeled after a school of thought. Most important for a poet was to "sing his song, in his own mode and to sing it well." Lazarević concluded that Petković Dis "sings his song" although he is not alone in this task. In a similar vein, poems were written by Sima Pandurović, Dušan Malušev, and sometimes by Dimitrije Mitrinović and Svetislav Stefanović. Isidora Sekulić and L. Mihailović wrote in a similar manner in prose. However, Lazarević stressed that Petković Dis wrote several poems that should remain in literature. They were Predgradje (Suburb), Tišina (Silence), Bol i Stid (Pain and Shame), Himna (Hymn), and especially Nirvana. [52]

Apparently the collection *Utopljene duše* attracted wide attention. Views of the critics varied and caused an impression of controversy. An unknown critic wrote a review without signature discussing this fact. The critic was probably a member of the editorial board since he addressed Petković Dis as "our collaborator" with obvious pride. The critic summed up the situation and added that Petković Dis' book attracted numerous yet varied responses. Jovan Skerlić published in *Srpski Književni Glasnik* a negative opinion. Skerlić, as a proponent of moral health and nationalism in literature, censored what he believed to be the moral atrophy. Skerlić did not believe in Petković's bohemian and disenchanted attitude. On the other hand, Svetozar Stefanović wrote about visionary qualities in Petković Dis' literary creations in the journal *Brankovo kolo*. Stefanović acknowledged Petković's poetic talent and considered him as the true and "God given poet." In the journal, *Savremenik (The Contemporary)*, Dragutin Domjanić perceived Petković Dis' poetry as a vision of a solitary and dark lake permeated with dreams. Above the lake there is a somber cloud and all around there is peace and sorrow. Domjanić concluded: "This is a desolate yet a good book." In the journal, *Bosanka vila,* Dimitrije Mitrinović portrayed Petković Dis "as our legitimate poet, decadent in his morals and in poetic form." According to Mitrinović, Petković Dis had lively dynamics and tone in his poetry, which was proof of his great talent. However, his expression is not always clear. In addition, Dis' poetry was reviewed in the Croatian journal, *Pokret (The Movement)*. The reviewer, Stjepan Parmačević, pointed out the sincerity of the poetic expression and melodic quality of the verses.[53]

Petković Dis' collection of poems, *Utopljene duše*, stirred a very lively response. The numerous critical reviews testified that the book was regarded as a notable literary event. The diverse interpretations of the significance of the poems explained also the criteria and opinions of respective reviewers.

Dimitrije Mitrinović contributed often to the journal, *Bosanska vila*. In an article with a programatic connotation, he discussed the role of tendency in literature. Mitrinović thought that a literary work may comprise an expressed tendency, but is purely artistic, patriotic or any other, if it displays sufficiently artistic qualities: "If it is truly literary, then it should be sufficiently artistic in order to be artistic notwithstanding the tendency, and it should carry within innnermost poetry even if it is the poetry of pain, sin, darkness, ugliness, and humor."[54]

Mitrinović thought that Serbian literature in Bosnia should have a specific character and social value. That did not mean that political articles should be written in literary forms like stories or patriotic songs. In such instances, patriotism prevailed to such an extent that these works ceased to truly remain poems or stories. Furthermore, Mitrinović thought that one should not think that a literary work would become national if it presented "only one side of general national life." Aleksa Šantić often found a fortuitious balance between artistic and patriotic tendencies in his poems. In a similar fashion, Petar Kočić managed to produce recurringly poetically inspired passages that were successful and that were "beautiful because they were Serbian, Bosnian, and from Krajina." Mitrinović also tried to advance his idea about the necessity of cultivating a feeling of Yugoslav cultural interdependence. However, Mitrinović understood the term Yugoslav in a broader sense, as established during the preparations of the First Yugoslav Art Exhibit in Belgrade in 1904. This historic exhibit brought together artists from Slovenia, Croatia, Serbia, and Bulgaria. The artists felt that the term Yugoslav identified their aspirations. Mitrinović reiterated that Bosnian and Serbian literature should consider Croatian literature and Croatian people as their own. Later on, an effort should be made to establish closer ties with Slovenian and Bulgarian literature.

Mitrinović also gave credit to the editors of the journal *Bosanska vila* for their dedicated work. The editors managed during a period of 25 years to fulfill their national function very well, especially in view of difficulties experiences in an occupied region. The journal started first with the collections of ethnographic and folkloric material. It included also publications of speeches with a patriotic connotation held during the yearly celebrations of Saint Sava. In addition, the journal published reports of varied choral societies and reading rooms that were fostering nationalistic activities. These were the beginnings of the journal, mainly directed towards preservation of a national unity. Later on, *Bosanska vila* became a forum for writers from Bosnia as well as from Serbia. The journal also gave decisive support to young writers from Bosnia and Hercegovina. Some of these writers, in the course of time, became respected literary figures.

In a certain period of time, some remarkable literary contributions were published in *Bosanska vila*, which helped to establish the fame of the writers and that of the journal. The works of renowned writers like Janko Veselinović, Stevan Sremac, Simo Matavulj, and many others were published on the pages of *Bosanska vila*. This helped to strengthen the reputation of the journal. There were also less favorable times when the journal experienced a "low tide" due to the scarcity of appropriate literary material for publication. The critics were keen to notice such fluctuations. Mitrinović explained that, in such an instance, a critic addressed a plea to the Bosnian writers to help overcome the crisis. The critic suggested that the writers should rally around "the miserable *Bosanska vila*" in order to help improve the existing literary policy.[55]

In another shorter article, Mitrinović stated that the literary works written in folk style still enjoyed a large following. It seemed to him that anthologies of modern works would not attract a large public. In comparison, the stories and poems written in folk style would sell much better since these works were more popular.

Mitrinović tried to discourage the widespread belief that the category of folk literature should be interpreted as contrary and even contradictory to the category of modern literature. In a mildy mocking fashion, Mitrinović noted that the public would rather read the collected works of Veselinović which could be published under a meaningless title, such as, *Jes, jakako, o brale, o nano (Yeah, Oh Brother, Oh Ma)*. The same could be true for the would-be publication of collected poems of Milorad Petrović under a similar title, *Sjajni mjesec, eto tako, to sam bio ja (Bright Moon, in this Way, That Was I)*.

Mitrinović concluded that there existed a firm conviction that the modernization of society meant the defeat of the people and inherent national ideals and individuality. Contrary to this belief, Mitrinović trusted that Serbian literature could fall under the strong influence of modern trends and still remain Serbian.[56]

On the pages of *Bosanska vila,* Mitrinović often maintained the importance of the Yugoslav idea. Mitrinović supported the spiritual unity of Serbs and Croats in a review of the poetry of Vladimir Nazor. Already in the opening lines, in discussing the verses by Nazor, Mitrinović wrote:

> Mr. Vladimir Nazor is our poet. He is Serbian yet he is
> a Croatian poet. He is a poet worthy of being honored
> sincerely and should be read with pleasure and often . . .
> . He is a man from a race that has feelings . . . (he is)
> Slovenian, Croatian, Serbian, that is *ours* in the manner of
> expression used by our great sculptor Ivan Meštrović.[57]

Mitrinović thought that Nazor's poetry instilled the fighting spirit and wish to win. His verses have some of the dynamic traits that permeate the sculptures of Meštrović. In particular, Mitrinović singled out Nazor's hymn of life as poetry of "the winner and of an honorable man."[58]

In comparison to the serenity of Nazor's lyrics, Serbian poetry did not have, at the time, such a healthy glow. Mitrinović endeavored to present a comprehensive review of the existing state of Serbian and Croatian poetry in a series of interesting observations. Thus, Mitrinović stated that, in Serbia, Sima Pandurović deplored the wounds inflicted by life itself. Mihovil Nikolić wrote about similar attitudes. These feelings were familiar to Mitrinović and he liked the poetry of both poets. Veljko Petrović started writing stories and Mileta Jakšić withdrew. Nestor Žučni, was the pen name of Proka Jovkić. He lived for a long time in California and was not a real and true artist. Rakić discovered in his last poems some patriotic and lyrical accents. Šantić was turning his attention to dramatic works. Mitrinović voiced his fear that dramatic form would not allow an expression of gentle force that emanated from Šantić's lyrical poems, especially in his patriotic poetry.

According to Mitrinović's evaluation, the situation in Croatia was not better. Kranjčević was dead and Tresić had stopped writing poetry. Begović went to Hamburg to study dramaturgy. Domjanić wrote poems occasionally with mild erotic connotations. Only Nazor still continued to write verses:

> Only Nazor, far in Kastava, unknown and single, holds the flag and sings. He is here, Serbs! Croats! Here is a poet among us! Love him, read him! He is celebrating life and victory, he is the one who loves the sun and wind, Nazor the cricket and singer of joy.[59]

Pera Slepčević often contributed to *Bosanska vila*. At one point, Slepčević observed a new development in contemporary dramaturgy. The dramatic form that was evolving was very likely spurred on by wishes of many artists to explore new avenues. Slepčević thought that this new form of drama could best be described as folk drama. This wish for novelty was present in other art forms. One should remember that the German composer, Wagner, at one time exclaimed, "Kinder macht Neues."[60]

The advent of this new form of drama inaugurated a distinct democratic content which was opposed to former presentations of eminent individuals. In the former drama, it was customary to portray gods, kings, heroes, and much later, ordinary citizens. Instead of monologues of noble personages from Shakespeare's dramas, Hamlet or Richard III, Ibsen's dramas introduced a different discourse in that respect.

Folk drama presented a populistic content where the voice of the people was heard. As forerunners of folk dramas Slepčević quoted the *Empire of Darkness* by Tolstoy and *On the Bottom* by Gorky, *The Weavers* and *The Spiders* by Hauptmann, and *Trust in Home* by Schönherr. Slepčević quoted among Serbian dramas *Gorski vijenac (Mountain's Wreath)* as weakest in its dramatic aspect yet strongest as an artistic work.[61]

Slepčević stated that drama corresponded best to contemporary and hasty life filled with tensions. Perhaps this fact could explain the popularity of drama as a literary form. However, in some literary works, there existed a blur of boundaries that delineated dramatic, epic or lyric creations. Slepčević thought that Verharen's poetic work approached drama. Some of Hofmannstahl's dramatic works could be understood as a set of lyrical poems. Tolstoy's drama, *The Empire of Darkness* could be linked to a novel. The dramas of Maeterlinck as well as *Hännelin's Road to Heaven* by Hauptmann were as much lyrical poems as dramatic works. The event of the folk drama was an interesting phenomenon since it occurred parallel to existing individualistic tendencies. Slepčević was not sure about the future of this literary form.

Sima Pandurović, a poet, wrote a leading article for *Bosanska vila* under the characteristic title of "Tedious Literature." Pandurović stated that at the present time there were no clearly established literary movements in literature. Some of the writers were still influenced by the Russian Utilitarian School of the 1870s, akin to realism and depicting "histories of lesser people." These writers have not yet found a way to separate themselves from their old models and their dependency was shown in the form and content of their work. Pandurović pleaded for taking more freedom in the process of creating new works in order to surpass these limitations:

> It is necessary that these horizons be broadened and that those who write take a closer look at everyday appearances in depicting the past and in entering into all avenues of life. It is necessary to differentiate literary forms, to take indispensable excursions into the unresearched areas of experience and phantasy. . . . It is necessary (to have) more freedom and less stereotypes.[62]

Pandurović thought that only in such a manner would there be a possiblity for the appearance of really lasting works that would entertain and provide pleasure to several generations. The artists should rely more on their instinct and ignore the requirements of their environment and dated ideas from 40 years ago. One had to discard obsolescent influences and introduce original ideas, personal impressions, and in-depth observations to develop one's own style. A talented mind should have freedom to explore. If the freedom was limited, as a bird in a cage, one could discern that the poets considered that there was not room in the arts for banalities. The verses of Jovan Dučić, Milan Rakić, Veljko Petrović were examples of this period.[63]

Svetislav Stefanović maintained that poetry also contained sub-

stantial criticism. If poetry did not repesent criticism, then it did
not fulfill the essential task of poetry. Analogous to this statement, if
criticism did not possess poetic sensibility, it could not be considered
as real criticism. Stefanović mentioned that these thoughts occupied
him for a long time. This article gave him a chance to present his
ideas in writing for the first time.[64]

Stefanović quoted the artistic concept of Richard Wagner as an
example of a new and different comprehension. The borderlines between varied art forms should disappear in the future, including those
dividing criticism and fine arts. Stefanović supported the opinion of
Oscar Wilde, stating that criticism was art, and he further advanced
his own belief about art fulfilling the task of criticism. The critical
character of the fine arts was deeper and more discreet. Stefanović
pointed to the literary works of Anatole France in order to corroborate
his thesis about art as criticism. France's works displayed a profound
criticism of different aspects of human existence within a varied social
and economic framework. Stefanović thought that France's literary
thought was permeated with criticism, starting with his inspiration,
as well as character and style of his works.

Stefanović, a poet himself, wrote *The Letter to a Critic* as a result
of his contemplations about the true meaning of poetry. Stefanović
stressed the belief that fine arts, including poetry, elucidated human
spirituality as a creative force in shaping varied human activities.
Poetry was perceived as truthful and even as criticism, debating the
notion of *l'art pour l'art* ideology. In the unruly period preceding
World War I, poets aimed at expressing concern rather than engaging
in a delightful exercise in words.

Sima Pandurović wrote another editorial for *Bosanska vila*, which
was published in 1912 under the title *Modernism in Literature*. Pandurović shared his concern about the tasks facing him and his generation of writers. The writers tried to solve the existing dichotomy
between the categories of Nationalism and Modernism. Pandurović
felt that the time had come for the writers to unite their literary
schools and associations in order to encourage collaboration. The
impending political situation made it necessary to understand the
national plight:

> The assignments that face the coeval literary generation can
> be reduced to these words: modernization and nationaliza-
> tion of literature. The stipulation is that in the organized
> work of literary schools and literary associations, one has to
> oneself establish and work with individual freedom. . . .
> In that way, national and modern literature should be es-
> tablished, both large and integral, and it should become one

of the cornerstones of the national and modern state of our nation.[65]

Pandurović wrote often for *Bosanska vila* in the capacity of an informed and eloquent literary critic and theoretician. In addition to his thorough knowledge of the literary and cultural situation, Pandurović, with a profound sensibility of poet and writer, anticipated possible solutions to present problems and pointed to perspectives in further development. The editors of the journal appreciated the depth of Pandurović's observations and often printed his articles on the front page of the journal in the form of an editorial. Thus, Pandurović's opinions seemed to be supported and upheld by the editors. In his editorials Pandurović addressed most often the tasks and problems facing writers. However, in his editorial in the May 1914 issue of *Bosanska vila*, his attention was focussed on the reading public. Pandurović noticed that the number of readers had increased steadily but it was not large enough to give the necessary support to a continuing literary development. In comparison to other more numerous European peoples, the public was still small and uneducated. Pandurović thought that this situation should change in a relatively short time. Thus, the intellectual and moral needs of this new public ought to help the literary development with an increased interest and dissemination of literary works. The increased revenues should help to separate the literary works from other activities and receive all due attention. All these changes should beneficially affect the literary endeavors.

However, Pandurović was aware that the subsequent and possibly accelerated development did not depend on the public alone. At least one third of this task should be shouldered by the writers themselves, who, unfortunately, besides their writing, performed diverse other jobs too numerous to mention. The writers thus dissipated their energy and did not give all that they could in proportion to their talent. That was the reason why they did not reach all the public they could. Yet, the writers themselves often voiced their belief that the small and uneducated public should be blamed alone for all the difficulties in the literary field.[66]

The publication of the *Antologija novije srpske lirike (Anthology of Newer Serbian Lyrical Poems)*, written by Bogdan Popović, was an exceptional accomplishment. Pandurović was prompted to review the collection for the readers of *Bosanska vila*. In his review, Pandurović expressed his admiration for the artistic perfection achieved in the *Anthology*. For the last 100 years in Serbian cultural and literary life there had not been another anthology of poems that could be compared with Popović's selections. Popović accomplished a remarkable deed thanks to the meticulous and conscientious efforts, first, in selecting, and second, in properly placing poems in a well chosen order as to enhance with such juxtaposition every poem in his *Anthology*. Popović, as esteemed professor of comparative literature and aesthetics, used his knowledge in selecting the poems for the *Anthology*, which resulted in an exceptional work.

However, Pandurović had some disagreements with Popović's periodization. Popović divided Serbian poetry into three periods. The poet, Milan Rakić, was placed in the second period that covered the time span between 1880 and 1900. Pandurović agreed that the second period of lyric poetry justly started around 1880 with the advent of poetry by Vojislav Ilić. Milan Rakić, on the other hand, although he was born in 1876, published his poetry only in 1902 for the first time. Therefore, the placement of Rakić in the second period did not correspond to the truth of the matter.

Pandurović thought that Popović's *Anthology* did not receive the attention that it deserved. Jovan Skerlić was the only one to review the book in *Letopis Matice srpske (The Annals of the Serbian Queen Bee)*, and there were no other seriously written reviews or comments. Pandurović stressed that the selection of poems was superb. Not one poem that was included in the *Anthology* should have been omitted. Pandurović also expressed his hope that Popović's work would be continued in the future.[67]

## The Founding of the University of Belgrade

The higher education statute in Serbia was enacted in 1863 with the founding of the first institution of higher learning, Velika Škola (Academy) in Belgrade. In that year, Prince Mihailo M. Obrenović III proclaimed publicly and approved "The legislature on the founding of Velika Škola (Academy) as a scientific institution for higher and professional education." On that occasion, three colleges were established—College of Philosophy, College of Law, and College of Technical Sciences. The Academy developed quickly and efficiently to prepare students for future professional and scientific employment. The success achieved was due to the leadership and dedicated work of scientists and professors who were themselves trained abroad.[68]

In the course of time, the increased enrollment as well as the growing need for highly trained professionals pointed to the necessity of expanding the Velika Škola into a university. Many well known scientists and professors pleaded for the necessity of such a scientific and educational institution. Dr. Svet. Radovanović discussed the possibility of founding a university in Belgrade. In a booklet published in 1901, Radovanović stressed that the thought about a university was not new—it was on the cultural agenda and already discussed

50 years ago. In order to justify the rekindling of this question, Radovanović noted that the presence of a university could provide a powerful instrument in political and economic affirmation and advancement. Serbia and Montenegro were the only two independent countries in Europe without a university.[69]

The booklet by Dr. M. Jovanović–Batut, published a year later in 1902, was written in a similar vein. At the time the author was the rector of the Velika Škola in Belgrade. Jovanović–Batut raised the question about the impending needs that the university could ameliorate.[70]

The opening of the First Yugoslav Art Exhibit in 1904 presented an affirmation of the achievements of Yugoslav people in cultural and artistic fields. The exhibit also had a national and political connotation which promoted the union between the South Slavic people. Gauging public awareness on the importance of further development in cultural and artistic fields, Professor Petar M. Vukićević thought that the right moment had come to remind the public about the importance of the founding of a university as a vanguard for future growth. While Velika Škola was meant to serve the educational goals of Serbia, the university would serve the Yugoslav community in a broader national configuration.[71]

Vukićević described the enthusiastic and accelerated work which, accompanied with good will, solved many of the unfinished tasks:

> The numerous problems and goals associated with our cultural development and social life, as well as those that are political and national, are permeated with aspirations for duration, progress, and perfection. Our future depends on the correct solution of these complicated questions which are solved today only with training and science. . . . Velika Škola, as it exists at present, does not perform this task. . . . It is necessary to perfect the school and change it . . . transform it into a school of a higher rank, into a university.[72]

Vukićevic stressed the need for a number of bright and well trained scientists in "all areas of the sciences and in scientific applications." It is necessary to cultivate educated generations from many South Slav regions. The new project of the legislature, relating to the future university, was prepared in this spirit. The project was scheduled to be submitted to Parliament for further discussion.[73]

The obstacles that prevented the transformation of the Academy into a university derived mainly from disorderly political and economic circumstances that prevailed in Serbia at that time. It was only with the introduction of the Constitution and a democratic regime that the legislation for the university was finally accepted on 19 February 1905. Instead of the former three colleges in the Academy, the university would have five separate colleges—College of Theology, College of Philosophy, College of Law, College of Medicine, and College of Engineering. In addition, two separate courses were planned, one in agriculture and the other in pharmacy.[74]

Prior to the founding of the university, Velika Škola attracted a number of outstanding scientists who taught and, at the same time, continued to excel in their research. Jovan Cvijić taught geography and geomorphological mathematics and differential equations; Jovan Žujović taught geographic maps; Sima Lozanić taught chemistry and electrosynthesis; Sava Urošević taught mineralogy with petrogrpahy; Milan Nedeljković taught astronomy and meteorology.[75]

After the founding of the university, Lozanić became its first rector while Jovan Cvijić acted as the first dean of the College of Philosophy. Lozanić delivered a speech on the occasion of the inauguration of the university:

> It is known that the German and Italian universities became prime agents which prepared their respective unifications by cultivating the national consciousness. Therefore, I believe that our university will peform the same service for the Serbian people and for the unification of Yugoslav countries.[76]

Besides the teaching of duties by the scientists that were dispatched with great dedication, these scientists introduced Serbian scientific thought to the realm of Europe during this period.[77]

Shortly after the founding of the university, there followed a reorganization in grouping of interdependent subjects, minimizing the differences in curriculum as compared to European universities. The College of Philosophy was advanced from a solely educational institution to include research projects. The pursuit of research was granted due to the exceptional authority of the professors serving as faculty members. Thus, the following scientists and humanists taught at the College of Philosophy at the time of its founding in 1904–05: mathematicians, Bogdan Gavrilović and Mihailo Petrović; archeologists, Nikola Vulić and Miloje Vasić; Slavists and philogists, Aleksandar Belić, Ljuba Stanojević, and Radovan Košutić; ethnologists, Jovan Erdeljanović and Tihomir Djordjević; literary theoreticians and historians, Bogdan Popović, Jovan Skerlić, and Veselin Čajkanović; philosopher, Branislav Petronijević; biologist, Ivan Djaja; seismologist, Jelenko Mihailović.[78]

The enrollment increased steadily. However, as the student body increased, the former ideological unity ceased to exist. Rather, a new atmosphere was characterized by a diversity of opinionated clubs and groups. This spiritual climate among the students was described in an article published in 1910. There were not any active cultural-patriotic organizations to help promote closeness. The only honorable exception was the well known choral society, Obilić. On the other hand, every new student quickly joined one of the numerous clubs or political parties. There were more political factions and clubs than recognized political parties in the Serbian Parliament. The anonymous writer of this review must have been a student himself or one who had recently graduated since he wrote knowledgeably and with conviction about this situation.

The writer had the impression that students had lost in their views and in their ideas the wide horizon that used to be the hallmark of university youth at the beginning of the century. Very likely this impression was corroborated by the writer's still vivid memory of two major cultural events organized largely by the students in 1904–the Youth Congress and the opening of the First Yugoslav Art Exhibit which marked the centennial celebration of the Serbian uprising.[79]

The second decade of the twentieth century was marked by an increased enrollment of young women at the university. Women started to participate in academic life and their presence soon became noticeable. Coeducation became the topic of the address by Bogdan Gavrilović which marked the annual celebration of Saint Sava. Gavrilović addressed the audience with his speech, "The Social Role of the University." The speech, a valuable interpretation of the role of an institution of higher learning, was later published in the pages of *Srpski Književni Glasnik.*

Gavrilović made an historical digression in the opening paragraph of his speech. He reminded the audience that the Velika Škola (The Academy) was already more than 100 years old, founded during the reign of Karadjordje. Gavrilović reminded the audience that at the occasion of the founding itej Obradović. It was noteworthy that Dositej spoke about humanist, Dostej Obradović. It was noteworthy that Dositej spoke about the great importance of education, a notion very likely shared by many. Gavrilović chose to quote in his speech Dositej's words, "We should strive to deliver our souls from the spirit

Gavrilović concluded that one of the most important tasks is all societies and all periods is the education of the male and female children and adolescents. Lately there had been much discussion about the education of women. Gavrilović noted that women contributed as equal partners in their professional capacity at the university:

Women have entered the university and we can see today
that they fulfill their function in a complicated social ma-
chinery, just like men, even better in some instances, according to their special endowments. The importance of this fact
is formidable in the sociological aspect. The fear that the
great design in scientific work will be basically changed with
the arrival of women has disappeared, and science has gained
very much because of this occurrence.[80]

Gavrilović emphasized that many women excelled as propagators
of national and social ideas. In particular, it was noted that women
had great predispositions in raising and educating children, far more
than men.[81]

It is noteworthy that another professor at the University of Belgrade addressed women's role in society. Dr. Tihomir Djordjević
was the invited speaker of the Women's Patriotic Society in Šabac.
Djordjević addressed the Society, giving a lecture entitled "About the
Serbian Woman" on 27 November 1911 in Šabac. This lecture merited the attention of the editors of *Srpski Književni Glasnik* and was
published in the journal in 1912.[82]

At the very beginning of his lecture, Djordjević established that
it would be impossible to speak about one singular type of Serbian
woman, since in Serbian society there existed several very different
types of women. Therefore, he decided to change the title of his
lecture, "About a Serbian Woman," which only referred to one type
of woman in Serbian society, since his research indicated that there
are in fact many and different profiles of women in Serbian society:

We have several types of women, and there is a great dif-
ference among them. There is a large scale, starting from
patriotic Serbian women who are considered as lower class
creatures and are without rights, an economic necessity and
containing factory or labor force, and the cultured Serbian
women who have become writers, artists, and fighters for
ideal women's rights. This scale is large, even among most
cultured people, but never sinks as low as it is in the case of
our society.[83]

In his lecture, Djordjević focussed his attention on three types
of Serbian women: patriarchal, semi–patriarchal, and cultured. The
patriarchal women lived in traditional environments in the villages. In
order to improve their difficult lives, a great deal of attention should
be directed toward procuring some of benefits for the peasants. One
should remember that the women in the villages represented the true
force that provided life sustenance for the broad masses of Serbian

people.[84]

Professor Slobodan Jovanović traced further the development of the diverse functions of the university in his festive address on Saint Sava's celebration in 1914. Jovanović commenced his speech by commemorating the students killed in the Balkan wars. The tremendous participation of the youth in the Balkan wars was unheard of before. Unfortunately, there were many students among the victims and their names will be emblazoned forever on the walls of the university.[85]

Jovanović thought that important tasks awaited the university in the new and enlarged Serbian state. In the first place, the university, as the strongest cultural center, should help the cultural consolidation. While the population from the old kingdom already had a century of peaceful development and access to education, the newly liberated regions had been, until recently, treated like slaves. A political union in the new state could not be achieved unless the cultural differences were alleviated.

Jovanović stressed that two important goals had not been fulfilled—the College of Medicine and the College of Law had not yet opened nor had the agricultural department. The university building, endowed by Captain Miša Atanasijević, was presently too small and additional classroom space had to be rented. The Serbian Institute, one of the most important, could not accept more than ten new students. Students enrolled in the Institute of Chemistry had to wait for an additional year to be accepted.[86]

The number of faculty teaching at the university was determined by the legislature. The old Academy, Velika Škola, did not have the imposed limit for the number of professors. However, the university had a fixed number of full professorships, and this number was too small as compared to the real teaching demand. The number of docents was larger since the docents performed some of the duties assigned to full professors elsewhere. In spite of the heavy teaching load, docents received meager wages; their salary lagged behind that of high school teachers. Jovanović pleaded for recognition of the work of some docents and asked that a number of docents be advanced to full professor, thereby increasing the number of professorships at the university.[87]

Jovanović did not forget the plight of students in need of financial support. In order to alleviate the burden of deserving students, Jovanović emphasized the importance of individual endowments as well as founding of dormitories for students and providing stipends. The university should not remain exclusively a government institution but rather become a joint venture between the government and the people, since it is the center of national education. It should be supported by the "sacrifices and contributions of all of us."[88]

## Chapter 4

## Musical Arts in Serbia at the Beginning of the Twentieth Century

The revived interest in the historical past appeared not only in pictorial art but in other arts forms as well. Jovan Skerlić contemplated this fascination with the past while discussing, in retrospect, the historical and general cultural development in Serbia at the beginning of the nineteenth century. Skerlić called attention to the misfortune of many small nations that were still in bonds of serfdom and poverty during the nineteenth century. The outlook was bleak, and there was little hope for betterment. In this context of resigned misery and dissatisfaction with the present, the historical past seemed to instill the feeling of self–esteem and national pride. Skerlić concluded that these were the reasons that the Serbs, as a people, "became hypnotized with the memories from the past."[1]

With a gradual betterment of political and social circumstances, the wish for strengthening the national consciousness became enhanced. The past was reexamined and the old glory and victories of ancient rulers were recalled. Historians and philologists brought fresh insight into the historical past with their current research. The past became the ideal for the future. Skerlić thought that the heraldics and epigraphics, together with the medieval knighthood and dusty parchments, replaced the initiative and belief in life. The emperors and kings were revived, and the lives and deeds of Dušan, Simeun, and Zvonimir were explored. The enchantment with the past spurred imperialistic tendencies expressed in "the orgies of the romantic imagination."[2]

Bogdan Popović, a literary and art critic, gave another proof of the widespread feeling of patriotism and of nationalistic feelings in his review of the First Yugoslav Artistic Exhibit that took place in Belgrade in 1904. Popović also noticed that a general characteristic of Serbian pictorial art, as well as all art forms, was a search for inspiration in a national historical past. Folk epic poetry of medieval times, the bard with his stringed musical instrument, gusle, and historical events still delighted the artists and their audiences. Popović concluded that Serbian art was in its essence "patriotic."[3]

Popović was aware of the danger of exaggerated devotion to patriotic feelings. Therefore, in his programmatic article in the first issue of *Srpski Književni Glasnik,* he stressed that a literary work should not be praised only because the writer was a native son. On the contrary, true patriotism required fortitude to declare shortcomings, if there were any, even if it meant to draw the wrath of the coevals. One should recognize the true value of good literary works, but also should not hesitate to criticize the lesser works. Popović pointed out that the influence of literature was formidable at times and that literary works changed moods and influenced social movements. Events in real life were sometimes, to a certain degree, duplications of events described in literary works. Popović expressed his hope that the discussions in literary journals would enable Serbian literature to justly take a place in world literature, according to the talent of Serbian writers.[4]

A similar outlook of national consciousness was shared by artists in the musical field, including composers, conductors, and performers. Guided by the spirit of national and patriotic pride, it was decided to commemorate the fifteenth anniversary of the founding of Beogradsko pevačko društvo (Belgrade Singers' Society) in an elaborate manner. The celebration was scheduled to take place in May of 1903 in Belgrade. An invitation to the celebration was extended to many choral societies as well as to renowned musical pesonalities. The choral societies were also invited to participate in a competition that lasted three days. At the same time, a congress of musicians was scheduled to convene. The Belgrade Singers' Society, under the artistic leadership of Stevan Stojanović Mokranjac, the composer, prepared a special concert for this occasion. Mokranjac hoped to present an exceptional program on "the history of Serbian song," tracing the development of artistic music from the epic songs.[5]

On the first day of the celebration, 25 May 1903, The Belgrade Singers' Society scheduled the official groundbreaking ceremony for the future Umetnički dom (Fine Arts Home). The event was supposed to be attended by King Aleksandar Obrenović and other high dignitaries. However, the King declined the invitation at the last moment, fearing for his safety, and decided to send as a substitute the court marshal.[6]

The presence of eminent personalities at the opening ceremonies attested to the leading position the Society had attained in the field of music during the 50 years of its existence. The wish of the Society to establish a fine arts center of monumental proportion was obviously readily supported and regarded as justifiable. The Society planned to establish its headquarters in the building. Most importantly, the Society provided special facilities for the Serbian Music School within its building. Stevan Stojanović Mokranjac was the founder of the Serbian Music School in collaboration with Cvetko Manojlović. At the time of its founding in 1899, the Serbian Music School was regarded as a forerunner of the future Serbian Conservatory. These plans pointed to farsighted policies of the Society. In addition to very demanding performing schedules, the Society was actively involved in establishing educational goals in the field of music. The planned building included additional concert halls and adjoining facilities for the performing arts. In order to raise the necessary funds for the building, shortly before the beginning of the celebration, lottery tickets were sold. The lottery did not bring in enough revenue due to the unexpected political upheaval created by the sudden violent death of King Aleksandar Obrenović on 29 May, which was just four days after the groundbreaking ceremonies. The magnificent and spacious fine arts home remained an unfulfilled dream.[7]

Mokranjac arranged the program for the historic concert in four parts, corresponding to four stylistic periods. The concert was held in the National Theater on 25 May 1903, the first day of celebration. The concert was preceded by a festive speech by the director of the First Singers' Society, Spira Kalik. Mokranjac presented the Serbian epic song as the oldest level of musical culture. The epic song, *Smrt majke Jugovića (The Death of Jugović's Mother)* was performed with accompaniment of stringed instrument, the gusle. In the next stage of musical development, *Two Songs from the XVI Century* were presented, which were arranged by Petar Hektorović. Hektorović included these songs in his work, *Ribanje i Ribarsko pogovaranje (Fishing and Fishermen's Talk)*, which was published in 1556. These songs were arranged by Mokranjac for mixed choir. The last number, in the first part of the program, was *Three Folk Songs*, arranged by Franciszeck Mirecki, after the lyrics of Vuk Stefanović Karadžić in 1815. These songs were also arranged for mixed choir.

As a fifth and sixth number on the program, Mokranjac presented choral songs of Nikola Djurković and Atansaije Nikolić, denoting these musicians as composers with a "foreign basis." Mokranjac wanted to stress that these composers did not use the national musical idiom in their compositions.

In the second part of the program, Mokranjac performed the compositions of Kornelije Stanković, and Aksentije Maksimović and Mita Topalović, his followers, who started to compose in the national spirit. Mokranjac then presented selected choral works composed by "prominent Slavs who used Serbian songs." They were Vaclav

Horejšek, Gvido Havlas, and Davorin Jenko.

The concert concluded with the compositions of the "Newer Serbian School," which included the famous *Hej trubaču (Hear ye, Trumpeter)* for male choir and *Molitva (Prayer)* by Josif Marinković. The concert included the specially composed *Himna o pedesetogodišnjici (Hymn for the Fiftieth Anniversary)*, by Mokranjac, based on the poem bearing the same title, by Aleksa Šantić. Šantić was at that time the best known and beloved poet. His willingness to write a hymn praising the Society gave additional proof of the esteem that the Society enjoyed.

The last number on the program featured the choral cycle, *Peta Rukovet (Fifth Handful)* by Mokranjac. This vocal rhapsody was composed in 1892 for mixed choir, and marked the high point of the first period of Mokranjac's compositional work. In the subtitle, Mokranjac indicated that all ten songs of the composition originated in his native region. This Rukovet presented a magnificent richness of melodic, rhythmic, and dynamic reflections rooted in the national musical idiom.

On the second day of the celebration, the competition of choral societies took place. Twenty–three choral societies participated from Serbia along with some Serbian choral societies from the regions still under the domination of the Austro–Hungarian monarchy.[8] Jury members were Cvetko Manojlović, Boža Joksimović, Petar Krstić, and Stevan Mokranjac, who were from Belgrade, and Franja Gal, from Subotica.

The Congress of musicians and members of choral societies convened on the first day of the celebration, 25 May 1903. The question of the founding of a federation of choral societies was considered as most important on the proposed agenda. On some previous occasions, the question of the federation had already been discussed. The former president of the Society, Steva Todorović, was the first to devote his attention to a planned collaboration of choral societies. The minutes of the special convention held in 1889 testified to a discussion about this matter.

During the congress of 1903, Stevan Mokranjac made a proposal to found a federation of choral societies, in the name of the Belgrade Singers' Society. Mokranjac also submitted the bylaws of the future federation which he had prepared earlier. The bylaws were accepted in principle by the members of congress. According to the bylaws, the federation would organize one congress annually, while a festive congress, The Glory of the Serbian Singers' Federation, would meet every three years. The meetings of the congress would include concert performances of the choral societies. The bylaws, as submitted, were officially accepted by the membership in June of 1905. At that occasion, the election of the members of the board were completed. Steva Todorović became president, M. Cukić became vice president, Stevan Mokranjac became the director, Mil. D. Šoškić became the treasurer, Miodrag Ibrovac became secretary, and J. S. Davičo became the librarian.[9]

Kosta P. Manojlović wrote about the 50th anniversary in his monograph, *Spomenica St. St. Mokranjcu,* dedicated to the memory of Stevan Mokranjac. Manojlović wrote his monograph in retrospect some 20 years later concluding that this celebration presented the artistic highlight of the Belgrade Singers' Society, as well as of Mokranjac as composer. In the years to come, Mokranjac paid increasingly more attention to the administration of the Serbian Music School. The school progressed rapidly under Mokranjac's watchful eye.[10]

The news about the foundation of the Federation brought new inquiries about further collaboration. Thus, in 1906 the Croatian Singers' Society addressed an invitation to the Federation for cooperation in the musical field. The invitation mentioned that the Croatian Singers' Society established good professional contacts with the Czech and Slovenian Singers' Societies. Therefore, the Croatian singers wished to establish similar friendly ties with the "Singers' Society of our brethren Serbs . . . only through mutual acquaintance and togetherness will it be possible to fulfill the goal that we all strive to achieve, i.e., the cultural union of all Slavs."[11]

The musicians were also ready to help the celebration of the centennial of the uprising during 1904. A concert, with a specially chosen program, featured works of South Slavic composers. The concert, A Yugoslav Evening, was held in the National Theater in a sellout performance. The opening number was the overture, *Ljiljan i omorika (The Lily and the Pine)* by Stanislav Binički, a composition that enjoyed high esteem at the time. The orchestra, which was conducted by Petar Krstić, performed *Smeša pesama (Medley of Songs)* by Josif Marinković, arranged for orchestra.

Obilić, a choral society of students from Belgrade University, performed *Slavija,* a composition for male choir by Josif Marinković, based on the lyrics of Jovan Ilić.

Representing the musicians from Bulgaria was M. Ceren who performed Bach's *Toccata* and Schubert's *Trout,* arranged for piano by Heller.

Mira Devova was the singer representing the musicians from Slovenia. Devova sang *Zvezde zarijo (The Stars are Shining)* by Prochazka, *Sing Me the Song* by Tchaikovsky, and *Solveig's Song* by Grieg.

The reviewer noted the well trained voice and diction of the artist as well as the well deserved success.

The Croatian musicians were represented by the Mladost (Youth) choral society. Their performance was distinguished by the purity of intonation and brilliance. The choir performed two choral compositions—*U letnji suton (In the Summer Dusk)* by Vilko Novak and *Jadranski zvuci (The Sounds from Adria)* by Franjo S. Vilhar.

According to the reviewer of this concert, the most accomplished performance was that of Petar Stojanović, violinist. Stojanović played his own composition with piano accompaniment, *Pesma bez reči (The Song without Words)* and *Polonaise* by Henri Vieuxtemps. The concert was concluded with the Slovenian Choral Octet singing the composition, *Strune (Violin Strings)* by Davorin Jenko, and *Dragi i mladi (Dear and Young)* by Anton Nedved, the Czech composer. The singers of the Octet were well received and applauded.[12]

## The Role of Stanislav Binički in the Musical Life of Belgrade

At the beginning of the twentieth century, Stanislav Binički was a very well known personality in the musical world of Belgrade. After completing his studies at the Music Academy in Munich in 1899, Binički became co–founder of the Serbian Music School together with Stevan Mokranjac and Cvetko Manojlović. Following the founding of the school, Binički became its vocal music instructor.

During that year, Binički organized the Military Orchestra as the first symphonic body in Serbia. He often conducted the orchestra of the National Theater. In 1901 alone, he led the orchestra in 82 performances.[13]

A special event required Binički's collaboration in the production of a recital of poetry by Vojislav Ilić. Due to the great popularity of Ilić's poetry, the National Theater decided "to present for the first time Vojislav's verses on the Serbian stage." For this purpose, *Pesnik (The Poet), Radoslav,* and *Periklova smrt (Pericle's Death)*, all dramatic poems, were chosen. This project was accomplished and the recital took place on 12 May 1901.[14]

Binički's music was praised in a review published in *Kolo*. The reviewer stated that Binički's stage music corresponded beautifully to the gracefully flowing verses by Ilić. It was also noted that Binički understood the milieu of classical Greece in the time of Pericles, as described in Ilić's verses.[15] However, some other reviewers had different opinions. Dragomir Janković thought that Binički's music should have been played only as an overture before the recitation of the verses. The music, in fact, presented an obstacle for the actors while reciting the verses.

Binički's association with the National Theater resulted in his collaboration in a number of theatrical plays. Binički wrote incidental music for two dramas by Branislav Nušić. They were *Ljiljan i omorika (The Lily and the Pine)* and *Put oko sveta (The Voyage around the World)*. For the dramatic work *Ekvinocio (The Equinox)* by Ivo Vojnović, Binički wrote the overture and intermezzo.

The incidental music for drama, *The Lily and the Pine*, presented Binički's first attempt of this kind. The premiere of the play with Binički's music took place on 21 November 1900. Bnički's score was favorably compared to previous attempts of some other composers. The incidental music by Davorin Jenko for the dramatic work, *Pribislav and Božana*, or the music by Josif Markinković for the play *Sudjaje (The Witches)* did not achieve as much success. Binički's incidental music came closer to operatic genre than any previous musical score.[16]

The success of this venture led Binički to write his first opera, *Na uranku (At the Dawn)*. The libretto for the opera was written by Branislav Nušić upon the request of the composer. The premiere took place on 23 December 1903 in the National Theater where it was conducted by the composer. The main roles were sung by the famous singers Sultana Cijukova–Savić and Žarko Savić.

The opera was written in one act and was preceded by an overture. The plot took place in a Serbian village occupied by the Turks. True to its milieu, the music was based on the Serbian folk idiom with oriental influences, such as the opening chant of the muezzin. Binički aimed to closely connect the dramatic and musical development while keeping the dramatic divisions of the scenes. Binički had an opportunity to perform the overture earlier in April of 1903 with the Military Orchestra. The complete opera was staged in the National Theater, and it gained historic importance as the first performed Serbian opera.[17]

Only one year earlier, during 1902, two operatic works had been written in Serbia, which were *Ženidba Miloša Obilića (The Wedding of Miloš Obilić)* by Božidar Joksimović and *Pitija (The Pythia)* by Vaclav Vedral. However, neither of the works was performed. In addition, the first version of the opera by Petar Konjović, *Ženidba Miloša Obilića*, had a similar fate. Konjović composed his opera in 1903 using the libretto by Dragutin Ilić, the poet. Konjović offered his work to the National Theater but it was not accepted.[18]

Binički's most important contribution was in the field of performing arts. Binički founded the Belgrade Military Orchestra in 1899, the first symphonic body in Serbia. Only one year later, Binički organized the Music of the Royal Guard. These two instrumental bodies gave performances of important oratorios as well as symphonic and operatic works. However, Binički did not neglect choral music either. At different times he conducted the choral societies of Stanković, Obilić, and Jakšić. Binički performed a number of important classical works of music with the members of the Stanković choral society and the Music of the Royal Guard. In addition, Joseph Haydn's *The Creation* was performed in 1908 and Beethoven's *Ninth Symphony* in 1910. Binički went with his orchestras and choirs on a concert tour to Russia in 1911.[19]

Binički became director of Stanković, the newly established Music School, in 1911. In addition, shortly before the outbreak of World War I, Binički prepared and conducted the first operas at the National Theater. He was helped by his wife, the singer Miroslava Binički, who played piano accompaniment for the rehearsals and recitals, and who also conducted the choir. Binički selected the following operas for eventual performance in Belgrade—*Il Trovatore, La Tosca, Der Freischütz, Mignon,* and many others. During the war years, Binički retreated with the Serbian army through Albania and went to Corfu. He was evacuated to France with the surviving members of the Royal Guard. While he was in France, he conducted several concert tours in gratitude for the help that was offered, thus promoting Serbian music. After the war, Binički returned to Belgrade, and he became the first director and conductor of the newly founded Opera at the National Theater in 1920. Binički stayed in this position until 1924.[20]

The founding of the Opera at the National Theater in Belgrade represented the fruition of efforts to build a musical culture during the first two decades of the twentieth century. Many obstacles arose during the process of its rapid growth while it was trying to emulate the example set by some European countries which had a longer tradition in education and culture. The lack of an educated public led to the belief that a gradual approach should be taken, and it was therefore decided to present operettas at first. As an advanced musical and dramatic form, opera should be presented only when the public was sufficiently prepared and attracted to theater. However, the operatic performances were severely criticized by the musicians and critics. Many polemical reviews were published in the pages of *Srpski Književni Glasnik.* In 1904, Milan Grol wrote a lengthy review summarizing the situation in his article "The Question of the Operetta at the National Theater."

> Perhaps it has become banal to use patriotic, sentimental, and literary reasons in order to convince the public that this art is not suitable for a theater that started with *Romeo and Juliet, Scapin's Pranks, Zaire,* and *Hernani,* to per-

form, after 50 years of its existence, the *Mikado* or *One Day in Tintin,* and that in this theater which housed plays by Shakespeare, Molière, Sterija, and Djura Jakšić, they should have their place, and not Offenbach's mazurkas and Zeller's verses from Prater.[21]

Grol concluded that the Austrian waltzes and the low class entertainment of the Japanese Tea House should not be on the repertory of the National Theater. The National Theater, as a national institution, had an obligation to fulfill in the areas of literature, fine arts, and education. Serbian poets were producing translations of *The Doll* and *The Student Prince.* The drama department did not stage a single performance of Molière or Shakespeare during the last year, while during the same period three operettas were performed. Furthermore, renowned artists like Zorka Todosić and Raja Pavlović were not further cultivating the repertory based on the folk music of Marinković and Mokranjac. Instead they were "killing themselves with a barbaric language and music fit for a nightclub, as well as losing any real meaning, accent, direction, and beauty of music."[22] In a similar fashion, Ilija Stanojević, one of the best actors in the National Theater, could not manage to create an important role as, for example, in a newly staged play by Molière. Instead he prepared three operatic caricatures, one of which was the role of the Fly from Orpheus in Hell.[23]

Due to the more and more outspoken criticism of the operatic productions, the administration of the National Theater decided to conduct a conference with the key personalities involved in musical life. The conference was attended by Josif Marinković, Stevan Mokranjac, Božidar Joksimović, Kosta P. Manojlović, Stanislav Binički, and Petar Krstić.[24] Dušan Janković presented the conclusions that were reached at the conference in the journal *Delo.* He paid special attention to the ideas of Josif Marinković. Marinković pointed to the pernicious influence of foreign light music on the development of Serbian music in general. In order to remedy the situation, Marinković thought that one should not start the reform from the top. The majority of the people could not truly participate in the musical arts since they did not have an introduction to a proper musical education. There should be a shift in emphasis on musical education starting from elementary school. Children in elementary grades should receive a solid foundation so that they do not learn to sing by rote but by reading the musical text. Children should be able to read the notes and understand basic musical theory. The high schools have teachers with a musical education. There is, however, a lack of good textbooks and song collections for high school students. Marinković stressed that he served more than ten years as a conductor of the Obilić student choir. During that time, he realized that not even one tenth of the students had some knowledge about music theory or singing. Therefore, Marinković concluded that one should start the systematic development of that musical education which is already in the elementary schools and then continue it through high schools. Such an approach would result in a true comprehension of musical art and feeling for the necessity of cultivation of this art. Marinković noted that choral societies often used their singing as a tool in arranging excursions, banquets, and similar entertainment. Members of these societies do not consider music as a spiritual commodity. If musical education continued to be misleading, there would be a steady influx of both youth and public that would not hold the musical arts in their proper esteem. Furthermore, Marinković suggested that in lieu of nonexisting Serbian music in the National Theater, a Slavic repertory should be introduced. Marinković reasoned that compositions by Slavic composers should be more appropriate than the music from operettas.

> After such a well prepared speech by Marinković, nobody had to add anything more. One of the board members repeated several times that the elimination of operetta would bring material loss since the operetta filled the house. In reply, the dramaturgists pointed out that drama performances filled the house as much as the operettas, and they presented proof with statistics. After that exchange, it was concluded that operettas should be eliminated.[25]

Petar Krstić also attended the conference and wrote a report that was published much later in *Srpski Književni Glasnik.* Krstić stated that the administration of the National Theater hoped to hear opinions from leading figures in the musical field about the operatic repertory. The question was asked whether the operetta should be cultivated in a milieu that wished to be abreast of new and contemporaneous cultural events.[26]

Krstić noted, with obvious satisfaction, that it was the first time the musicians were invited to a conference dealing with musical matters. It was customary to negotiate musical questions involving subsidy by high ranking personalities, especially if such matters came under governmental jurisdiction. Even in the case of requests or proposals by musicians the decisions were made by ministers of education or perhaps warfare without consulting with qualified musicians.

Krstić concluded that the fine arts in Serbia perpetually had a role similar to that of Cinderella. The state agencies were not offering all that they could, while, on the other hand, various private artistic agencies directed their efforts to ventures that were damaging to national music and its development. Since Belgrade represented the center of Serbian culture, many artistic movements spread from there to the periphery of the land. There was a tendency to emulate all that was taking place in the cultural field in the capital. However, Belgrade accepted much from the West, not thinking about the consequences, while neglecting a selective approach in order to choose only the best for young Serbian art. Krstić reported that a unanimous decision was reached at the conference declaring the operetta as harmful. It was also decided that operettas should not be part of the repertory of the National Theater.[27]

Krstić stressed that Serbian people love song and dance, as well as theater. One needs only to compare the statistical data about theatrical plays. There should be an effort to improve the criteria and taste of the public, and not to perform the local Viennese popular music of the lowest kind or crude slapsticks. The National Theater should select the dramatic repertory that fitted a theater with a governmental subvention and choose the music repertory carefully.[28] Artistic music, be it operatic, symphonic or vocal, could have a beneficial influence on the younger musicians, presenting examples of the old or new musical literature. In this case, there existed a richer or more numerous repertory of Serbian artistic music, and if the National Theater staged some 30 or 40 theatrical plays with singing—similar to successful ones like *Sudjaje (The Witches), Potera (The Pursuit)* or *Vračara (The Fortuneteller)*—then it could be allowed to perform one or two operettas. Without sufficiently valuable domestic or foreign works, however, it presented a grave mistake to introduce any weak and crude comedies.[29]

Krstić refuted the opinion that operatic music could facilitate the understanding of the more advanced artistic music. In order to prove the futility of such an assumption, Krstić offered a parallel with a literary approach. It would be equally inappropriate to suggest for a beginning literary education the reading of a selection of cheap, sensationalist fiction instead of the works of well known writers. Krstić made some remarks concerning the lack of program policies in the National Theater. He stated that all well established theaters have a certain artistic profile safeguarding one type of programming without any exceptions. As an example, he named some theaters that staged only comedies or dramas. Krstić was concerned that the National Theater did not contain a specific artistic criterion concerning the programs:

Our theater is probably the only one in the world where

all the possible and impossible stage works are performed. We perform all that exists in theatrical art: tragedy, drama, comedy, vaudeville, comical plays, enchanted plays, historical drama, etc., from the following world literature: Serbian, French, German, Russian, Italian, Norwegian, Greek, Romanian, Spanish, Czech, and Hungarian, starting from Sophocles and ending with Ibsen and Gorky.[30]

The National Theater did not have an operatic choir with solo singers and orchestra, a fact that also spoke against the introduction of operetta. Among the solo singers, only two could read music. They were Zorka Todosić and Raja Pavlović. All the others learned their parts by rote. The majority of the actors were trying to fulfill the requirements of operatic acting to the best of their knowledge by reciting their parts and sometimes just singing along in the manner previously introduced in theatrical plays with singing such as *Djido* and *Potera*. Since these actors were not even able to perform operettas proficiently, it would be very hard to upgrade them into opera singers. All other actors who did not sing could then be transferred into ballet dancers. Krstić concluded with a sarcastic tone that with two to three decrees "we could get all that the cities of world have accomplished in the course of years and decades."[31]

The National Theater should not concern itself with pecuniary matters in wishing to produce more and more revenues for the budget office of the government. If it were only for money, there existed a quicker way to produce additional income. One could invite a circus or variety show. Krstić continued in a derogatory mood when he wrote:

> One should enter the temple of Serbian theatrical art to observe the descendants of one Vasa Čarapić being entertained with *Bird Catcher* by Zeller or by *Geisha* by Sidney. Even if the national culture is on a low level . . . one has to take care and cultivate it since that is what supports every nation.[32]

Krstić stressed that operetta had a pernicious influence on domestic musical productions. For the last eight years, right after *Sudjaja* and *Potera* had been written, there was not one single new theatrical play produced with singing. The play, *Ljiljan and omorika* by Stanislav Binički, was the first one produced after this extended hiatus. Krstić thought that, for the given historical and social development, theatrical plays with singing offered the most suitable dramatic genre. Krstić believed that the love of the Serbian people for music presented another reason for the popularity of this work. Usually one could hear from the public the plea "for songs and instrumental music" in the repertory. Therefore, the administration of the National Theater should try to influence the Serbian writers and induce them to write new and original theatrical plays with singing. These plays were very appropriate for depicting dramatic content based on national substance. In Serbian folk songs, stories, fairytales, and such, one could find an abundance of material that could be presented on the stage. Krstić even thought that "in a theatrical play with singing one can accentuate the national element more than in a historical or social drama."[33]

Krstić mentioned further that the National Theater, under the leadership of Milorad P. Šapčanin, tried to encourage the writers to produce new plays with singing. Perhaps one should sponsor a competition for a Serbian play with singing since in that way one could obtain not only the prizewinning work but also a number of others. The prizewinning play would attract the public to attend its performances. There was, therefore, an impressive record of a large attendance at such plays. One should only compare the receipts from the performances of popular plays like *Djido, Šokica (The German Girl), Potera (The Chase), Saćurica i Šubara (The Cape and the Fur Cap).*[34]

Theatrical plays with singing from foreign repertory should be ranked in second place. Among these plays, a selection from Slavic literature would be a better choice since the Russian, Czech, Polish, and Slovenian writers were more familiar to the public. These plays, which were close to the type known as Singspiel or Märchenspiel, could serve as an example to the writers. Krstić thought that the less complicated operas by Weber, Mozart, and Pergolesi could be performed as well since these works corresponded to the abilities of the present performers. Krstić concluded:

> According to all of the above mentioned, there ought to be singing in our National Theater, however, there should be no operattas. Singing will provide variety in the repertory since the theater should please a heterogenous public. Theater should be a nursery garden in order to help create drama and comedy as well as opera in the distant future.[35]

Krstić, as composer, practiced what he preached as a music critic. He composed a great number of plays with singing which dealt with national history and literature, such as, *Kosovska tragedija (The Kosovo Tragedy), Ajša, Koštana, Dorćolska posla (The Dorćol Affairs), Novela od Stanca (The Novel by Stanac).* He also wrote two plays in the spirit of German 'singspiel', which were *Knjeginja*

*Maja (Princess Maja)* and *Snežana i sedam patuljaka (Snow White and the Seven Dwarfs)*. Krstić composed two operas, *Zulumćar (Oppressor)*, based on the drama by Svetozar Ćorović bearing the same title. Towards the end of his life, Krstić wrote his second opera, Ženidba Janković Stojana *(The Marriage of Janković Stojan)* with the libretto based on folksong. However, Krstić did his best in choral works *a capella*, sometimes under the influence of folk music idioms. In this group of works, the cycle *Seljaničice (Little Peasant Girls)*, which was based on the verses of Milorad Petrović, attained a special place. In the second group of choral works, based on Krstić's original invention, the most accomplished were the ones composed using the verses by Jovan Dučić, Vojislav Ilić, and Gustav Krklec. Among the orchestral works that Krstić composed, *Skerco (Scherzo)* was often performed. The first performance of this composition was in 1903 under the baton of Stanislav Binički.[36]

Petar Krstić started his many–sided musical career around the turn of the century, similar in this respect to Stanislav Binički and Božidar Joksimović. In his desire to advance the musical life of Belgrade, these young composers, who were at the very start of their professional careers, acted as pedagogues, performers, and organizers. Sharing the renewed feeling of national consciousness, these composers attempted to enhance the compositional and technical knowledge in order to raise Serbian music to the levels achieved so far by European composers. In particular, Krstić, Binički, and Joksimović stressed in their music an adherence to the national musical idiom. They were attracted to the national folk epics and to their historic past, and they hoped to achieve a unity between the dramatic content and an autochthon musical language. Through their works and station in life, these composers were confirming the opinions of Bogdan Popović and Jovan Skerlić and revealing the patriotic character of Serbian art.

The premiere of *Čučuk-Stana* in the National Theater in 1907 introduced the young composer Stevan Hristić, who was a new name in the musical life of Belgrade. Hristić was at the time in his last academic year of studies at the Conservatorium of Leipzig. In order to attend the premiere of his first stage work, Hristić temporarily interrupted his studies and went to Belgrade to assist in rehearsals and preparations of this performance. He was obviously well informed about the popularity of theatrical plays with singing. That was very likely the reason that led him to the composition of a musical score based on folk music idiom. The theatrical play of the same name by Milorad Petrović–Seljančica was Hristić's choice for the plot. Petrović was a well known and popular writer at the beginning of the century.

Milan Grol, a theater critic, wrote the review of the premiere of *Čučuk-Stana* for *Srpski Kniževni Glasnik*. Grol addressed words of appreciation to the young composer on the performance of his first major work for the stage. However, Grol expressed his criticism concerning the dramatic plot that reminded him of some pastoral plays, but without deeper coherence:

> The little and naive love story is sprinkled with songs, dances, and pranks of a village joker. The writer produced a dramatic potpourri since he was not able to set the well known historical personality in this naive, Arcadian situation . . . . In *Čučuk-Stana*, the differences between the two historic periods and geographic regions were obliterated. Thus, at the end of the idyllic first act in which the present day village of Šumadija is supposedly representing the village Sikole from Krajina during the first uprising, the writer introduces the fight of Hajduk Veljko with the Turks . . . At the end of the second act, after the attack, Stana Pljestićeva, with a gun in her hand, goes to Veljko to complain. In the third act . . . Veljko, delighted with the courage of the heroic girl, presents her with an apple and asks for her hand in marriage, with the blessing of a priest who is present, as if by accident.[37]

Grol objected mostly to the uneven quality of the dramatic text. Next to the very successful scenes, such as the scene where an apple is presented to the girl, where a sincerity and expressiveness was achieved, there are the scenes that present Veljko and his fighting friends, the renowned "bećari" (batchelors) who were considerably weaker due to the declamatory tone and verses containing banal epithets and awkward rhyming. In a similar vein, there was the presentation of the belly-dancers observed by Veljko in a lifeless and stiff pose.[38]

Grol pointed out that Hristić's music was harmonious and much more interesting. Grol thought that Hristić showed his artistic temperament, as well as a feeling for folk music and an ability for the development of musical themes and motives. The score also showed a flair for interesting instrumentation.[39]

The question of the founding of the opera company was often discussed by the younger musicians. Petar Konjović, the composer, remembered that Stevan Mokranjac accepted the proposal of a young musician and called a meeting in order to discuss the opera question under the auspicies of the National Theater. Among the participants were renowned critics and personalities like Jovan Skerlić and Milan Grol.[40]

During the conference, the discussion was centered around the musical repertory of the National Theater that derived mainly from theatrical plays with singing. Simultaneous with the changes of the administration of the theater there were changes in the repertory. The public was fond of musical performances and therefore, on occasion, an operetta was featured. The performances of the operettas threatened to spoil "the better and more appropriate musical education in the field of scenic music." Such an artistic policy was not considered feasible in a theater that should concentrate on the cultivation of national art. Mokranjac himself was in favor of the foundation of the opera company and supported the proposal of his younger colleagues. The main opponent of the opera was Milan Grol.[41]

Grol repeated the same argument in his article under the title "Opera in the National Theater." He thought that the time had not yet come for the founding of a new and complex theatrical form. The reasons were numerous, such as a not yet sufficiently large and well versed public, the lack of well trained actors, and the established expectations of the public concerning the customary repertory of the National Theater. Besides, there was a shortage of necessary funds for the establishment of the opera as well as a need for trained opera singers. Therefore, Grol was questioning the validity of such an undertaking since it was not certain that an operatic public existed at all.[42]

All leading personalities of the theatrical and musical life agreed on one point—the National Theater should cultivate art of high ethical value. The theater as well as the opera should elucidate and ennoble the public and it should not only serve as entertainment. The public at large obviously had another opinion about the performances of operettas in the National Theater, since operettas were performed, as a rule, before a capacity audience. However, the adherents of the operetta did not often express their opinions in writing. An exception was an article signed with the pseudonym Anonim appearing in the daily paper, *Politika*. The unidentified writer reviewed the performance of the operetta *Dolls* by Edmon Audran, and he stated that the theater was never as much filled with the public as this specific evening. This fact was even more amazing since it had been more than three years since the premiere of the operetta, yet the performance still attracted many theater patrons. The reviewer noted that he too appreciated national obligations that were set for the theater and that he understood the futility of the performances of the operetta. In spite of an awareness of higher ethical tasks, the reviewer, hidden behind his fictitious name, admitted that he enjoyed the performances of the operetta like any other citizen.[43]

## The Celebration of the Twentyfifth Anniversary of Mokran-jac's Professional Activities—A Change of Musical Credo

Stevan Hristić wrote a lengthy review honoring the contribution of Stevan Stojanović Mokranjac. Hristić pointed out that the year 1909 marked a period of 25 years of Mokranjac's dedicated work in the building of musical culture. The historical development of Serbian music almost symbolically coincided with the celebration of Mokranjac. The building of musical culture appeared to decline since there was widespread apathy toward culture and fine arts, a consequence of the long Turkish domination. During that time, Mokranjac managed to bring Serbian music to a relatively high level of accomplishment, especially taking into account the general circumstances. The field of vocal music represented the focal point of Mokranjac's compositional activities. Together with his contemporary, Josif Marinković, Mokranjac created works that would outlive their creators as well as many later generations. The name of Stevan Mokranjac would take its place in the history of the country, together with some other immortal names of founders of Serbian fine arts and literature.[44]

Hristić stressed that the most valuable of Mokranjac's contributions was the collection of Serbian folk songs. In order to accentuate Mokranjac's merits in this field, Hristić compared Mokranjac's work with the distinguished accomplishments of Vuk Karadžić. Hristić drew a parallel between Karadžić's epic and lyric folk song collections and Mokrajac's collections of Serbian spiritual and secular folk songs. Mokranjac not only noted down the songs, but his research of these collected songs led him to present a harmonic system based on characteristic motives of folk music. Mokranjac achieved beauty in his harmonization of folk melodies. His arrangements were "full of soul and poetry." He was able to project the depth of exalted feelings and the serenity of Serbian folk motives. *The Tenth Rukovet (Tenth Handful)* presented proof of his exquisite feeling for the latent harmony of Serbian folk songs. The musical content of the song of Kara–Mustafa in the *Sixth Rukovet* by Mokranjac was as powerful as the poetically inspired lines of Žal'za mladost (Lament for the Lost Youth) in Koštana by Borisav Stanković. Mokranjac accomplished what others had previously failed to do. He introduced the inflections of folk music idiom into Serbian artistic music.

> Mokranjac gave life and artistic style to Serbian music, which was until then spoiled by ignorant persons . . . . He collected the material for musicians and for composers in order to enable the research of melodic qualities from specific parts of Serbia, and to form on this base a whole movement, a

school, an epoch of Serbian artistic music . . . Furthermore, his material is important for music theoreticians, who may create from these motives a whole system of origin, harmony, and forms of Serbian music . . . And even when Serbian music produces a Tchaikovsky, Smetana, Dvořak, Grieg or Schumann, the name of Mokranjac, as well as his merits, are not going to decrease.[45]

As a young and well educated composer who was full of confidence and with a newly acquired diploma from the Conservatory in Leipzig, Hristić noted that Mokranjac, in his artistic path, had almost reached his final end. Although this statement contained a measure of truth, it reflected to a degree the insolence of an impatient youth who thought that the new generation should transcend the existing limits of musical style. The future of Serbian music should be in the development of large forms of vocal and instrumental music and in the creation of original musical works, while safeguarding the national spirit. In all likelihood, Hristić foresaw his part in such a development along these lines.

Hristić concluded that Mokranjac did not contribute only in the field of collection of folk songs and their arrangement, but equally in the field of musical education. Mokranjac was the founder of the Serbian Musical School. In addition, Mokranjac, a long time conductor and artistic director of the Belgrade Singers' Society, achieved remarkable success. Under his leadership the Society enjoyed a reputation as the best Serbian choral society. It would be a hard task for any musician to maintain Mokranjac's level of perfection and to follow in his footsteps.

On the occasion of Mokranjac's celebration, Hristić's tribute contained in its essence the summing up of Mokranjac's artistic merits, measuring the scope of his legacy as if a final judgment should be passed, although the composer was still alive. Next to lavish praise, the article contained a pejorative note, especially in the statement that Mokranjac reached the final phase of a dated genre as a composer of shorter musical compositions for choir. Hristić thought that the compositional output of Mokranjac was secondary in importance, since it was his belief that Mokranjac achieved the most as a folk song collector. The role of the young generation of composers was to create larger and more complicated vocal forms that would help establish the national school of music.[46]

It is interesting to note a similar outlook by another young musician, Miloje Milojević who was a member of Hristić's generation. Milojević expressed a similar view in his review of the choral collection, *Muški horovi (Male Choirs)* by the Slovenian composer Anton

Ferster. Milojević noted that he was familiar with such choral music since Ferster's music represented a style shared in the past by many musicians. At the time of the Davorje Choral Society, such choral music must have been the most popular since it was often performed by singers and also enjoyed by the public. However, new times had arrived and "the modern soul became more complicated." Therefore, Fester's music could only elicit the respect that a young person can feel before an older and honorable colleague. Milojević recommended that the collected choral compositions, as accomplished works, be designated for all male choirs. Choirmaster should pay attention to Ferster's work, especially due to the fact that there still existed a public with appreciation for this musical style. As for the younger, contemporary public, these choral works had little to offer.

While declaring the music of Anton Ferster as valuable yet surpassed in the given moment, Milojević had only words of praise for another collection of vocal music from Slovenia. This collection, under the title *Osam solo pesama (Eight Solo Songs)*, comprised solo songs composed by a group of younger Slovenian composers, Anton Lajovic, Emil Adamič, Josif Pavčić, and Vladimir Flegel. Milojević felt an expressed kinship with the music "of our days and our souls."[47]

Stevan Hristć turned his attention to the question of the national musical style in a review of a concert featuring works of Tchaikovsky. The concert, considered an important cultural event, took place in the National Theater. Hristić thought that Serbian artistic music was only in a formative stage. Other nations, with a higher level of development, had already passed through a similar stage. The Russian composers, Berezovsky, Bortnjansky, Dragomizhsky, Varlamov, Serov, and Glinka were part of such an historical development. The works of the following composers anticipated the arrival of composers that created the Russian school of music: Tchaikovsky, Balakirev, Musorgsky, Borodin, Rimsky-Korsakov, Glazunov, and others. Therefore, Hristić concluded that Serbian composers were in a more fortunate position since they could benefit from the example set by two Slavic people with a distinct musical profile—the Russians and the Czechs. Their example could eliminate unnecessary any wanderings and struggles to find the path of development for Serbian music. This path should incorporate the national and general Slavic spirit.[48]

Hristić, as a critic and music writer of grat acuity, advocated the importance of creation of a national musical language. However, the premiere of his biblical poem, Vaskrsenje (Resurrection), which was based on the text by Dragulin Ilić for soloists, mixed choirs and large orchestra, revealed Hristić's predilection for Italian verism. In order to distinguish his work from oratorio form, Hristić described

Vaskrsenje as a biblical poem.

Miloje Milojević wrote the review of the premiere of Hristić's poem which took place in the National Theater on 3 May 1912.[49] Milojević praised the efforts of the conductor Stanislav Binički who prepared and rehearsed the large body of performers. The choir of the Stanković Singers Society took part as well as Miroslava Binički, Vojislav Turinski, J. Predić, and Bajković. The Orchestra of the Royal Guard was joined by faculty members of the Serbian Music School. Milojević quoted the words of the composer who declared the musical score of *Vaskrensje* as being dramatic in character. Milojević noted that it was possible to draw a parallel with the music of *Salome* by Richard Strauss. The choral interludes have an expressed epic character. Therefore, he wrote that *Vaskrsenje* presented a mixture of drama with epic elements. The solo parts revealed the influence of the Italian tradition known as *bel canto*. In this respect, the aria of Magdelena especially pointed to the influence of Puccini. Milojević concluded that Hristić should return to the folk music idiom, following the example he set in his first compositional venture, the music for the theatrical play with singing *Čučuk Stana:*

> Hristić should return to the road he started in *Čučuk–Stana*, since a work could be . . . written well, yet with no meaning for the people . . . if it does not reflect its spirit. I am able to state that Mr. Hristić, as a well versed composer, has written music with musical talent, clearly and lucidly . . . . I have to add that one can be a Serbian composer only, when intelligently arranging elements of folk music and creating on the basis of its idioms, new rhythmic, harmonic, and melodic principles are used that will be artistic and national at the same time.[50]

Hristić continued to write reviews with insight and acuity of perception. In his review of the concert in the National Theater under the baton of Dragutin Pokorni, in April of 1909, Hristić had an opportunity to describe the general musical situation in the theater. Hristić noted that though the attendance was excellent, the musical art was "in a sorrowful situation." The reason for this deplorable state was due to the fact that the employed people in the theater did not have a proper musical education. Hristić stressed that it is not enough "to love the theater" or "to love the music;" it is more important to have a professional artistic knowledge. According to Hristić, the conductor, Pokorni, "loved the music" in the above quoted context. The proof was the programmatic concept of the last concert held in April that aimed to impress the public.[51]

For the opening number, Pokorni chose the overture to *Rienzi* by Richard Wagner. Hristić thought that this overture was not appropriate for serious concerts since it pointed to the influence of Meyerbeer, Weber, and others in Wagner's musical realm. Wagner's themes show many reminiscenses based on musical themes of these composers. Moreover, this overture was often played in parks and open air concerts, as well as at some inexpensive places where the public was seated "at tables covered with chequered tablecloths and with beer mugs." The second piece was the Second Violin Concerto by Ludwig van Beethoven featuring the violinist Frajt. The soloist was a fine musician with a promising future and performing career. Afterwards, Pokorni conducted a potpourri from the opera *Tosca*, consisting of arias, instrumental introductions, and interludia. Hristić thought that such a performance was not doing justice to the composer or to the public. Music written for specific scenes and situations lost some of its intrinsic value when performed outside the intended dramatic and musical context in a form of a medley. Hristić thought that the performance itself was not impressive enough. In the second part of the concert, the performance of Dvořak's *Terzetto* brought a lovely change of pace, thanks to the performance of Saks, Nejdela, and Zorko. The final piece presented another potpourri from the opera *Herodiade* by Jules Massenet. The failure of this piece was due to the same reasons as that of the potpourri from *Tosca.* It was sinply a lining up of well known arias and interludes, which deprived the listener from the coherent context that justified and enhanced their musical and dramatic content.[52]

At the end of his review, Hristić addressed his most serious remark concerning the program policy conducted by Pokorni in the National Theater. In a mildly sarcastic tone, Hristić stated that Pokorni wanted "to educate" the Belgrade public by applying a gradual approach. That is the reason for the introduction of operettas in the repertory as a first preparatory step before presenting opera performances. He should have started with less pretentious works, such as *Cavalleria Rusticana* by Mascagni and *Pagliacci* by Leoncavallo. However, a peformance of *The Bartered Bride* by Smetana was a total failure. Hristić stated that the orchestra performed the best it could since it was only a small instrumental ensemble. One should wish for a larger orchestra as well as for implementation of musical performances of domestic composers.[53]

Miloje Milojević also debated the opera question in his review of the guest appearances of the Operatic Company from Zagreb. In the course of their stay in Belgrade fom 17 May to 1 July 1911, the Company performed the following operas: *Aida* by Verdi, *Mignon*

by Thomas, *Il Secreto di Susanna (The Secret of Susanna)* by Wolf–
Ferrari, *Madame Butterfly* by Puccini, Tiefland (In the Valley) by
d'Albert,    Bartered Bride by Smetana,    and    *Eugene Onegin*
by Tchaikovsky. The Croatian composers were represented with the
opera *Povratak (Return)* by Josip Hatze, as well as with the operetta
*Barun Trenk (Baron Trenk)* by Srećko Albini. Milojević thought that
the Opera did not come to educate the Belgrade public, since it did
not wish to assume the role of a stern teacher while giving guest performances. The Opera came with good will and a first class repertory
which was selected with taste and knowledge.[54]

Milojević praised the decision of the National Theater in Belgrade to extend the invitation to the Zagreb Opera Company in order to "delight the intelligent public with the highest artistic form,
with music drama." At the same time, young people had an opportunity to see a fine production of selected operatic works. Milojević
concluded that the Zagreb Opera left an impression of a highly professional body and that the Serbian opera could not be established
overnight, even with large subsidies. To achieve this goal, musical
education should be stressed and special attention should be given
to the young professional artists. The music schools should become
recipients of subventions. Milojević thought that by applying such
measures, in some five to six years, a well trained cadre would emerge
with more appreciation for professional work in their native land. In
the meantime, a new repertory should come forth which would be created by Serbian composers that would enrich the opera scene. While
waiting for all these plans to come to fruition, Milojević suggested
that the Zagreb Opera should be invited many times.[55]

While the performances of the Zagreb Opera filled the National
Theater and public interest grew, the Opera Company of the Croatian National Theater from Osijek was less successful. During 1911,
some of the performances of this Opera Company had to be cancelled.
Milojević concluded that it would be impossible to give any serious
artistic credit to the Opera Company from Osijek.[56] This unfavorable impression was even augmented by the inevitable comparisons
with the splendid guest appearances of the Zagreb Opera earlier in
the same year. An agreement was made for future collaboration with
the Zagreb Opera on a yearly basis. Milojević was in favor of guest
appearances, although he had reservations about the educational success of these performances among a public lacking musical experience.
It would be impossible to request a special repertory since the Zagreb
Opera came from another milieu and musical tradition. Their repertory was suitable for the needs of their public. However, guest appearances in Belgrade would offer pleasures, especially to those who

have a deeper understanding.[57]

Milojević thought it was necessary to start a systematic plan of musical education designed for those who do not have enough knowledge and understanding of music. It is very difficult for the uneducated public to understand music with such a heterogeneous profile, that is one evening to listen to an Italian opera with *verismo* style, and another evening to a national opera, be it Italian, French, Russian, German or Czech. Instead of the false sentimentality of the grand opera of Wagner, the Serbian public should be presented with the opera–comique of the eighteenth century. Milojević believed that this operatic form, although highly accomplished in its artistic concept, was also sufficiently clear and easy to understand. The musical texture of the comic opera is characterized by a natural flow, grace, and spontaneity. Milojević reasoned like a pedagogue whose concern was the education of a broader public. Therefore, he argued that the presentation of comic operas would accomplish a gradual introduction to the complex and diverse operatic literature that consequently evolved. However, comic opera contained elements that led to the origin of operetta. The easy and spirited double meaning of light conversations and the moral or physical defects of protagonists were traits that were shamelessly exploited in operettas, thereby gradually losing all good taste.[58]

In conclusion, Milojević listed comic operas that would accommodate the needs of the public as well as serve as a possible guideline for the future repertory of the National Theater. Milojević gave the following operas as suitable for this purpose: *Richard Coeur-de-Lion* and *Les Deux Avares* by Gretry, *La Serva Padrona* by Pergolesi, *Il Matrimonio Segreto* by Cimarosa, *Bastien und Bastienne* by Mozart, *Le Cadi Dupé* by Gluck, *La Molinara* by Paisiello, and *Doctor und Apotheker* by Dittersdorf. Milojević thought that the National Theater had artists who could interpret these works that are indispensable for the beginner's stages of musical understanding. This repertory of comic operas will be attractive to the broader public since operetta had created a following among the musical public.[59]

The administration of the National Theater in Belgrade obviously listened to Milojević's suggestions and decided to present *Bastien und Bastienne* by Mozart. The premiere of the pastorale took place in December of 1911. In a review of this performance, Milojević declared that he was pleasantly surprised when he heard that there was a plan to present several comic operas of the eighteenth century. He admitted that he did not believe that his suggestion would be so quickly accepted and that at first the comic opera by Mozart would be performed. Milojević further insisted that his suggestion was motivated by the wish to help solve the opera question.

Milojević noted that there had been many plans for the solution of the crises in the National Theater. It was even suggested that for a period of time no musical works should be performed. Then came the motion to limit the musical performances to theatrical plays with singing, like *Djido,* based on the play by Janko Veselinović with music by Davorin Jenko, or *Dorćolski posla* by Ilija Stanojević with music by Petar Krstić. Finally, operettas were introduced as lucrative and easy to understand.

> And when this effort failed, opera was introduced of the verismo style, loud and effective, and that did not fail to reach the goal. There were many attempts, but no results . . . . This question became a heated issue on the occasion of the engagement of the Zagreb Opera. The operetta is not any more an alternative. The Osijek Operetta . . . showed clearly that this artistic form cannot serve pure art and cannot fulfill the artistic needs of an intelligent public. Then came a new proposal—to start with the comic opera of the eighteenth century, French, German, and Italian. There is strength of a mature kind in comic opera and only with the help of this form . . . can the artistic sense of a young public be developed.[60]

However, the performance of *Bastien and Bastienne* did not fulfill the expected results. Milojević tried to find the real reasons for this failure. The performance could have fared better with a different interpretation. There was a lack of "rhythmical gesture on the stage." The acting was stiff and banal. Bastienne, in an affected manner, "sighed and looked to the ground . . . whimpering and fidgeting with her apron." Mozart wrote this pastorale when he was only 12, and therefore this work was in all its beauty also naive and childish. The Belgrade public so far knew musical drama only as presented in a coarse and crude style of the veristic operas.

Milojević remembered that he saw this work by Mozart in Munich under the baton of the famous conductor and composer, Felix Mottl. Mozart's work was classed as Singspiel, that is a theatrical play with singing.

At the end, Milojević mentioned that there are even more interesting works from the eighteenth century, like *Les Deux Avares* by Gretry, or comic operas by Johann Schenk. Schenk, a longtime friend of Beethoven, composed comic operas, and Milojević singled out, in particular, *Der Dorf Barbier (The Village Barber).*[61]

The premiere of the theatrical play, *Kosovska tragedija,* based on the drama by *Žarko Lazarević* with stage music by Petar Krstić, took place in during 1913. Milojević, in his capacity as music critic for *Srpski Knjiševni Glasnik,* wrote about this performance. Milojević thought that the music by Krstić was of an uneven character and there was not sufficient cohesion between the spoken parts and musical sections. The spoken words should have been interwoven in a melodic entity since the declamation itself breaks the flow of a musical and dramatic form.

Krstić accented the pathos in the overture and in the lyricism in the monologues, bu the noted the omission of a dramatic aspect. Krstić's musical style was prevailingly homophonic. Polyphonic style, essential for stressing dramatic action, was not developed enough. Milojević hoped that Krstić would produce a better work if a suitable dramatic plot was found.[62]

Milojević suggested a new musical and artistic program during the same year. The renewed feeling of patriotism on the eve of World War I was reflected in Milojević's article about Serbian music. In the introduction, Milojević reminded the readers about the well known value of Serbian folk poetry. Many writers wrote laudatory reviews about Serbian folk poetry, including the German poet and thinker Johann Wolfgang Goethe. The ornamental arts and crafts, as well as wood carvings, were gaining recognition thoughout the world, while Serbian music was still confined to its borders. In other countries with established musical centers, the public with refined taste had great demands of musical performances. The simple and short folk melodies could not offer enough musical satisfaction. Milojević concluded that it is not enough to harmonize folk melodies. One should arrange them and elaborate the motiv material. Even more importantly, the young composers should examine folk music and research its principles. Only then would it be possible to create real national music. The examples of composers of different nationalities could help in this endeavor. Among composers succeeding in this task, Milojević named Grieg, Sibelius, Rimsky–Korskov, Grechaninov, MacDowell, Suk, and Smetana. There was also another way of achieving recognition— Richard Strauss possessed originality of artistic power, a trait that Milojević admired most.[63]

In order to reach the goal of national musical language, Milojević encouraged the collection of folk songs and instrumental music. Furthermore, Milojević warned against the incursion of foreign influences on indigenous folk music. In order to implement these requirements, Milojević pleaded for the introduction of courses on folk singing in elementary schools as well as for the organization of folk singers' societies. As an added condition, Milojević asked that "the Serbian composers should pass through some kind of folk music purgatory and cast off all in their musical composition that does not coincide with the national spirit." Serbian national music, born in the artistic spirit of native composers, should evolve into folk music but be arranged for a higher artistic goal.[64]

Milojević obviously believed that, in the creation of national music which was based on the folk music idiom, the decisive role was played by musical invention and originality. Only then could the musical compositions achieve a unique artistic contribution.

### The Founding of the Serbian Music School

The first decade of the twentieth century marked an upsurge in music and fine arts education. New professional schools were opening their doors to students. Great attention was given to the education of talented youths as a token for further betterment of cultural and artistic growth. The new generation of young artists, returning after their studies abroad, joined in an effort to sponsor the education of budding art students. As a rule, these young professionals were not only interested in developing their own artistic expression but were generously extending their collaboration in many areas of art education.

At the turn of the century, the Serbian Music School was founded in Belgrade. The initiative came in 1899 from Stevan Mokranjac, who was aided in this effort by Cvetko Manojlović and Stanislav Binički. The activities of the school were followed with attention and discussed on the pages of the prestigious *Srpski Književni Glasnik*. The annual recitals were held in the National Theater, thereby assuming a special place in the cultural life. Among the varied reviews about the concert appearances of its students and reports on the school achievements, attention should be paid to the well written article by an anonymous writer in 1908 which was published in *Glasnik*. In the opening remarks, the writer stated that the publicity about professional schools and academies presented a remarkable contribution to the cultural history of a country, especially if dealing with the development of a young nation.

> It is interesting to deal with the fate of some cultural institutions and follow them in their development. Sometimes insignificant beginnings started by private intervention lead to foundations of professional schools and academies. This is especially interesting among young nations when they are in the first stages of their spiritual advancement. Monographs about these institutions are nothing other than scattered yet precious pages of the cultural history of the country.[65]

The writer further declared that the school, which was founded nine years ago, was presently at the peak of its growth. The existence of the school was not accidental but was tightly connected with the history of the Belgrade Singers' Society. This Society acted in many respects as a pioneer in the musical field. In the course of time, it became well established and gained more recognition. As a result of the Society's activities, the need was felt for well versed music professionals, composers, and performers. It was necessary to educate the broader public in order to be able to follow the newly composed works of "higher music." At this time, the Serbian Music School was founded with Mokranjac as its first director. The rules and bylaws of the School, which were incorporated since the founding in 1899, stayed valid until 1909. It testified to the farsightedness of its founders. The school started with 30 students, and in its second year was increased to 50. The number of students grew constantly, and by 1908 there were 126 students. When the faculty was also increased, new rules had to be formulated.

In the meantime, a few of the graduates of the Serbian Music School became teachers of music in the middle schools. The reviewer noted that two years earlier the government decided to give subsidies to the school in the amount of 2,000 dinars. This financial help enabled the founding of a special course for teachers. Two young women initially finished this newly established course. The set requirements for admission to the teachers' course stipulated that the student should have previously finished six grades of high school in addition to some musical training on the piano or violin. The Serbian Music School was structured into three levels: Preparatory, Lower, and Higher Level. Each level lasted three years. According to the curriculum, the following courses were offered: choral singing, form analyses, history of music, solfeggio, theory, harmony, counterpoint, instrumentation, and reading of scores. The writer of the review mentioned the names of the faculty and the courses they taught. Mokranjac taught singing and all levels of music theory. Cvetko Manojlović, Jelica Krstić, and Ruža Šafarik taught piano. Jovan Zorko and Jovan Ružička taught violin. Rendl taught violoncello, double bass, and flute, and Petar Konjović taught history of music.

The reviewer also mentioned that the yearly examinations were conducted before a special deputy of the Ministry of Education. Afterwards, a student concert was presented in the National Theater in order to inform the public about the work accomplished. The writer of the review thought that the beginners and very young children should not participate in these recitals. The success of the school should be judged on the strength of the older students, and the entire concert would gain by a more sophisticated approach. Among the participants of the concert in 1908 the reviewer singled out the singer, Sofija Predić and her interpretation of the aria of Agathe in *Freischütz* by Weber. Her singing revealed a pleasant, soft, and melodious voice in addition to good training reflected in diction and word accentuation. Even more praise was given to the interpretation of the Violin Concerto Op. 23 by Viotti. The young violinist, Dimitrije Golemović, showed his ability "to be consumed with the music he played." He had a sufficiently serious attitude and training to master this difficult composition.[66]

The concert held at the end of the next school year, 1908–09, was reviewed by Stanislav Binički. Binički stated with pleasure that the Serbian Music School had as much success as it was possible to have in a milieu where little attention was paid to music. The concert featured two new songs for soprano and piano accompaniment by Stevan Hristić. These two songs had obviously influenced the reviewer favorably. In conclusion, Binički commented that the concert was not attended by a large number of people. Parents and friends of the performing students were the core of the audience. Binički thought that it was a pity that the public of the capital city showed such little interest in a fine musical event.[67]

The final concert of the following school year 1909–10 was reviewed by Jovan Zorko. It drew high praise for the school and for its students. The progress was visible from year to year thanks to the dedicated work of its faculty in spite of the insufficiently improved teaching conditions. This time, only the students of the more advanced levels were presented. Zorko singled out the participation of the choir which was comprised of students under the baton of Stevan Mokranjac.[68]

Miloje Milojević wrote a review of the concert held in 1911. Milojević presented the role of the Serbian Music School in the context of the general cultural development. He stressed the fact that the members of the school's faculty were artists trained in musical centers abroad. Therefore, the school had a dual function: young students received the necessary musical instruction while the school provided a steady occupation and source of income for composers and peforming artists who served as its faculty. Creative work alone or a career in the performing arts could not be profitable enough to sustain a bare existence. Therefore, the school provided a complementary source of support while, in turn, the pedagogical work of fine young artists helped in the process of furthering a musical education. The future growth of the school depended to a great extend on the quality of its faculty. The school also was helpful for the general public. It appeared that the school was the most powerful factor in the creation of Serbian national musical culture.

Milojević pointed out that the concert performances left the impression that some students had reached a professional level of musical knowledge. Milojević suggested that more concerts should be introduced, like three public performances with a larger programmatic scope as well as several recitals for smaller audiences. These concerts could provide added experience to the students, and the public would have more opportunity to follow the progress of the school.[69]

The teachers at the Serbian Music School soon formed an Association for Chamber Music. The members of the Association were Ivanka Milojević, singer, Ruža Šafarik and Rajna Dimitrijević, pianists, Jovan Ružička and Jovan Zorko, violinists, V. Rendl, violoncellist, and M. Buzin, clarinetist. The Association again proved the artistic qualities of the faculty members of the Serbian Music School.

The young musicians of the Association endeavored to enrich the musical life of the capital. The membership decided to gear its repertory toward the cultivation of classical and contemporary music. Special attention was given to the inclusion of Serbian and Slavic music literature. The Association also wanted to present a number of prominent foreign artists at their concerts. In October of 1911, the Association had already organized the first concert in the hall of the Second Belgrade High School before an overflowing audience that included eminent personalities of cultural life. Rajna Dimitrijević, the pianist, played *Nocturne in F sharp major* by Chopin, the *Preludium in G major* and *Dans les Bois* by Liszt and Beethoven's *Sonata Op. 53 in C major*. Dimitrijević completed her musical studies in Vienna under the tutelage of Professor Ludwig. Ivanka Milojević, the singer, presented a "modern repertory that until then was seldom heard in Belgrade." She sand the *Lieder* of Hugo Wolf and Johannes Brahms as well as selected compositions by Miloje Milojević and Petar Konjović–Božinski. Milojević graduated from the Music Academy in Munich where she studies under Bianka Bianki. The concert closed with the Piano quartet in E flat major by Robert Schumann. The reviewer stressed that the chamber music presented the most delicate art since it is not pretentious but subdued and modest yet strong in its intimate fashion. The attending public gave its approval by a prolonged applause. The reviewer concluded that this applause also signified that there could be a better future for the cultivation of chamber music.[70]

The Serbian Music School marked another milestone in 1912. The total number of students climbed to 207. The largest number of students attended the piano division, numbering 104 students. The violin division had 77, while 18 students studied voice. Five students graduated in 1912 from the teachers' course. There were 11 music teachers on the faculty of the school. The school provided a well rounded musical education as opposed to the instruction of private music teachers concentrating on developing playing or voice skills. There were courses in aesthetics, theory of music, harmony, counterpoint, history of music, and musical styles, as well as methods developing technical skills in music interpretation. Such education enabled students to interpret a musical work with greater comprehension. The programs of the school concerts testified to a careful selection of teaching materials encompassing works ranging from the classical to contemporary style. Featured composers were Bach, Scarlatti, Gluck, Viotti, Spohr, Mozart, Chopin, Liszt, Glinka, Tchaikovsky, and Godard.[71]

The reviewer stated that the Ministry of Education realized the importance a of musical education, and raised the subsidy to the school to 10,000 dinars. This amount should be increased in order to bring new faculty to teach all the instruments featured in a symphonic orchestra. Another suggestion pointed to the need for forming courses for an operatic studio and for acting. If all the suggestions could be implemented, then the school should become a state institution of learning, like the Glazbena Matica in Zagreb.

The final examination was treated as a serious professional qualification. Every year the deputy from the Ministry attended these examinations. In 1912, the designated deputy was Dr. Tihomir Djordjević, docent at the Unviersity of Belgrade.[72]

## Establishment of the Stanković Music School

At the beginning of this century, musical life in Belgrade was rapidly developing. New demands for expanding the music repertory brought into focus a need for trained musicians, in particular orchestra players. In Belgrade, the only symphonic body at that time was the Orchestra of the Royal Garde. The orchestra was perpetually engaged in endless performances of various kinds. They played for festive parades and balls, at the Royal Palace, in movie theaters, at the National Theater, and in concert halls. The orchestra took part in the symphonic concert of 24 February 1912 under the direction of Stanislav Binički, which was performed as a benefit for the future building of the Stanković Music School.[73]

Miloje Milojević, a music critic, reviewed the performance and noted that the players of the orchestra were unevenly trained. Some were amateurs and some were professionals and teachers of music. As an instrumental body, the members of the orchestra managed to create an interesting profile. The orchestra received numerous demands, and the players became overworked and tired. Milojević addressed words of praise to these musicians who "played with a marvelous endurance the music for *Egmont, Dorćolska posla (Dorćol Affairs),* and *Vilarovi Dragoni (Vilar's Dragoons).* Yet the same musicians did not find time to perform the dramatic fairy tale *Veče na moru (The Evening at the Sea)* by Petar Konjović Božinski. Obviously Milojević held in high esteem Konjović's composition and reproached the orchestra and its conductor for not paying attention to the fine symphonic work of a young Serbian composer.

> The Orchestra of the Royal Guard is sacrificing itself, and we feel that very well . . . The time has come for us to receive a civilian orchestra . . . in order to perform a musical and civilizing mission. An orchestra is the base for the highest musical development. Musical life is becoming more intense. Joint efforts may bring it to a higher level.[74]

The Stanković Singers Society felt that the time had come for the opening of a second school of music in Belgrade. The founding of the Stanković Music School took place in 1911. It testified to the expanded need for professional musicians, in particular performing artists and orchestra players. The Stanković Singers Society was a well known musical institution which had been established in 1881. The Society gave numerous concerts upholding the cultural life in Belgrade. On the occasion of its twentyfifth anniversary of artistic existence, the Society bought a building in Knez Miloš Street in Belgrade. Since the existing building did not have a large concert hall, the Society commissioned the architect, Petar Bajalović, docent at the University of Belgrade, to remodel and enlarge the building. Bajalović submitted plans that were accepted and with the reconstruction the building was expanded to include a concert hall with a gallery and a seating capacity of 360.

The Society invited Stanislav Binički to serve as the first director of the newly established school. The festive opening of the school was marked by a number of concerts in the new concert hall of the school. On the first day of the opening, on 9 February 1911, the Stanković Singers Society arranged a concert with compositions of Jenko, Stanković, Binički, Mokranjac, Marinković, Milojević, Krstić, and Božinski. The next, on 10 February, the members of the faculty gave a recital with the participation of Miroslava Binički, Jelica Krstić, Šopović, Miler, and Petar Krstić. They performed the following compositions: Quartet by Beethoven, *Preludium* by Rakhmaninov, *Sparks* by Moszkovski, *Sonata for violin and piano* by Frank, a selection of songs by Schubert and Delibes, and the Piano Quintet by Brahms. On the third day, 11 February, the students presented a recital. There were 120 students enrolled in the second and third year.[75]

The ethno–musicologist and composer, Vladimir R. Djordjević, a practicing music teacher, was well aware of the existing need for music textbooks. Therefore, he paid special attention to the methodology of teaching music, writing the needed textbooks, and providing instrumental and vocal music collection for use in the schools. Djordjević was appointed in 1898 to serve as a music teacher in the newly founded Serbian Royal Male Teachers' School in Jagodina. Already at the end of the first school year, Djordjević submitted a report containing his views about the possible improvement of musical education. His report, *Prvi zahtevi za pravilno učenje pevanja (The First Requirements for the Correct Teaching of Singing)*, was approved by the director and faculty and was included in the yearly report of the school for 1989–99.[76] Consequently, Djordjević received invitations from several teachers' associations requesting him to lecture on methodology of teaching music in public schools. Thus, his lecture, *Iz metodike pevanja u narodnoj školi (About the Methodology of Teaching Singing in Public Schools)*, was published in 1901 in a volume, edited by Josif B. Stojanović, dealing with teaching in public schools .[77]

Djordjević wrote a very successful book, *Škola za violinu (Violin School)* in 1896 which eventually appeared in nine editions. In addition, Djordjević composed two more collections of violin pieces, *Trideset srpskih igara za violinu (Thirty Serbian Dances for Violin)*, in 1905, and *Violinski album (Violin Album)*, in 1910.[78]

Among his numerous choral compositions, Djordjević composed several albums for use in public schools, such as *Zbirka dečijih pesama za učenike osnovnih škola (Collection of Children's Songs for Pupils of Elementary Schools)* in 1904, which appeared in two editions. He also composed *Zbirka odabranih pesama za školsku omladinu (Collection of Selected Songs for School Youths)* in 1909, which had five editions.[79]

It is interesting to note that Djordjević's first work presented a collection of folk melodies from Kulin village. These were published in the Pobratimstvo journal in 1892. While serving as a teacher in this village, Djordjević started collecting folk melodies. He continued collecting folk melodies and dances throughout his life. The most important publications in this field of endeavors were the two collections of Serbian folk melodies, *Srpske narodne melodije (Južna Srbija)*, published in 1928 with an introduction in French by the noted Belgian ethnomusicologist Ernest Closson.[80] The second collection, Srpske narodne melodije (Predratna Srbija) was published in 1931.[81]

The appearance in 1912 of the textbook on the theory of vocal music for middle school by Isidor Bajić received a fine review. Miloje Milojević wrote a review which appeared in *Srpski Književni Glasnik*. He was a regular contributor on musical matters to this journal. Milojević thought that Bajić's textbook merited attention as the first textbook on vocal music based on modern principles. Bajić was active as a composer and as a music teacher of the well known Serbian High School in Novi Sad. Therefore, Bajić knew that the students needed a theoretical textbook on vocal music. Milojević noted that, due to circumstances, Bajić had an opportunity to attend a special course in Berlin where he acquainted himself with contemporary methods in vocal instruction. Bajić called special attention in his book to the musical dictation and practical requirements of class instructions. The book included a collection of folk songs. Milojević thought that the introduction of folk songs in this textbook was appropriate and reflective of the spirit of the times. Milojević only criticized the inclusion of some songs, such as *Idem šorom (I Walk down the Alley)*, *Moja mati i tvoja (My Mother and Yours)*, as well as some others which were not suitable for this purpose in either the melodic or literary aspect.

Musical education was an important part of the curriculum in the Theological Seminary of Saint Sava since its establishment under Veselinović, its rector. Stevan Mokranjac taught at the Seminary and conducted the choir for a period of time. According to the recollection of Kosta P. Manojlović, a former student at the Seminary, Mokranjac was respected and loved by his students. Later, when Mokranjac retired from his position, Jovan Zorko continued in Mokranjac's footsteps. The Seminary choir gave choral recitals and slowly attracted a following among music lovers.

Miloje Milojević wrote an interesting and vivid review of the recital of the choir on 28 November 1911. The concert took place in the National Theater, and it demonstrated once again exceptional artistic qualities. Milojević noted that the repertory of the choir was broadened and had, as a result, become "musically more interesting." This recital included both secular and spiritual music. Milojević praised the insight of Mokranjac and the rector of the Seminary, Veselinović, for making such a change in the repertory reflective of their concordance in ideological and artistic concepts.[82]

This recital featured the first performance of the choral composition, *Porečko mome (The Girl from Poreč)* by Petar Konjović–Božinski, written a few years earlier, but not previously performed. The choral societies noted that the composition presented "unsurmountable difficulties." Milojević expressed his appreciation to the conductor and members of the choir for performing this outstanding composition permeated with the true "national artistic expression." This was a contemporary work unknown until then to the public, and the efforts of the conductor and choir were commendable. Among compositions of spiritual music, the *Tropar Svetoga Save (The Trope of Saint Sava)* and *Dostoino* by Vladimir Rebikov were performed.

In his review of the recital, Milojević used the opportunity to write a discourse on musical education in the middle schools. It was customary to accept the belief that the scope of instruction should be limited to preparation of two to three choral compositions for the recital at the school's celebration of its patron Saint Sava. It was also customary for the school orchestra to perform at this celebration. Milojević thought that the appearance of an orchestra was not necessary. He even thought that teaching instrumental music at the school should be eliminated. Milojević reasoned that every music teacher did not have to be a violinist or need to be able to teach double bass or the flute. In music education, solfeggio exercises were neglected, and too much attention was given to theoretical definitions. It was Milojević's opinion that "It did not matter whether C–E is a major third and C–E flat a minor third; one should be able to sing these intervals."[83]

The music teachers, as a rule, were overworked and burdened with a large amount of teaching and of choral and orchestral rehearsals. Many school principals understood the plight of the teachers and tried to help them. Among the school's faculty there were also composers who were also teaching a heavy load, since "one could not live in Serbia by only composing." However, many musicians suffered greatly under these circumstances. In conclusion, Milojević pleaded that the instruction of music be limited to vocal music only in order to alleviate the difficulties of the music teachers in Serbia.

The efforts of the Serbian Music School, and subsequently of the Stanković Music School in the field of musical education, started to produce visible results. Already in the course of the first decade of the twentieth century former students were starting their professional activities. Among the former students of the Serbian Music School, Miloje Milojević was one of the best known. In 1908, Milojević became the music critic of the prestigious journal, *Srpski Knijževni Glasnik*. Milojević joined the editorial staff of *Glasnik* upon the invitation of Bogdan Popović, his former professor at the University of Belgrade and the founder of the journal. Milojević strove, in particular, to implement higher artistic standards in musical life in general.

As a music critic, Milojević gave encouragement to composers to pursue their credo in music without compromise, demanding the same standard of excellence from themselves and from others. Milojević also contributed as a music pedagogue by teaching in the Serbian Music School and in IV Belgrade High School. As a member of the Chamber Music Association, he often accompanied his wife, the concert singer Ivanka Milojević, in recitals. Milojević was active as a composer as well. During 1905–10 he composed a series of piano miniatures. In 1911, Milojevicć enriched Serbian vocal literature with exquisite choral compositions, using the verses of the popular poet Vojislav Ilić, *Dugo se polje zeleni (The Long Field is Greening)* and *Slutnja (Premonition)*.

As a music critic, Milojević recorded with perseverance musical events that merited attention. His criticisms, as well as his studies and essays on diverse musical topics, became valuable historical material. Milojević's review of the piano recital by Jelica Subotić may be cited as an example of the style of his writing and his fresh observations. Subotić, an outstanding former student of the Serbian Mucic School, gave her piano recital in the National Theater on 16 December 1913. Milojević reminded his readers that Subotić had given many concerts previously in Belgrade.

> Miss Subotić has been giving concerts for many years. She received her training under the skillful hand of Cvetko Manojlović. Six or seven years ago she had already received tumultuous applause . . . for her interpretation of Chopin as well as Beethoven . . . Shortly after her graduation abroad she returned to present the results of her work and receive from us the same praise and exaltation.[84]

According to Milojević, Subotić had the predisposition of a good pianist and soloist with inborne musicality. When she appeared as an accompanist, she was able to collaborate and become a true partner of the ensemble. After graduation from the Serbian Music School, she continued her studies abroad, as did others who pursued the completion of their musical studies.[85]

Furthermore, Milojević noted that there existed an distasteful custom practiced by the public attending concerts in Belgrade. There persisted the belief that a singer or pianist from abroad would present greater pleasure than a native artist because the former came from Europe. However, after the recitals of domestic artists, the public was often pleasantly surprised and even elated. Enthusiastic praise was expressed and then proclaimed that it is a real pity that native artists are seldom acknowledged sufficiently.

Unfortunately, after their return from serious studies abroad, the

young artists were forced, due to circumstances, to serve more as
teachers than as "regulators of artistic taste of the intelligent as well
as broader public." Therefore, Milojević pleaded for the organized
action to unify young artists aspiring to such goals. One ought to
enable young artists to support their existence as concert artists and
help organize their concert appearances. The integration of young
and promising musicians into the educational system of the middle
schools, receiving modest salaries, could not help foster their careers
as performing artists.[86]

Many young artists extended their stay abroad after graduation
due to the unfavorable conditions for their work at home. The violinist and composer Petar Stojanović chose such a road. He stayed in
Vienna where he enjoyed the reputation of a fine violin pedagogue.
On a few occasions Stojanović appeared as a guest artist in his native land. Miloje Milojević wrote a review of Stojanović's recital in
the National Theater in Belgrade on 28 April 1914. Milojević noted
that the artistic concept of the program testified that Stojanović mis-
judged the public in Belgrade. Since Stojanović lived abroad he was
misinformed about the concert life and its public in the capital city.
Stojanović thought that it was necessary to simplify his transcriptions
of the popular songs and compositions full of romantic sentimentality.
He played the once well known song, *More mi je ljubav tvoja (If It
Were for Your Love)* by Davorin Jenko. Milojević noted that this
song at the time was only familiar to grandmothers or tender hearted
spinsters. Stojanović played *Zujte strune (The Strings are Humming)*
also, a composition that entertained young girls of the previous generation. The concert program was disappointing to many, and it was
the reason why the concert was not well attended.

Milojević thought that it would have been far more interesting if
Stojanović had included some of his own compositions, even if these
works were not rooted in the folk music idiom. As an example of
such compositions by Stojanović, Milojević mentioned the *Concert for
Violin in D minor*, compositions for violin, *Adagio man non troppo*
and *Scherzo in Ancient Style*.

Milojević concluded that Stojanović's fate presented an example
of an artist who spent his life in a foreign milieu where his name would
be recorded only on the last pages. In his own country, his name would
have been in the forefront since Stojanović was a talented artist. He
should have spent his life among his people helping to develop the
young musical art.[87]

Besides Stojanović, there were numerous outstanding artists working and living abroad in different art fields. Many among them have
earned recognition, like Paja Jovanović, Vlaho Bukovac, Ivan Gro-

har, Anton Ažbe, Branko Popović, all painters, and Josip Plečnik, architect. Their presence in their native land was highly desirable since they could provide enrichment with their participation in many areas of cultural life. Thus, with their collaboration in various exhibits, concerts or architectural projects, they could have influence the artistic and cultural appreciation of connoisseurs and the wider public alike. As educators, they could have helped elucidate a new generation of artists and intellectuals instilling in them aspirations for completion of yet unfinished goals.[88]

A special difficulty was the backwardness of some newly liberated provinces during the Balkan Wars. In Belgrade, the cultural and artistic growth reached new peaks of development. Similarly, the Serbian land that enjoyed independence from Turkish rule had slowly established its schools and attained cultural and economic growth. The discrepancy between the provinces, which were occupied until recently by the Turks, was overwhelming. Most of all, there existed an obligation to improve the education of the younger generation in these provinces.

Milojević vividly depicted the existing situation in a review of the choral recital of the Singer's Society, Car Uroš, from Uroševac in 1914, on the eve of World War I. Milojević noted that in the recently liberated town of Uroševac, formerly known as Ferizović, choral singing was cultivated. Vocal music, and especially choral singing, had an important national and social significance in many townships throughout Serbia.[89] Milojević noted that Ferizović was a neglected Turkish provincial town. Yet, the choir directed by the conductor, Nigl, sang surprisingly well. The members of the choir were dressed in colorful folk costumes. The program started with the intonation of the national anthem. Then followed the *X Rukovet (X Handful)* by Morkanjac, and a selection of compositions by Marinković, Binički, Joksimović, and Bajić.

While deliberating about the choral societies in general, Milojević stressed that special attention should be given to the musical education of future teachers and clergymen. The students should be instructed in sight reading and solfeggio in order to enable them to learn new compositions with less effort. Such an education would eliminate memorization by rote of the same repertory. The concert program would be able to include more interesting and serious selections. However, Milojević was aware that old customs and habits were hard to change.

> The province, with its stereotyped habits and stereotyped physiognomy, has always been the winner. Under the burden of narrow views, insufficient spiritual education, and patri-

archal customs, our citizens in the provinces never thought that there existed more freedom, never guessed that there is more to life than to take a siesta . . . on soft rugs . . . in the shade of a leafy walnut tree, in the mild sunset, and then to think about which restaurant one should go and where is the best beer . . . . Nothing has changed much in the provinces. There are Gypsy bands and singing of questionable songstresses. However, these forms of entertainment are being suppressed, thanks to the well organized traveling theater companies, a result of a new regulation by the theater.[90]

## Chapter 5

## Theatrical Life in Serbia in the Beginning of the Twentieth Century

In 1906, the well known theater critic, Milan Grol, wrote a valuable assessment of the current theatrical situation in Serbia. His evaluation appeared in the prestigious literary journal, *Srpski Književni Glasnik,* since Grol was a frequent contributor providing essays and articles in connection with the theater and its repertory policies. Grol contended that there had existed a serious crisis during the last 12 years in the theater company and its repertory as well as in alienating the public. In truth, the theatrical public in Belgrade had outgrown its old attitude towards theater, although it was not ready to accept the new repertory. Grol thought it would be desirable to find an acceptable solution. The theater company itself was not prepared well enough for a demanding dramatic repertory, such as the plays of Shakespeare, Schiller, Dumas fils, Musset, Ibsen, Gorky, Chekhov, and Sudermann. Furthermore, the introduction of opera under existing conditions, he suggested, would serve only to undermine the chaotic circumstances in the National Theater.[1]

Grol recalled that during a special conference held at the National Theater the decision was reached not to introduce operetta performances in disproportion to actual needs. The introduction of shorter and more modest classical operas in one act with relatively simple staging and a small cast would correspond better to existing requirements for a musical repertory. There were suggestions for performances of plays from diverse Slavic literatures with accompanying music. In spite of these recommendations about the repertory, the administration of the theater engaged foreign operatic singers to perform *Cavalleria Rusticana* by Mascagni.[2]

The members of the company of the National Theater were also very much concerned about the crisis that the theater was experiencing. The actors formed a club with a goal directed at preserving Serbian theatrical art. Since they were also concerned about their own position, they sent a resolution to the administration of the the-

ater. The public, informed of the difficulties facing the actors, sided
with the beloved actors, and they engaged in demonstrations during
a staging of Gorky's drama, *On the Bottom,* on 7 February 1906. Due
to the general commotion and shouting, the performance had to be
cancelled.[3]

Discussion about the crisis in the National Theater grew and
gained new ground. The actors succeeded in attracting public attention, while presenting their interpretation of the controversy. The
National Theater, in a response from Dragomir M. Janković from the
administration, presented the other side of the case.[4] Janković wanted
to turn attention to the major concerns that influenced the level of
repertory as well as the level or artistic interpretation. A majority
of the requests from the actors, as presented in the resolution, were
justifiable, he believed, and particularly those requests concerning the
lack of protection for the families of the actors. Janković dismissed
those claims that were written in anger and without reflection. The
efforts of the administration were directed mostly towards saving the
pension fund from default. The position of the artists, he noted,
would be improved if the state would guarantee their pensions.[5]

The pension fund had started in 1879. In order to improve the
existing shortage of funds, the administration had recognized the necessity of revising its policies to meet the current situation. The
minister of finance accepted the administration's new proposal and
agreed to form two commissions to examine the requests. Janković
thought that actors should serve as members of the commissions in
order to reach a fair solution regarding the pension fund and the
protection of families in accordance with new developments in the
theater.[6]

In addition to the requests for improvement of the financial position of those actors who were members of the National Theater,
there were other not so valid criticisms. Milan Grol commented that
the resolution of January 1906 discussed the role of the director and
dramaturge in the theater as well. The actors felt that the position
of the dramaturge should be terminated as being redundant. Grol
did not agree with such an action and pointed out that the directors
were in most cases also actors more interested in their acting and less
with directing. Often they lacked the thorough literary knowledge
needed in order to direct the repertory policy. The dramaturge was
needed since he would offer valuable advice and much needed collaboration with the directors at the theater. Grol concluded that the
request for improvement of material conditions was justified while the
request directed against the dramaturge was unjustified since "everybody appreciated how much progress depended upon knowledge."[7]

These discussions, which were led with great eloquence and persuasion, resulted in an increased subsidy.

In 1907, Dragomir Janković addressed himself again to this question and stated that the increase in funding would improve the salaries of the actors. The question of the pension fund remained, however. Janković pointed out that artists, sculptors, and musicians with credentials were accepted as civil employees of the state and taught in the middle schools. They also received pensions. But actors did not belong to this category. They did not have pensions. There were, nevertheless, excellent actors in Belgrade who could be compared with the composers, Josif Marinković and Stevan Mokranjac, or to the artist, Paja Jovanović and the sculptor, Djordje Jovanović. Such an eminent actor was Toša Jovanović.[8] The pension question persisted.

The 1906–07 theater season started under a new administration. This change was apparently brought about by the criticism surrounding the resolution of 1906. The united actors defined, in the resolution, the shortcomings of the previous administration as well as the real need for betterment of the salaries and general conditions. Some improvements were incorporated due to the increased subsidy and changes in theater administration.

In 1908, Milan Grol contended that two major issues had not been resolved—the pension fund for the actors and the definition of the roles of director and dramaturge in the theater. The actors thought that the director should enjoy independence in his work and that the role of the dramaturge in the theater should be limited to purely literary aspects.[9] Grol thought that the greatest shortcomings of both administrations was the squandering of funds in cultivating the operetta. Experience had shown that the work involved in preparing an operetta demanded unnecessary exhaustion of both energy and of a small budget. Yet the old practice continued. Grol stressed his belief that the operetta was directing the work of the theater in the wrong direction, demoralizing taste, and "bringing shame to the National Theater." Among the existing improvements in the theater, Grol mentioned an increase in the budget of the orchestra and an increase in honoraria for guest appearances.[10]

Awareness of the existing crisis in the National Theater brought many suggestions about possible solutions. Several articles appeared in the journal *Pokret* on this topic, followed by possible solutions which appeared in the fifth issue of the journal in 1910. This journal was published sporadically by an association of young writers from Vojvodina. Its editorial policy aimed at eliciting a livelier interest in the improvement of cultural and social life. The National Theater occupied a position of greater importance, according to the opinions expressed in many of the articles. The editors wished to inform the readers about a possible reorganization and other solutions that might help solve existing problems. It was important to provide all such information before the meeting of the Society of the National Theater.[11]

Peter Konjović, a composer, wrote the leading article for *Pokret* about the existing crisis under the title "Why is it necessary to talk about our National Theater?" Konjović showed an interest in the theater even by his own preference for operatic genre early in his artistic career. In 1903, Konjović composed his first opera, Ženidba Miloša Obilića. In the course of time, Konjović composed four more operas. He also served as director of the theaters in Osijek, Split, and later, Zagreb.

In his article, Konjović addressed the question of the National Theater from a broad and well defined point of view. The question of the theater should be understood only as a part of the cultural life of the Serbs in Vojvodina. Konjović hoped to establish one single objective for the development of all institutions aiming for unification.

> This work . . . should be understood as part of the cultural policy that could involve all segments of our conscientious people. If we proceed in this direction cautiously but in a clear and balanced course, more and more of our people will approach a good and artistic book in order to learn about true artistic forms, and be influenced by thought, taste, and refinement. Then will our literary and artistic efforts receive a wider field of works, and at the same time we will be giving to society a better look at our culture and national consciousness.[12]

Konjović further noted that the National Theater lacked an ideological program as demonstrated by the heterogeneous and tasteless repertory and wretched diction and acting of the actors. There were too many adaptations of Hungarian vaudevilles that bordered on absurdity. The staging of well known Shakespearian tragedies were marred by capricious changes, poor scenery, and pathetic declamation. Plays of the romantic style were overly sentimental. Konjović concluded that the repertory of the National Theater did not adhere to a stable program and did not show definite direction or style due to the fact that the administration was guided by insufficiently prepared amateurs who were "lovers of the arts." Rather, such responsible functions should be performed by trained professionals and should be distinguished by a serious approach and sincerity in the presentation of true works of art.[13]

At the beginning of the century, one of the often discussed topics dealing with the theater in Serbia was the apparent lack of trained young actors. The director of the National Theater, Dragomir M. Janković, was well informed about the existing situation in Belgrade. Since there was no special school devoted to the training of young actors, Janković proposed that special attention be addressed to the traveling theater companies. Among the actors in these companies there were likely to be found some fine talent. Janković noted that, in both France and Hungary, traveling companies were regularly reviewed in order to find talented individuals. The Hungarians allotted considerable funds to their traveling companies.[14]

Some traveling theater companies were very successful. Janković singled out the Actors Society in England, headed by Frank R. Benson. The Society performed not only plays of Shakespeare, Sheridan, and Goldsmith but also Greek tragedies. In addition to his studies at Oxford and his extensive experience, Benson possessed natural talent as an actor. He taught diction and dramaturgy to young actors and created a kind of "travelling group." In one engagement, Benson's company gave 18 performances in 15 days during the last festivities in Shakespeare's birthplace. Benson believed that dramatic plays had a distinct democratic character and that the true function of a drama was to uplift and delight the people and to offer refined entertainment.

Janković was in agreement with Benson's philosophy of the role of dramatic plays. Drama should not become a monologue of highly educated individuals or of those who follow the whims of fashion. Most certainly it should not resemble a commercial enterprise. Janković believed that great success could be achieved with a good traveling company organized according to the model provided by Benson. The repertory of such a traveling company should be planned with the help of the National Theater. The theatrical plays of regional folk style as well as several plays of the standard repertory would be appropriate. For such a venture, a good director was essential in order to build a good company with relatively few difficulties. However, Janković concluded with a note of resignation.

> Since the time of Joakim Vujić—blessed be his memory— up the the present time, nothing was done for our traveling theater companies. No special regulation exists. In the new proposals of the bylaws concerning the National Theater, an effort was made to sanction such activities . . . The National Theater has no right to supervise the work of these companies and to suggest guidelines . . . . In spite of my research, I could not find out how many companies there were . . . In conversations with old leaders of companies

such as Fotije Ilić and Djura Protić, I realized that , based on their experiences, one could compile a considerable amount of material about Serbian ambulatory theatrical art.[15]

Furthermore, Janković described the difficult life of traveling actors who took their tent from one place to another and tried hard to succeed, only to earn enough to have food.  Since these companies were in direct contact with the people, they were ready for compromises.  The repertory consisted of adaptations of novels and "dramatizations of all kinds of events."  The best known traveling company, Sindjelić, offered in miniature the repertory of the theater in Belgrade.  *Mam'zelle Nitouche,* with music by Hervè, was the only operetta that was currently performed.  Great caution should be exercised, the critic observed, with the repertory of the National Theater since the provincial theaters imitated trends set in Belgrade.

The National Theater in Belgrade followed a custom of entertaining the public between acts of the plays with incidental music. Since the public became fond of these musical interludes, Peter Krstić pleaded that the National Theater should enlarge the orchestra in order to be able to play more intricate musical scores.  Krstić noted that the same custom of providing musical entertainment during intermissions was practiced in the Viennese theater, Deutsches Volks Theater. He felt that the orchestra in the National Theater in Belgrade should upgrade its repertory to play overtures and suites and try to avoid light or dance music.  Until recently, the Military Orchestra, with 25 players, was engaged to play.  A smaller ensemble had replaced the Military Orchestra.  Krstić added sarcastically that the current ensemble was inadequate and smaller than the ones in "Prater's dance saloons where Viennese cooks, coachmen, and caretakers are entertained."  Kristić concluded that Belgrade, as the capital city, should have an orchestra with 40 to 45 players.[16]

The role of theatrical performances in the first years of the twentieth century often went further than presentations of purely artistic messages.  These performances were often a means of displaying patriotic and national aspirations.  The same ethical and patriotic function was often achieved by musical performances, particularly choral recitals as well as art exhibits with historical national themes.

In 1909, the guest appearances at the National Theater in Skoplje achieved the mission of strengthening the feeling of spiritual union and rekindling the hope for liberation of Macedonia from Turkish domination.  Such a tour was vividly described for readers of *Srpski Književni Glasnik* by a reporter identified only by the signature X. The reviewer, a well informed and very eloquent writer, revealed insight and knowledge as well as a flair for writing in his delightful review.[17]

On his departure from Belgrade one cold October evening, the reviewer, by a strange coincidence, found himself on the same train with a large group of actors from the National Theater. He had decided to take this trip because it meant a fulfillment of a pledge and a "cherished vow." The actors started singing as the train was leaving the railway station. As the reviewer walked through the different cars of the train, he saw in the last car some stage apparel—emperors' crowns, armor, swords, and daggers. He could not discern whether they were made of precious metal or of plaster. All these make-believe trappings were symbolic tokens of a common past. The reviewer understood these reminders of past glory to be tools that would help save and conquer, as a figurative essence of "the new campaign for the South."[18]

Deliberating about this theatrical paraphernalia and fake glitter that sparkled in the darkness of the compartment, and to justify its presence, the traveler wrote that these vain accessories reminded him of the time when the real swords of brave knights rattled over the cobblestone streets of Kruševac, the place of residence of the honorable Prince Lazar.

> The blind Serbian bard sometimes used hundreds of verses to dress up Miloš and his two blood brothers in their lordly outfits . . . these verses of impoverished poets presented at the best the grande style of our past . . . and a taste planted in us for beauty and space . . . . We went to the South to conquer a future with our past since all these crowns and daggers should have their battles . . . I forfeited the belief of my generation that our history and folk soul derived from peasant stock and that my heart felt the necessity for more space and beauty.[19]

By early morning as the train approached Skoplje and the surrounding Šar mountain came into view covered with new white snow, the view reminded the traveler of Prince Marko who had fallen asleep into eternity. The suburbs of Skoplje left a pitiful impression compared with the beauty of Šar mountain. Even the center of the city had "miserable buildings and shabbily dressed people." The reviewer felt disappointed since there was no trace of the city and former glory of Emperor Dušan.

> There is only the bridge on the Vardar River . . . and the people . . . . One's eyesight is blinded by the poverty, famine, terrible disorder, filth, and depressed faces. The city, at a crossroad from Roman times, is situated in one of

the richest parts of Europe, having a population of 50,000, yet it has nothing to show to Europe, save the quay along the Vardar.[20]

This dismal impression was further emphasized by the gray skies and muddy ditches. However, the reviewer noted that the new theater building left a pleasant impression with its two tiers of boxes, a tribute to Pasha's desire for contemporaneity. The building served for cinematic shows as well. The audience presented an interesting gathering. In the second tier, the street vendors were seated wearing their white caps. They expressed their approval by whistling, especially during the performance of Koštana. The more educated public was seated in the orchestra, the men wearing red fezzes. The ladies, seated in the boxes, had huge hats with feathers, very likely bought in Vienna, Budapest or Thessalonika.

Among the plays staged, Koštana by Borisav Stanković enjoyed hugh success. The famous Ilija Stanojević "Čiča" enraptured the public with his interpretation of Mitke. Less successful was the performance of *Ljubavno pismo (The Love Letter)* by Kosta Trifković, *Pod starost (In Old Age)* by Branislav Nušić, and *Les Precieuses Ridicules* by Molière. The performance of the play, *Djido*, by Janko M. Veselinović was dragged out and uneventful. However, the folk costumes were attractive and the musical numbers were well peformed. The public was greatly impressed by *Zidanje Ravanice (The Building of Ravanica)*, a historical play. The whole play resembled a liturgy. It developed at its own slow and majestic pace and reminded one of the speeches of the clergy and also of the chanting of epic bards, guslari. The history of a great people was presented with personages from the Kosovo epics, the Emperor and Empress, the young Jugović brothers, and the old Jug–Bogdan, Miloš Obilić, Rade Neimar. The historical costumes were delightful and rich, and the actors subdued their diction and did not talk too loudly. The reviewer thought that this play had shown the possible direction for future plans. The presentation of Koštana with Mitke's drinking bout was not a good choice for a guest appearance. The reviewer thought that Molière's play also did not fit the occasion.[21]

The National Theater in Belgrade celebrated the fortieth anniversary of its founding on 5 November 1909. The celebration, which was attended by the highest state and church dignitaries, demonstrated the important role of this institution in public life.

The special festive program commemorating the founding was held in the National Theater. The program opened with a Prologue written by the poet, Velimir Rajić, in the style of a *tableau vivant* commemorating the moment of the groundbreaking ceremony which took place 40 years ago.

> Against the backdrop of a Turkish mosque, Turkish houses, and the green river banks of the Danube, Metropolitan Mihailo and Prince Milan, surrounded by dignitaries, were laying the foundation at the location of former trenches.

The celebration was attended by theater directors from many other South Slavic towns. Thus, this occasion generated talk about possible future collaboration among these theaters.[22]

*Podvala (Deceit)*, a play by Milovan Glišić , was chosen for the festive performance since Glišić wrote this play in 1869 at the time the National Theater was erected. The reviewer stressed that this was not the only reason for choosing this play. More important was the fact that Glišić's play was the predecessor of a number of similar plays which later became the most popular theatrical genre. This play presented a series of unrelated scenes from folk life which did not have the form of a classical drama. The characteristic of the personalities presented in the play were recognizable types and they were regularly featured in other plays. Later, music was introduced, and these plays became known as theatrical plays with singing. Although they lacked real dramatic action and tended to be drawn out, they still represented successful achievements of Serbian drama. The reviewer concluded that there had been actors who appeared in plays by Shakespeare, Ibsen, and Dumas as well as writers who wrote plays other than folk plays. Yet, the plays with singing became the only real measure of the success of writers as well as the actors who appeared in the performances.[23]

Glišić's play was discussed at another festive occasion—the opening of the School for Actors at the National Theater, which was, for many, a dream that finally came true. The new school formally opened a few weeks after the celebration of its founding on 21 November 1909, and presented a continuation of the festivities associated with the anniversary celebrations. The opening speech, delivered by the director of the National Theater, stressed that the 40 years of existence of the National Theater had been a period filled with important events and important memories. Progress in the theater went hand in hand with progress in other fields of art. Yet on the day of celebration the critics pointed to the shortcomings of the program. There were suggestions that a tragedy by Miloš Cvetić or drama by Branislav Nušić should have replaced the comedy *Podvala* by Glišić.[24]

The director admitted in his speech that while the National Theater did not fulfill all expectations, despite its successful beginnings, it had raised high hopes in its first years of existence. Therefore, renewed support and improved working conditions should be offered to the theater company. The main question regarding the recruiting and education of young actors remained as well as the general development of theatrical arts. The opening of such an artistic workshop should help revitalize the National Theater. A school for actors was opened by the initiative of the administators and actors in accordance with their existing needs and experiences. This initiative ensured the establishment of the actors' school on a solid foundation. A knowledge of the spoken language and clarity of enunciation and diction were considered as an obligatory part of the education of an actor. In order to refine acting, knowledge of literary epochs, dramas, and theater were necessary as were the history of acting, costumes, stage design, dancing, fencing, and music.

> This long road in the development that a good actor can fulfill on his own takes place only in a long and strenuous career . . . in today's world of more complex and greater requirements . . . . It would be redundant to explain the usefulness of a systematic education of Shakespeare's interpretations.[25]

Later in his speech, the director described the curriculum at the school for actors. Instruction and exercises were to be divided into four–month segments during a two–year period. The annual examination, which was planned for the month of May, would consist of performances of selected scenes, roles, or plays. The lectures were designed for all of the participants, consisting of 24 of the younger actors/beginners at the National Theater. The practical work and exercises were to be conducted in separate groups under the leadership of three directors. Depending on their performance, the young actors would be accepted or promoted. There was a provision for possible specialization abroad.[26]

For the first examination, which took place on 1 and 3 June 1910, the following plays were performed: *Kir Janja (Master Janja)* and *Svirači iz Kremone (The Players from Cremona).* Grol in his review argued that the administration of the new school tried to present the examination performances by the students as matinees where they charged admission. Grol was confident that they would be successful although it was unrealistic to expect that after a few months all mistakes would be corrected.[27]

Grol listed the names of professors and the subjects they taught during the first school year. Milan Predić, the dramaturge, taught Logic and Aesthetic Analysis of the Literary Text as an introduction to reading and discussion of the text itself. Dr. Nikola Vulić taught

History of the Ancient World. Dr. Veselin Čajkanović taught History of Drama and Theater of the Old Greeks and Romans. Dr. Vojislav Djordjević taught Psychology of Mimics and Gestures. Fighting techniques were taught by Erb. The directors and dramaturges of the National Theater instructed the young actors in the practical applications of the art of acting.[28]

Unfortunately, when the school closed its doors a short time later the need for reopening such an institution was soon intensely felt. Branko Lazarević, the literary critic, wrote in 1912 about the necessity for furthering the education of young actors.

> Our actors only seldom possess in the first place a general discipline and, secondly, an acting discipline. They appear on the scene by accident . . . . an actor who only has an instinct for a characteristic trait but did not acquire any kind of acting instruction, in comparison to an actor who has the one and also the other, loses very much . . . Not one of our acting talents was cultivated according to a plan, method or system. They act . . . in the same manner as a bird sings or a stream babbles, they act by instinct or as it just occurred in their mind, or by accident.[29]

Lazarević thought that the state of acting in 1912 was similar to the state of literature 10 or 15 years ago. At that time, it was assumed that a poet was born and that his gift of creation was inborn. He did not need to work at or to learn his craft, "One should only drink and wait for inspiration." Accordingly, inspiration will certainly then lead to exceptional creations. Lazaravić thought that this "romantic" theory was harmful since it ruined the literary work of talented people. This same theory, if still considered valid among the actors, should be proven as false. Lazarević singled out few exceptional actors and actressses. Thus, Ilija Stanojević would be judged a remarkable actor on any stage as would Sava Todorović. Dobrica Milutinović would be considered, with his appearance and voice, an outstanding personality in any theater. Zorka Todosić had become very well known by performing the works of Sterija Popović. Lazarević thought that these actors were truly capable of demonstrating in their presentations of dramatic personalities the all important characteristics. They were able to create a role in the sense of intuitive comprehension of the very essence of the portrayed personality. However, they were successful only in one particular repertory, and after careful observation one could detect even among them a lack of acting knowledge. Lazarević was especially weary of the unproven theories of inborn talents which assumed that already at birth one is endowed with a gift of becoming a poet. Thus, Ilija Stanojević could portray Kir Janja with insight, and yet could truly be disappointing in a French play.

> Our actors, in the most elegant French salons described by Hervè, Bataille, and Capus, place their hands deep into the pockets of a smoking jacket all the way to their elbows and move around in a very dubious and fashionable way, or they sit around as if in a cafe of the third order . . . Therefore, one should cultivate and educate them, and especially by the help of a School for Acting and other institutions, cure them of the theories of "birth" and "creation."[30]

As a result of all these reasons, Lazarević pleaded for the reopening of the school for acting, even for expanding its scope and defining qualifications for enrollment. Lazarević thought that the school should accept only those who have a well–rounded general education. In the case of the exceptionally talented acting students, this first prerequisite could be waived. The older actors should also attend the acting school since they also have much to learn.[31]

In his article published in 1911 in *Srpski Književni Glasnik,* Lazarević also described an important project of collaboration between Serbs and Croats. The administration of the National Theater invited members of the Belgrade National Theater as their guests at performances so the actors from Belgrade would have an opportunity to return visits. This exchange of guest appearances was helpful for the development of the national program as well. Lazarević reminded the public that a similar collaboration was already operating in the areas of science, fine arts, and politics. There were already visible results, but there would be even more success in the future since the program was well planned and executed with dedication. It was planned that all Yugoslav actors visit all Yugoslav theaters to create closer ties and a better understanding. All these efforts would lead to a greater professional quality of artistic work. The guest appearances of Ivan Rajić and Josip Štefanec in Belgrade marked the beginning of this collaboration. Both actors came from the Zagreb Theater which was considered one of the finest among the South Slavs and had already enjoyed several years of successful organization with a definite goal. Lazarević noted that Radić and Štefanec were good actors and educated although with little natural talent. Štefanec distinguished himself in the role of Damjan in the drama, *Smrt majke Jugovića (The Death of Jugović's Mother).*

All this was in contrast to the National Theater in Belgrade. In Belgrade, in the past ten years, many changes had taken place in the administration, repertory, directing, and staging. In some ways, a real revolution had taken place. "The Zagreb Theater gave the impression of gradual growth, established plans, and orderliness."[32] In conjunction with the collaboration between the Serbian and Croatian theaters, Milan Begović gave a public lecture entitled, "Our Modern Theater," at the National Theater on 18 May 1911. Afterwards, it was published in *Srpski Književni Glasnik* as an important explanation of the goals and objectives of the theatrical arts among Serbs and Croats alike.[33] Begović stated that he was not considering the revival of the national theater in the sense expressed once before in national drama, *Poslednji Zrinski (The Last Zrinski)*, and other similar plays. Such nationalism, no matter in what art form, is only an exterior mark "without the soul" and real understanding of specific people. Begović wished that contemporary art could preserve the people, their name, and their identity, as well as the historical past. If this goal could be achieved, then such art would be understandable to many—to the English, American, Japanese, and finally to the South Slav people as well. The essence of the existence of a nation could be preserved if presented from a universal point of view. It would remain understandable even if its language were lost and the nation itself perished. The old Greeks experienced such a fate. Although the majority among the present day coevals did not know their language, their deeds, and their future, their innermost soul remained alive and understandable in what remained after them, in their epics, lyrics, architecture, and sculpture.[34]

Begović recollected with pleasure the success of Meštrović whose works were delighting Europe. At that time, the dramatic plays by Vojnović were little known outside Yugoslavia. The reasons were mainly due to a technical nature—that is, translations, publishers, publicity, and also popular demand, depending on the whims of fashion. Begović noted that Hungarian plays enjoyed popular acclaim at that time.[35]

Begović noted that Josip Kosor wrote *Požar strasti (The Fire of Passion)*, a drama that delighted many. Yet his work was not shown on the stage of any foreign theater. Afterwards, Kosor wrote another drama which was even more impressive than the first. There were hopes that this drama would be performed. Begović expressed his dissatisfaction about the difficulties that writers faced when he wrote:

> The fear from the unknown, my dear gentlemen, that is our curse! Nobody has the power to reach into the poetic treasury of another world, from an unknown author or an unheard style. However, one has to reach out . . . . Still, this is not only a question for individuals. It matters to all

present and future writers . . . that which is our cultural calling.[36]

Begović then named some important people in the theatrical world. Joca Savić, once a high ranking director of the Royal Theater in Munich, was considered among the best known professionals in Germany. Stjepan Miletić, who was affiliated with the Croatian Theater, started to write an excellent Pentalogy. *Knez od Semberije (The Prince of Semberija)*, a drama by Nušić, had the potential to become a masterpiece of modern theatrical art if performed by a well trained company. Begović concluded that it was necessary to pay more attention to domestic creations and study new avenues of art development when he wrote, "Let us take a handful from the treasury of our spirit to create something that will carry our fame. A strong desire to find new ways in the arts ought to be our cultural goal."[37]

*Pozorišni godišnjak (The Theater Annual)* for 1911–12 contained more information about the collaboration among Yugoslav theaters.[38] Among the important events of the year a guest appearance of the National Theater in the neighboring capital of Bulgaria was mentioned. The National Theater gave performances in Sofia in May of 1912. A reciprocal appearance of the Bulgarian Theater was soon to be scheduled. The collaboration among South Slavic theaters was part of a carefully planned cultural policy implemented in the first decade of this century.

Among the guest appearances of foreign artists on the stage of the National Theater, the presentations of the members of the Comedie Francaise were singled out. Castelnova, the Italian operatic company, presented a number of performances. There was a guest appearance by the Russian actress, Haliutina–Andreeva. A renewed contract with the Croatian Opera Company was later cancelled by the Croatian state officials.

In addition, *The Theater Annual* recorded an interesting attempt by Luka Popović to establish a Serbian Theater in the United States. During the same theatrical season, the founding of the Serbian Dilletante Theater in Sarajevo took place.

The repertory of the National Theater in Belgrade was also scrutinized in the *Annual*. It was noted that the administration of the Theater cultivated with much vigor the performances of plays with singing. It was suggested that a competition be offered sponsoring the writing of new theatrical plays with music. The reason for this decision was the great popularity that these plays enjoyed among the general theatergoers. It was known that plays with singing invariably filled the theater to capacity. In spite of the fact that the theater had started the new 1911-12 season "in a new and reformed situation," the repertory still featured plays with singing. In contrast, only one play by Shakespeare was staged. There was also a disproportion between performances of foreign dramas and the works of Serbian writers. Serbian drama was represented by performances of *Maksim Crnojević* and *Janković Stojan*. It appeared to the reviewer that the plays that were based on Serbian historical past were poorly presented in an artistic and dramatic sense. The public should be won over by true artistic qualities and not by relying on feelings of national compassion.[39]

The renowned theater critic, Milan Grol, contributed a valuable analysis of the repertory of the National Theater in *Srpski Književni Glasnik* in 1912. Grol argued that the repertory itself gave important information about the ideas that prevailed at the time. His review was a testimony of an informed contemporary about the theatrical and cultural aspirations, in general, of the environment he thoroughly knew.

> The most profound characteristic of a theater, of a theater company, dramaturgy, public, critique . . . that is all represented in the repertory. The repertory is the basis of all critiques be it artistic, financial, professional or of that of a layman.[40]

Grol pointed out that the state theaters and subsidized theaters in large cities had difficult tasks. These theaters had to perform the best plays from the world and national dramatic literatures. The Austrian Burgtheater and the Comedie Francaise had such responsibilities. However, national theaters in relatively small countries with small cities had even greater difficulties. These theaters were national institutions and at the same time the only theaters. The situation is even further complicated by the restricted technical and material conditions. Yet, these theaters aimed at presenting a varied repertory in order to please different tastes. Furthermore, such theaters are expected to continuously work on improving the artistic and national character. The theaters in Belgrade and Zagreb ought to present on a modest stage to the young and not too numerous public theatrical repertory in a harmonious balance of all genders, literatures, and centuries. There should be 12 to 15 new performances, and three times that many repetitions.

Grol stated that he was aware of the criticism about the repertory policy of the National Theater in Belgrade. In the era of Gabriel d'Annunzio, Leonid Andreev, Maurice Maeterlinck, Oscar Wilde, Bernard Shaw, and Knut Hamsun, the National Theater was still presenting plays by Victorien Sardou and Alexandre Dumas fils. There seemed to exist a necessity for a theater to present contemporary and fashionable plays for smaller groups of people out of sheer snobbery. These passing whims did not offer satisfaction to the broader and larger public that constituted the essential raison d'etre of a theater. Finally, these plays did not provide roles that could bring success to the actors. Apparently Grol was not in favor of the contemporary dramas, favoring instead theatrical plays that appealed to larger audiences.[41]

For several years the repertory of the National Theater included presentations of French vaudevilles that lasted in spite of their futility. The presentations of plays by Alexandre Dumas fils lasted even longer. On the other hand, the folk plays of Ludwig Anzengruber reached the National Theater only in 1906, already too late for the beneficial role that Anzengruber's dramas could have exerted on the formation of Serbian folk plays. Instead, Serbian folk plays continued to be produced adhering to the model provided by *Seoska Lola (The Village Carouser)* and similar other crude plays. Grol recalled that *Le Demi Monde,* a play by Dumas père, arrived on the stage of the National Theater in the middle of the 1890s preceeding Anzengruber's play by ten years.[42]

Improved conditions for artistic work, in particular for good directing, showed results, however. During previous theater seasons, the more successful and larger premieres hardly reached four or five performances in the same season. In the 1911-12 season, almost all premieres surpassed these numbers of performances. In spite of the visible progress, it was not yet possible to stage *Uncle Vanja, Three Sisters* or *The Cherry Orchard* by Chekhov. Grol thought that these dramas of a discreet and psychological nature were too refined for performances at the National Theater.

Popular plays with singing still constituted the largest part of the repertory. These folk plays did not present great difficulties for interpretation of characters and their psychological makeup. The plays with singing presented a theatrical form close to melodrama with simple heroes and plots, including laughter and weeping for the simple fantasy of the masses. Grol noted with distress that in the last three years Vojnović's play, *Dubrovačka trilogija (Dubrovnik's Trilogy)* was seldom performed. The plays by Vojnović offered many possibilities for success as well as many responsibilities for the actors and directors. Molière's plays were hardly ever performed, a fact that Grol deplored. Among Shakespeare's plays, only the most popular, such as *Othello, Hamlet,* and *Romeo and Juliet,* were performed.[43]

The arrival of Aleksandr Ivanovich Andreev at the National Theater in 1911 brought great improvements. Andreev served in a dual capacity as director and chief administrator. It was expected that Andreev would introduce the methods of Stanislavsky since he was a former member of the prestigious Khudozhestveny Theater in Moscow. The directorial methods of Stanislavsky had attracted the attention of informed circles since the triumphant guest appearances of the Khudozhestveny Theater in Germany in 1906.[44] During his first season at the National Theater in Belgrade from 1911-12, Andreev directed six plays, *The Tempest* by Ostrovsky, *Public Apartment* by Rishkov, and the two tragedies, *Macbeth* and *Coriolanus*, by Shakespeare. He staged the premiere of the drama *Gospodja sa suncobranom (The Lady with the Parasol)* by Ivo Vojnović. In addition, he reviewed the presentation of *Gabriel Borkman* by Henrik Ibsen. By the summer of 1913, Andreev had staged several important plays—*The Bethrothal* and *Uncle Vanja* by Anton Chekhov, *The Snake Maiden* by Victor Rishkov, and *Four of Them* by Gabriel Zapol'sky. *Kosovska tragedija (The Kosovo Tragedy)*, a drama by the young Serbian poet Žarko Lazarević, was also presented. In addition, Andreev directed the opera production of *Il Trovatore* by Giuseppe Verdi, trying his hand in an operatic performance.

During the 1913-14 theater season, Andreev staged the one act plays *Jubilee, Chirurgy*, and *Culprit* by Chekhov and dramatized *The Brothers Karamazov* by Dostoevsky. In addition, Andreev staged *The Death of Ivan the Terrible* by Aleksei Tolstoy and *Cyrano de Bergerac* by Edmond Rostand. During the same season, Andreev again took part in operatic productions and directed two operas, *Djamileh* by Georges Bizet and *Werther* by Jules Massenet.[45]

Starting in 1912, the National Theater engaged Milutin Čekić as director. He was born in 1882 and was the first Serbian professionally trained director from the German theater. He spent the 1911-12 theater season in a specialization in Berlin while waiting for a vacancy in the National Theater in Belgrade. Čekić was familiar with the innovative theatrical work of Reinhardt and other German directors associated with symbolism. He relied in his own work on architectonic solutions in scenography and demanded from the actors a psychologically justified and studious performance. In opera performances of *Freischütz* by Carl Maria von Weber and *Mignon* by Ambroise Thomas, Čekić collaborated with Balusek, an artist. For the plays that Čekić directed he often combined a background of painted scenery with a more modern adaptation of the classical stage. Čekić brought an enrichment with his directorial work to the National Theater and, in particular, advanced an approach to scenography.[46]

The 1913-14 theater season finished with *Allons Enfants*, a drama by Vojnović and *Običan čovek (The Simple Man)*, a comedy by Nušić.

These performances were also the last before the closing of the National Theater for restoration on 18 June 1914. However, only ten days after the curtain fell, the Sarajevo assassination occurred. After the outbreak of World War I, the National Theater was evacuated to Skoplje. Due to the general mobilization there was a shortage of actors and the National Theater from Belgrade soon merged with the National Theater from Skoplje. The theatrical work ended in July of 1915 shortly before the evacuation from Skoplje.[47]

## Chapter 6

## Cultural Progress in Serbia before World War I

### Advancement of Fine Arts

The affirmation of Yugoslav artists both in their country and abroad became more pronounced at the beginning of the second decade of the twentieth century. The renowned artists, Vlaho Bukovac, Paja Jovanović, Ivan Grohar, Anton Ažbe, Mirko Rački, Emanuel Vidović, Celestin Medović, Ljuba Babić, Vladimir Becić, and Branko Popović, lived and worked abroad. They visited their native land periodically. Thanks to the initiative of several prominent public figures as well as some artists and scientists, the Council for the Organization of Artistic Affairs was founded in Belgrade in 1913. The Council aimed to attract artists and facilitate their return to their homeland by trying to offer favorable working conditions. The sponsor of the Council was Crown Prince Aleksandar, and honorary vice presidents were Bogdan Popović, Andra Stefanović, Ivan Meštrović, and Josif Plečnik.[1] Nadežda Petrović, an artist, supported the founding of the Council with enthusiasm and joined the Council in the capacity of its first secretary.[2]

The Council prepared a printed program that defined the goals and related activities contained in ten propositions: 1) Founding of the Fine Arts College and Artistic Industry with a national character; 2) Extension of the existing art education at the University and in middle schools; 3) Founding of the Arts Gallery containing pictorial and plaster copies; 4) Founding of the Modern Yugoslav Gallery in Belgrade; 5) Enrichment of Serbian and Yugoslav national art and artistic culture; 6) Enhancement of Theatrical and Decorative Art; 7) Building of the Vidovdanski hram (St. Vitus' Monastery) by Meštrović; 8) The Council should serve as an Advisory Body to the minister of education in all artistic affairs of Serbia and Yugoslavia; 9) Founding of a special department in the Ministry of Education; 10) Founding of a Great Society for the advancement of Yugoslav art.[3]

Kosta Strajnić reported in *Srpski Kujiževni Glasnik* that the fine arts had achieved a leading role within the Yugoslav cultural community.

> Yugoslav fine arts, as one of the highest manifestations of the culture of Serbes–Croats, Slovenes, and Bulgarians, ought to be a harmonious organization of the best spiritual treasures of all Yugoslav clans, the building of a new and great civilization of Slavs in the Balkans. After the heroism and victories of the Serbian Army, Yugoslav cultural nationalism should continue the work worthy of the primeval Serbian state and national powers. Only the highest artistic achievements and a high level of culture shall enable the Yugoslav union to govern in the cultural aspect the Balkans and to uphold the Slav idea in the Balkans.[4]

The founding of a Fine Arts College was considered as the most important prerequisite for the betterment of artistic culture. The curriculum of the Fine Arts College was supposed to include, next to courses for painting and sculpture, special architectural classes. Plans for a division in applied arts included graphics and textile design as well as a modern foundry. The Fine Arts College should have played a leading role in influencing the industry of consumer goods, especially furnishings and carpets, implementing the national style.[5] Various folk artifacts, carvings, and embroidery were identified by many artists and art historians alike as sources for the creation of a national style in furnishings and decorative textiles.

The possible expansion of art education at the University was considered as an improvement of far reaching consequences. Two independent departments were planned, one for the study of aesthetics and fine arts and the other for the study of the history of Serbian and Yugoslav art. Plans were drawn for the reformation of art education in middle schools as well as an introduction of courses in art history with emphasis on the development of Yugoslav art.

The Council recommended the opening of a Yugoslav Modern Gallery and a museum of pictorial copies and copies of sculptures in plaster for educational purposes. A Yugoslav Modern Gallery was supposed to patronize the art works created by contemporary artists, both foreign and Yugoslav. The representative art works of Yugoslav artists that were already sold to different institutions would be collected and hopefully exhibited in the Gallery.

The Council paid great attention to the advancement of theatrical scenography in the belief that theater performances influenced to a great extent broad segments of the public. The Council believed that since Russian scenography was best developed, the young artists should be sent to specialize in stage design in Russia. Since the Russian people were a brotherly Slavic nation, their art methods should be readily understandable. Dramas, operas, and operettas staged in an appealing and fresh contemporary style should help in the development of a specific domestic style in directing and stage design.[6] The Council planned to support the building of the Vidovdan Temple designed and sculpted by Meštrović. The members of the Council admired the work of Meštrović and their evaluation verified the opinion they held of his artistic contribution.

> Vidovan Temple is Serbian and Yugoslav national art and represents the historic and legendary essence of Serbia and Yugoslavia . . . observed spiritually through myths of Serbian tradition. The Vidovdan Temple shall present a monument that shall last until Slavic thought is present in the civilization of the Balkan Peninsula since it presents the organization and harmony of all that is the highest and best, that is closest to the Yugoslav entity in architecture and plastic arts, and recreates in addition the greatest architectural and plastic works of art. The art of Meštrović represents Serbian national religion and the highest art of the Balkans, as well as the Vidovdan Temple, the synthesis of all Yugoslav efforts.[7]

The Council recommended the building of public artistic ateliers and of a Fine Arts Pavilion in Belgrade in order to enhance artistic culture in Belgrade. The Council advocated the arrangements of foreign and domestic art exhibitions in Belgrade as well as exhibits of Yugoslav art works abroad.

The Council wished to serve as an advisory body helping the minister of education in all Yugoslav artistic matters when the need would arise. In collaboration with the Council, different competitions would be sponsored in the area of painting, sculpture, and architecture—especially the one designed for large, representative buildings. The Council also suggested introducing a law about the conservation of old monuments of historic and artistic value. This law was geared especially towards protection of valuable monuments in the newly liberated lands that were until recently under Turkish domination.[8]

The Council addressed a written proposal to the ministry of education explaining the need for establishment of a Fine Arts College. Special emphasis was devoted to the architectural program. The public and representative buildings together with some private ones often had the architectural appearance of buildings from the first half of the past century when historical styles were copies. Some of the buildings were regarded as weak copies of the dated secession style. Monumental buildings, parliament, the theater, the royal palace, and the university, were the pride of a people and of a city in which they were erected. These buildings were a lasting tribute to the culture of their time according to their architectural worth.

In the proposal, the Council presented its views about the importance of folk tradition. All reformers of European architecture made generous use of elements of the old tradition that displayed decorative motifs and originality. The ornamental treasures of embroidery, woven fabrics, and various objects of the peasants' households became sources of inspiration not only for architects but also for applied and decorative art. Modern art aspired to create its own national style. However, the western nations did not enjoy a rich depository of folk tradition and the artists soon exhausted these sources. It was common knowledge that the Slavs possessed a wealth of folk ornaments. Thus, the Austrian architect, Joseph Hofmann, became famous throughout Europe with his interiors for which he used Slavic ornaments.

In the proposal, due attention was given also to the necessity of developing a distinct national style in music. The experts in the field of music pointed to the abundance of melodic motives. The originality and beauty of melodic motives from Old Serbia and Macedonia could help the future development of music:

> We have to consider our national honor and obligation to use an abundance of traditional material since foreign artists and authorities acknowledge the inexhaustible treasury of our folk tradition and predict a future in architecture as well as sale of our arts and since foreign artists use our motives . . . In order to arrive at our Serbian style, it is necessary to cultivate domestic talents in the European way so that they can create a national spirit.[9]

Elaborating further on these assumptions, the proposal stated that when French and German artists use Yugoslav motives they showed only their exterior part, whereas only a man from the native soil could penetrate to their essence. Yugoslav folk poetry could never inspire a German or French sculptor as it inspired Meštrović to give to his sculptures a profound and autochthonous expression. It was concluded that only a native could create a new and original style in architecture, fine arts, and music.

Dragutin Inkiostri tried to crate a new Serbian style. However, it was the opinion of the writers of the proposal that Inkiostri did not have enough professional training. Therefore, he decorated different facades, almost always of inferior value, with ornaments that he argued to be derived from national tradition. His ornamentation had instead for its basis the motives of the surpassed secession that was incoherently combined with folk motives.

In order to prevent confusion in the creation of a national style, it would be necessary to establish a College of Fine Arts and Applied Arts as soon as possible. It was suggested that applied arts, in particular, could play an important role in the manufacture of furniture, wood carving, weaving of rugs, and jewelry. The art of interior decorating should also be included. The Slovenian architect, Josif Plečnik, had been nominated as professor of architecture and applied arts at the Art and Trade School in Prague. Although there were many able architects in Serbia, not one among them dealt with applied art.

The Council members recalled that in well known art centers, such as London, Paris, Munich, Berlin, Vienna, Prague, and Krakow, such schools served as a core for the association of well known artists. It was justifiable to invite Yugoslav artists to teach in Serbia, they felt, since there were too few domestic artists. It was necessary that these artists instruct the youth in accordance with the curricula at European universities, but in "Slavic spirit." The well educated younger artists would surely help create a national art.

At the same time, the young artists, painters, and sculptors, who were recipients of scholarships, should aim toward getting an education in the applied arts. They should use the opportunity to specialize in any of the varied fields in that domain of applied art which suited their predisposition.

All these efforts would have as their goal the building of an artistic culture in order to renew Yugoslav art so that Serbia could lead in the Yugoslav and Serbian spirit. Belgrade would serve as the capital of the Balkans guiding the unification.[10]

## Education and Publishing Policies

The end of the first decade of the twentieth century and the years following until the outbreak of World War I were marked by considerable progress in the standards of education in Serbia. Jovan Skerlić wrote about this in his *History of New Literature* in 1914.[11] Skerlić compared statistical data that gave further proof of this cultural growth. Thus, in 1885, there were 534 elementary schools in Serbia, while in 1911 their number increased to 1425. The greater number of elementary schools presented almost a triple growth. While comparing the number of vocational school, Skerlić found a similar situation. In 1899, there were 19 middle and vocational schools in the entire territory of Serbia with 386 teachers and 6049 students. Eleven years later, in 1910, the number of schools rose to 49, with

723 teachers and 12,892 students.

The educational growth was especially apparent in Belgrade, the capital city of Serbia. The number of middle and vocational schools increased, and as a result, the increased enrollment in 1914 showed more students in Belgrade alone as compared with the total enrollment of students in all of Serbia 13 years earlier. In 1900, the College in Belgrade employed 58 instructors with an enrollment of 450 students. In 1913, the enrollment climbed sharply to 1600, and the number of teachers was increased to 80. Skerlić noted also the increased number of Serbian students attending institutions of higher learning in Austria, Belgium, Switzerland, Russia, and, in particular, France and Germany.

In his review of cultural progress in Serbia, Skerlić singled out the exceptional achievements of the Serbian Royal Academy. As an elected member of this institution, Skerlić was well informed about the dedicated work of fellow academicians. In the scientific field, the Academy achieved remarkable results and became a scholarly center in the Slavic South.[12]

Sklerlić noticed an increasing interest in foreign and domestic literature. The prestigious Srpska književna zadruga (The Serbian Literary Union) managed to attract around 11,000 members. In addition, different cultural and national societies, such as Kulturna liga (The Cultural League) and Narodna obdrana (The People's Defense) developed lively activities. Skerlić praised, in particular, the programs of similar societies in regions under foreign domination. Matica Srpska (Serbian Queen Bee), the literary and national association, supported and enhanced the spiritual life as well as the national spirit in Novi Sad and Vojvodina at the time of Austro–Hungarian rule. The Prosveta Society (Enlightenment), located in Bosnia and Hercegovina, exerted a similar beneficial influence. In Dalmatia, the Srpska Zora Society (Serbian Dawn) strove for similar support. The Matica srpska Society (Serbian Queen Bee) was founded in Dubrovnik in 1909 and followed the example of similar older organizations.[13]

Skerlić paid special attention to the publication of dailies and periodicals. While observing from a point of vantage, he noticed that in 1816 the only Serbian newspaper then was *Novine srpske (The Serbian Paper)* published in Vienna. Only six copies of this newspaper were dispatched to Serbia. However, in 1912, there were 302 various Serbian newspapers and periodicals published in Serbia and in towns and provinces outside Serbian jurisdiction. In Serbia proper there were 199 different publications, newspapers, and periodicals with a circulation of more than 50 million copies annually. In Belgrade alone, 126 publications appeared of which there were 24 daily papers, 20 literary, scientific, and political journals, and 82 professional papers. The literary journals had been previously satisfied with a circulation of 1000 subscribers. However, the situation improved and Skerlić noted that the number of subscribers had increased substantially to 3,000. Some popular books were published by advance subscription, attracting 30,000 to 40,000 subscribers. Various urban centers in provinces had their own literary journals and dailies. In Bosnia and Hercegovina, *Bosanaska vila (Bosnian Fairy)*, a literary journal, enjoyed popular appeal. *Pregled (Review)*, another journal appearing in 1910, was devoted to cultural and scientific questions.[14]

The oldest Serbian journal, *Letopis matice srpske (The Annals of the Serbian Queen Bee)*, successfully continued its chronicle of the literary scene. Starting from 1895, *Brankov kolo (Branko's Round Dance)* succeedded the publication of *Javor (Maple)* and *Stražilovo*. Another journal, *Srdj* was started in 1902/03 as the literary publication of the Serbs in Dalmatia, and *Dan (The Day)* was a literary journal published in Montenegro starting in 1911.

Skerlić thought that the progress in Serbian literary life was stimulated, in particular, by the appearance of *Srpski Književni Glasnik (The Serbian Literary Herald)*. Bogdan Popović, its founder and first editor in chief, was a prominent public figures in the cultural life of Belgrade. He was a renowned professor at the College of Philosophy in Belgrade and esteemed as a literary and fine arts critic. His journal was based on contemporary principles and values and was influenced by European examples, although he was keenly aware of national literary and artistic developments and the cultural scene in general. The journal influenced the general public by its editorial principles while its literary criticism helped shape Serbian literary thought. Founded in 1901, this journal managed to draw a sharp line between the nineteenth and twentieth century in Serbian literature and helped redirect Serbian literature in a new direction to create a lasting foundation for future growth. According to Skerlić, the rise of the newest Serbian literature was associated with the publication of *Srpski Književni Glasnik*.[15]

Skerlić stressed that the ensuing collaboration between Serbian and Croatian writers was one of the most important aspects of the new literary development. The Croatian books were reprinted in the Cyrillic alphabet and Serbian books were in the Latin alphabet. The editorial policies of *Srpski Književni Glasnik, Savremenik*, and *Bosanska Vila* were especially helpful in encouragint the collaboration between Serbian and Croatian writers. Starting in 1909, one Croatian or Serbian book was published every year in *Srpska Književna Zadruga* and *Matica Hrvatska (The Croatian Queen Bee)*. Croatian and Serbian writers published jointly their *Croatian–Serbian Almanac* in 1910/11. The result of this collaboration was that the Serbian readers understood better than they had before the Croatian writers, and the Croatian readers understood the Serbian writers better as well. This collaboration among South Slavs led to speculations of unification of Balkan countries into a confederation. Dr. Albert Galeb, private docent at the University of Geneva, published an article about this topic in the prestigious bulletin *Bulletin Mensuel de la Société de Legislation Comparée.* Galeb stated that there existed a great interest in Western Europe for the possible unification of the Balkan countries. Austria and Russia were particularly interested in the results of such a move. Germany paid a great deal of attention to this development while harboring intentions of possible expansion. The new confederation would present an obstacle to the German "Drang nach Osten." The writer concluded that the prospect of a Balkan confederation could not be achieved easily and quickly, considering the antagonism and conflicting interests among the Balkan countries as well as among the Slavic countries of the Balkan peninsula.[16]

### The Pan–Slavic Collaboration

Parallel to the aspirations for unification of South Slavs, there existed a desire for a Pan–Slavic commonwealth. The Pan–Slavic Congress, which was held in Sofia in 1910, strove to explore possible avenues of further collaboration. Recognizing the importance of this event, an historical evaluation of Pan–Slavic ideology was published in *Srpski Književni Glasnik,* which led to the Pan–Slavic Congress in Sofia.[17]

The Pan–Slavic movement experienced a strong growth in the 1860s and 1870s. However, as time passed, the movement lost its momentum and subsided to sporadic activities of the Slovensko blagotvorno društva (Slavic Philanthropic Society) which was centered in Petrograd. The tendencies for collaboration led by the end of the first decade of this century to a renewed Slavic movement identified as Neo–Slavism. The First Pan–Slavic Congress took place in Prague in July 1908, and was the result of the labor of many participants. However, the role of Dr. Kramarž was, in particular, noteworthy in helping to organize the Congress and most importantly to guide the collaboration among the Slavic people. Kramarž distinguished himself in the political life of his country, and he eventually became a representative at the Austrian Parliament. He concentrated his efforts on promoting the economic and cultural collaboration among the Slavs in order to abolish the deeply rooted hostilities that existed among the Poles and Russians, in particular.[18]

The Second Pan–Slavic Congress took place in June 1910 in Sofia. The representatives from Serbia were Kosta Stojanović, the former minister of education, as well as Božidar Marković and Pavle Košutić, both eminent professors at the University of Belgrade. At the final session of the Congress a resolution was passed concerning the founding of an association of Slavic publishers and bookstores, the writing of a Pan–Slavic dictionary, the establishment of a Pan–Slavic theatrical agency, and the organization of the Third Congress in Prague in 1912. An agreement was reached about the exchange of publications among the central libraries as well as about an association of Slavic Academies. A plan was established for the exchange of university professors and the preparation of a Slavic anthology. The Congress also took initial steps towards the organization of the first Pan–Slavic exhibition to be held in Prague in 1915. Bopčev, the Bulgarian representative, spoke at the closing session of the Congress. He ended his speech using a well known figure of speech "that the Neo–Slavic idea made a better marriage match than what was expected.[19]

Due to the circumstances, the Serbian representatives became mistrustful of Neo–Slavism. The reason for this change of heart was the impression made that the annexation of Bosnia and Hercegovina seemed to be an issue "of no great concern" among fellow Neo–Slavs, an impression that prevailed even during the preliminary meeting of representatives of Congress in Petrograd in 1909. The reviewer mentioned with a measure of pride that during all these meetings and Congresses the Yugoslavs stood together since the time they had initiated Yugoslav collaboration in 1904 on the occasion of the centennial celebration of the Serbian uprising against Turkish domination. The Yugoslavs had directed their work towards a cultural and economic union since that time. Thus, the Yugoslavs anticipated the Neo–Slavic movement by some four years.[20]

Collaboration in the cultural field resulted in new translations of literary works of the neighboring Slavic peoples. In 1904, the translation of a collection of short stories, *Kratke priče,* appeared by the Bulgarian writer, Ivan Vazov. This collection was translated by A. S. Popović and published in an established series under the title *Mala biblioteka* in Mostar. It was favorably commented on by Miodrag Ibrovac in the pages of *Srpski Književni Glasnik.* Ibrovac added that such translations are welcome since the Serbian reading public did not know the literature of other Yugoslav nations well enough. The Croatian writers were known to a certain extent while the Bulgarian and Slovenian were not known at all.[21]

The opinion of Ibrovac concerning a scarcity of translations of the Slovenian and Bulgarian people must have been understood by many as truthful and accurate. A collection of poems, *Iz jugoslovenske lirike (Out of Yugoslav Lyrics)*, translated by Vladimir Stanimirović, soon followed. Stanimirović translated from Slovene 24 poems of France Prešern as well as 22 poems by the Bulgarian poet, Ivan Vazov. The biographical and bibliographical notes for this book were prepared for the Slovene section by Anton Aškerc and Oton Župančič and for the Bulgarian section by P. K. Javorov. The collection was published by the Kolarac Endowment in Belgrade in 1909. In his short review of this collection, Jovan Skerlić recommended the book since it would provide an introduction to readers of literature of neighboring peoples. Skerlić believed that this translation would help to eliminate the paradox that Serbian readers knew the distant Scandinavian poets and the French writers better than they did the literary figures of neighboring nations.[22]

In anticipation of the Second Pan–Slavic Congress in Sofia in 1910, a representative poetic collection was published entitled *Slavic Anthology*. This anthology included a selection of lyric poetry from the literature of various Slavic people translated into Bulgarian. Serbo–Croatian literature was represented by 16 poets, Slovene with five, Czech with seven, Polish with six, and Russian with 38 poets. These poems were translated by the best Bulgarian writers: Ivan Vazov, P. R. Slaveikov, D. K. Popov, and St. Čilingirov.[23]

A translation of *Pregled istorije srpske književnosti (The Survey of the History of Serbian Literature)* by Pavle Popović into Russian won a special honor the the author. The translator, P. A. Lavrov, was a professor at Petrograd University. This translation also pointed to an increased interest in collaboration and a mutual understanding that existed at that time among the Slavic people.[24]

The Yugoslav Academy in Zagreb published the speech of its president, Tade Smičiklas, in its *Ljetopis (Annals)* of 1911, where the members were informed about the preparation of the *Enciklopedijski Jugoslavenski rečnik (The Yugoslav Encyclopedic Vocabulary)*. Smičiklas noted that Marko Crljen, a member of Croatian nobility, gave 20,000 crowns to the Academy with a wish to publish a vocabulary "that would be on the level of contemporary scientific knowledge and would depict the past and the present of the lands inhabited by the Croats, Serbs, Slovenes, and Bulgarians." The Academy accepted this offer and Smičiklas said in the conclusion of his speech:

> We know that the Croats and Serbs wish and work with
> a goal in mind to be one people in heart and soul . . .
> . The Slovenes are turning towards them in concord and
> brotherly unity, since Bulgarians seek cultural community.
> Therefore, we envisaged and founded the Yugoslav Encyclo-

pedic Vocabulary.[25]

Later, this project of the Yugoslav Academy attracted the attention of the Serbian Academy in Belgrade. The Serbian Academy wished to take an equal part in the preparations and share the costs. The Slovene association, Matica Slovenska, took the responsibility for this edition concerning Slovene participation. University professors in Sofia decided to direct their scientific efforts toward the support of the project.

Within the framework of the Pan–Slavic cultural collaboration, an exhibit called Serbian Women opened in Prague in 1910. It was arranged by the Women's Society with the help of the Ethnographic Museum in Belgrade. The theme of the exhibit dealt with various activities conducted by women in households throughout different regions of Serbia.[26]

The Tenth Congress of Slavic Journalists took place in Belgrade in June of 1911. A notice in *Srpski Književni Glasnik* informed the readers that the Congress convened in the Parliament. The floor of the Parliament was covered with handmade rugs from Pirot for this occasion. The festive opening of the Congress was attended by ministers of the administration and Metropolitan Dimitrije, and the academicians Jovan Cvijić, Ljubomir Stojanović, and Jovan Žujović. The Congress was opened by the Czech representative and "an old friend of Serbia," Josif Holeček, who presented a short history of the Slavic Journalistic Movement and pointed to future tasks of Neo–Slavism. Holeček paid special attention to the cultural ties between the Czech and Serbian people. From the Serbian side, Branko Lazarević greeted the guests and read a summary of the development of journalism in Serbia. The summary was based on a book written by Dr. Jovan Skerlić, *Istorijski pregled srpske Štampe (The Historical Review of the Serbian Press).*[27]

An editorial about the Congress of Slavic Journalists held in 1911 was published in the journal, *Bosanska vila*. The editorial was written by Milorad Pavlović and printed on the front page of the journal. Pavlović reported that Belgrade arranged a "royal welcome" for the participants of the Congress. Belgrade was the meeting place of Slavic journalists from the different Slavic countries: the Russians, Czechs, Bulgarians, Slovenes, and Wends. Poles who attended the meeting came from Poznan or from the regions under Austrian jurisdiction. Poles under Russian domination cancelled their participation.

In a concluding statement, Pavlović cited the important function that journalists perform in a society:

. . . the journalists, the eighth power, are not only representatives but also holders of public thought . . . . They should be apostles of the new times, the propagators of the idea of Slavic community . . . the idea of a Slavic union is spreading and getting more support.[28]

The movement toward a Slavic union and a wish to preserve the once glorious days of the Slavs were particularly cultivated by the Czechs. A group of 15 Czech scientists started the preparation of a monograph presenting the historical, cultural, and political development among the Slavs. The editors of the monograph were J. Polovka and J. Bidlo. The monograph was completed in 1912 and published in Prague under the title, *Slovenstvo: Obraz jeho minulosti a pžitomnosti (Slavs: The Presentation of Their Past and Present).* The monograph was accompanied by a map presenting the territories inhabited by the Slavs.

This monograph attracted attention due to the validity of its presentation of the multifaceted historical and political development, as well as the evaluation of the progress made in the fields of education, fine arts, and music. At the same time, the book supported the idea of a Slavic unification, a hope that was renewed and entertained by many. The monograph was reviewed by Dr. Jovan Erdeljanović for the readers of *Srpski Književni Glasnik* soon after its appearance in Prague.

Erdeljanović noted that the lengthy introduction to the book was written by Karel Kramarž, one of the followers of the ideology of Neo-Slavism. Kramarž supported a cultural and economic collaboration among the Slavs. The idea for the monograph originated during the First Slavic conference in Prague in 1908. At that time, a committee of 15 scientists was formed and "started to work with enthusiasm" almost immediately. It was the wish of the committee to identify the mutual ties of the various Slavic peoples through history. All important events from the historical past were documented with the founding of the states and their conversion to Christianity.[29]

J. Bidlo, who wrote the chapter about the historical development of the Slavs, stated that the idea of Slavic unity and Pan-Slavism appeared among the Czechs in the 1820s. Similar to Czech Pan-Slavism was the Messianic movement among the Poles in the 1930s. Among the Russians, congruent tendencies were seen as Slavophile. Bidlo considered the appearance of Neo-Slavic ideas one of the most important phenomena that was taking root among the Slavs. In order to fulfill this great concept of unification, several Slavic meetings were held, starting with the First Slavic Congress in Prague in 1908.[30]

A review of Slavic literature was compiled in a monograph by J. Mahala, where he presented the development of Serbian literature, reinforcing the opinions formulated previously in the works of Jovan Skerlić.

Franc Taborski wrote four chapters about Slavic visual art dedicating consecutive chapters to the achievement in the fine arts by the Russians, Poles, Czechs, and South Slavs. Taborski stated that the fine arts among the South Slavs remained backwards in comparison to those of other Slavic nations. His explanation for this backward state was due to the late development of a national identity. Taborski acknowledged the great talent of Ivan Meštrović, a sculptor who gained remarkable recognition in his field.[31]

The state of musical arts among the Slavic nations was presented by Zdeněk Nejedlý, a musicologist. Until the nineteenth century, foreign music was predominant in the Slavic nations. Musical works by native composers followed foreign examples. The Romantic Era brought the first efforts of liberation from foreign influence when the folk music idiom was introduced. At first, the works of Czech and Polish composers reflected this trend. Russian and South Slav composers approached a similar goal somewhat later. Romanticism initiated among the Slavs as well as the Germans a wish for the introduction of varied elements of folk songs and dances. However, the newly composed musical works contained only an exterior quality of the folk music idiom without rendering a true indigenous musical spirit. In spite of these shortcomings, these works served for the future development of Slavic music. The Czech composers truly advanced musical art with the advent of Neo–Romanticism since this art doctrine brought new perceptions advocating that a musical work should reflect the essence of folk soul and not only the superficial qualities and colorful effects. The main representative of this trend in Czech music was Bedřich Smetana who laid a solid foundation for the creation of music rooted in folk music idiom. Nejedlý concluded that the Czechs had acquired a leading position in contemporary music among other Slavic people. Czech composers contributed, in particular, to symphonic music and to musical drama.[32]

Nejedlý turned his attention to the development of Russian music. The Russians had for the foundation of their artistic music the compositions of Mikhail Glinka, imbued with the spirit of romanticism. However, the successors of Mikhail Glinka did not lead Russian music the way Smetana directed Czech music. Russian musicians were still attracted to superficially picturesque and colorful presentations while they neglected the ideological aspects. Nejedlý's evaluation of Russian music was not truthful and accurate. While praising Czech contributions, Nejedelý did not include in his evaluation the remarkable contributions of Musorgsky, Borodin, Skriabin, and Stravinsky.

The compositions of these outstanding musicians propelled Russian music to the leading ranks of musical achievements.

Still another writer in this monograph singled out the Czech contributions, this time with solid arguments. Antonin Jirak compiled a review of certain aspects of education among the Slavs. He observed that Czech people have a leading position according to the number of their schools and appropriate facilities. The worst conditions existed among the Wends who had an insufficient number of school, as well as the Polish minority in Germany and the Slovaks and Little Russians. Among the South Slavs, the Slovenes had the best folk schools. They had the smallest percentage of illiterates compared to the Serbs and Croats who had 20 percent. In Serbia, hardly one third of the eligible children attend school, and in Bosnia and Hercegovina this number was only 15 percent.[33]

It was noteworthy that this interesting publication contained a chapter on tourism among the Slavs. This chapter consisted of a number of short articles by various authors. Jan Hejret wrote a survey of Slavic journalism and J. Šejner wrote about the Sokol movement.[34]

An interest in a cultural exchange brought about the staging of a play by Ivo Vojnović, *Smrt Majke Jugovića (The Death of Jugović's Mother)*. The premiere took place on the stage of the National Theater and was reviewed by the poetess, Ružena Svobodva, who wrote about the moving impression the play left on the Czech cultural milieu. Svobodava claimed in this review that they were receptive to historical epics of the South Slavs as interpreted by Vojnović:

> The great, tragic song of the poet from Dubrovnik passed over the stage of Narodni Divadlo. Ivo Vojnović depicted Vidovdan, the day of the conclusive battle and defeat—he entered his poetic strength into the history of his people and merged with its heroic tradition without separation. He embraced tradition and tradition embraced him.
>
> What brought that about on our stage resounding the heroic songs of our Southern brothers? . . . to us who 20 years ago declared Russian literature as barbaric and who knew almost nothing about the life of our southern brothers shortly before they became famous? And did we not look at them from above, they who have been beheaded by the Turks, we whose souls were obscured by the Germans?[35]

Interestingly enough, the performance of *Smrt Majke Jugovića* was reviewed still by another theater critic. Milan Grol had the good fortune to attend the performance in Prague and accordingly furnished a report for a new journal, *Pijemont.* Grol was a longtime theater critic for the prestigious journal *Srpski Književni Glasnik,* as well as a theatrical administrator and historian. The title of his review showed his approach to the evaluation of the play and the methods used in staging, "Kako je u Pragu igrana Kosovska pesma Ive Vojnovića (The Kosovo Song of Ivo Vojnović" and how it was played in Prague. Grol could not avoid a comparison of the same performance as presented at the National Theater in Belgrade. The performance in Prague was obviously presented with greater artistic strength and decorative staging than the domestic production in Belgrade. Grol singled out in particular "the direction of the play and the rich decor." He praised the performance of Ana Suhanova in the lead role of the "magnificent production."[36]

Grol left another testimony of *Smrt Majke Jugovića* in his book which was dedicated to the development of the Serbian Theater. He had seen manyh performances of this play on the stage of the National Theater in Belgrade. On the eve of the Balkan Wars, a predominantly young public attended the play and responded to the lines recited by the actors with a great deal of enthusiasm. The actors themselves were often carried away by similar feeling of renewed national consciousness as they interpreted the moving scenes of the national defeat on the Kosovo field.[37]

In Vojvodina, which at the time constituted a southern province in the Austro–Hungarian Empire, the young and progressive Serbian people were guided by a mutual wish to uphold their ethnic and national identity. In 1910, it was in this spirit that the First Serbian Artistic Exhibit was organized in Sombor.[38] The opening of this Exhibit symbolically marked the beginning of a new cultural movement arising from national consciousness. There was a wish to present the latest development of the accelerated artistic growth in Belgrade and Serbia as well as a wish to establish ties with the Serbian cultural community. The Exhibit was declared the most important cultural and national event of the last ten years held in the town of Sombor. Prior to the preparations for the opening of the Exhibit, rumors were spreading that Vojvodina "was wasted in lethargy and was declining in importance in the general spiritual development of the Serbian people." Vojvodina was once in the forefront of Serbian cultural and literary life and the passive attitude that existed was lamentable to many. However, starting with the organization of the exhibit, the situation started to improve rapidly. As an old and prosperous economic and cultural center, an initiative was developed in many areas of cultural life in Sombor. The women's organizations, Srpsko devojaccko kolo (Young Serbian Ladies' Association) and Dobrotvorna zadruga Srpkinja Somborkinja (The Philanthropic Union of Serbian

Ladies from Sombor), took an active part in this movement. They organized a number of lectures with speakers not only from Vojvodina but they also invited writers and other speakers from Serbia.

The opening of the Exhibit took on a very festive character, since this was the first Serbian artistic exhibit ever presented in Hungary. Dignitaries and artists from Serbia and Vojvodina attended the Exhibit, which was opened by the Bishop from Bačka Mitrofan Šević, who, in his speech, expressed his opinion about the importance of such cultural missions. There were 114 art works exhibited representing 20 artists from Vojvodina, Serbia, Dalmatia, and Montenegro.

According to a reviewer's impression, the focal point of the exhibit was the painting, *Portrait of a Woman,* by Pavle Jovanović. Uroš Predić exhibited four panels from the altar that he painted for the church in Pančevo. The reviewer stated that these panels confirmed Predić as one of the best painters of ecclesiastic art. Predić also exhibited several smaller canvases. Beta Vukanović exhibited the painting, *The Gypsy Woman from Belgrade,* but this painting did not impress viewers as much as her earlier composition, *On My Terrace.* Rista Vukanović presented his portrait of *Captain D. I.* Among the younger generation of artists, Borisav Stefanović and Ljubomir Ivanović were mentioned as the most promising. Sima Roksandić exhibited a well executed bust of the the composer, Josif Marinković. Djordje Jovanović exhibited the bust of Dr. Vladan Jovanović, and Jovan Konjarek displayed the inspired sculpture, *The Last Sigh.*[39]

The Exhibit lasted one month and attracted a large number of viewers and brought excellent revenues. The reviewer concluded, therefore, that similar exhibits should be presented in other Serbian centers outside Serbia.[40]

The centennial celebration of the founding of the Serbian High School in Novi Sad was held in 1910. Tihomir Ostojić informed the readers of *Srpski Književni Glasnik* that the Serbian High School had grown to a total enrollment of 18,000 students during the past 100 years. The Serbian people and the city of Novi Sad could feel justly proud of their high school.[41]

Preparations for the commemoration of the centennial of the death of Dositej Obradović started in 1910 with the formation of the Council in charge of necessary preparations. The Council addressed the Serbian people "of all regions and of all ranks" with a proclamation published on the pages of *Srpski Književni Glasnik.* Dositej Obradović was proclaimed the foremost educator of the Serbian people and compared to the first Serbian Archbishop, Sava Nemanjić:

> Dositej Obradović was for the present generation the same
> that Sava was in former times—he was a great spiritual fa-

ther, a man who introduced the Serbian people to the ideas of the times and to contemporary culture. He was the first critical thinker among the Serbs who taught throughout his lifetime about the 'educated, rational, and a love for the truth.' More than anyone else, he saw to it that the Serbs were a great intellectual and spiritual whole despite their religious and state differences. He placed Serbian folk thought on a modern base, and he was the first to proclaim the principles of intellectual unity . . . . During this 100 year period Serbian literature only had a few writers who could influence entire generations.[42]

According to the program of the proclamation, among other projects, there was a plan to erect a monumental statue depicting Dositej, a new publication of collected works as well as the publication of a collection of treatises about Dositej, penned by well known literary and scientific figures, under the title *Spomenica (Memorial)*. The program suggested the creation of a special building to be called Dositejev dom (The Home of Dositej) to serve as a cultural center. The center would include auditoriums for lectures, concert halls, and space for exhibits. The Council proposed calling a congress of Serbian, and perhaps also Croatian and Slovene writers, along with educational and cultural societies. In addition to a celebration in the Serbian Royal Academy and University, a performance was planned in the National Theater to present the first act of *Damon* by Obradović together with a reading of his verses.[43]

The proclamation was signed by the President of the Srpska književna zadruga (Serbian Literary Association), Stojan Novaković, the Vice President, Ljubomir Stojanović, the Secretary, Jovan Skerlić, and a host of prominent personalities. The co–signers of the proclamation were also the representatives of cultural and professional organizations covering a wide range of social ranks, such as the Academic Singers' Society Obilić, the Stanković Singers' Society, the Association of Serbian Sisters, the Association of Serbian Engineers and Architects, the Belgrade Mercantile Youth Association, the Council of the Ladies of Princess Ljubica, and the United Guild Alliance.[44]

The Council carefully prepared the centennial commemoration that took place in 1911. The March issue of *Srpski Književni Glasnik* was dedicated to this memorable event. Jovan Skerlić, the initiator of this celebration, stressed in his editorial that the purpose was to pay homage to the memory of a deserving man to whom all Serbian people are indebted.[45]

The collected studies and articles in the March issue sought to present the role of Dositej in the South Slavic realm in accordance with current tendencies toward renewed ties among the South Slavs. Sima Pandurović, the poet from Hercegovina, dedicated three poems to Dositej, Vera (Faith), Život (Life), and Istina (Truth). *Dositej Obradović in Bulgaria* was a study written by the Bulgarian writer, Bojan Penev. Dr. Tihomir R. Djordjević, the well known ethnographer, described in his paper the ties that existed between Dositej and the Rumanians. The Dalmatian poet, Mirko Korolija, wrote a poem called Kancona o smrti Učitelja velikog Dositeja (Canzona about the Death of the Teacher, the Great Dositeja). Dr. Tihomir Ostojić from Novi Sad wrote about the poetic works of Dositej Obradović that were previously not sufficiently known. Professor Pavle Popović discussed in a short essay the ties that existed between Obradović and La Bryer.[46]

Within the framework of the centennial commemoration, a special session was held in Parliament. The key address was given by Andra Nikolić, a statesman. A mass was held in the Saborna crkva (the Cathedral) by the Metropolitan where a sermon was delivered about Dositej as a philosopher and educator of the people. The National Theater in Belgrade presented the play, *Mladost Dositeja Obradovića (The Youth of Dositej Obradović)* by Kosta Trifković.

It is noteworthy that the centennial of Dositej Obradović was commemorated in Prague. Šumadija (The Association of Serbian Students) arranged a festive program for this occasion. The highlight of the program was a speech given by Dr. Tomas Masaryk, the well known Czech statesman, entitled, "Dositej as Philosopher," where he presented Dositej as a thinker. In addition, the prominent Czech literary historian, J. Mahal, spoke about Dostej's life and works.[47]

The cultural and spiritual life of Serbian immigrants in the United States was scrutinized with increasing attention. The newly felt concern for Serbian communities in distant lands hoped to correct previous insufficient support. An article signed by the initial "L.," appeared in *Srpski Književni Glasnik* stating that the Serbian journal, *Sloga*, had published an important article dealing with the publication of Serbian books and periodicals. This journal was based in Pittsburgh.[48] According to this article, Serbs in America were predominantly workers who labored at strenuous and low paying jobs, and being exhausted after their daily work, read very little. They often chose to read a modest volume containing epic songs about Prince Marko or Miloš Obilić. Collections of religious stories were also very popular. These collections often included stories such as *Čudesa presvete Bogorodice (The Miracles of the Holy Virgin)*, *Srce čovečije (The Human Heart)*, *Hram Božiji (Temple of the God,)* and *Mati božija u paklu (The Mother of Christ in Hell.)* In addition, there were a number of popular prayer books, books about dreams, and sensational novels and poetry, such as *Pesme Nikole knjaza gospodara (The Poems of Prince Nikola, the Lord), Cipelice male grofice (The Shoes of Little Countess), Devojke sa ulice (The Girls from the Street), Kod ženskog raja (In Female Paradise)*, and *Prva bračna noć (The First Wedding Night)*. The writer of this article quoted the opinion of a publisher in the United States who tried to explain the popularity of similar editions as well as difficulties that the publishers faced when trying to publish literary works:

> If I would ever decide to publish an intelligent book for our people, I should be punished by God. All that I have published that was sensible and good was eventually eaten by worms in the depot, while the songs about Prince Marko, Miloš Obilić, and books about dreams and prayer books were sold like hotcakes.[49]

The writer of this article concluded with a warning—that the cultural and educational institutions in Serbia should pay better attention to those areas about the Serbian people that are left untouched and are in danger of going to waste.[50]

## The Renewal of Patriotic Poetry

In 1908, during the time of the Austro–Hungarian annexation of Bosnia and Hercegovina, a new spirit of devotion to ancestral lands became even more apparent. Jovan Skerlić, a literary critic of importance and a leading personality, declared with genuine enthusiasm that Serbian literature reflected a renewal of patriotism. He detected this spirit in the poetry of Aleksa Šantić, Veljko Petrović, Mileta Jakšić, Stevan Bešević, and in stories by Petar Kočić, especially in the famous *Jazavac pred sudom (Badger in Court)*, as well as in the powerful novels of Ivo Ćipiko, *Za kruhom (After the Bread)* and *Pauci (Spiders)*, when he wrote:

> The final arrival of realistic and healthy ideas in our poetry should be welcomed a hundred times. It is high time to express the necessary reaction to cheap decadency and shallow snobbishness; it is beneficial to stop the forced despair that Vojislav Ilić has already attacked—all this poetry of "Insincere Poems" and "The Hymn of Indifference" . . . . Our poetry should remain poetry. When describing the conditions of our people in our poetry, that is good and provides great hope.[51]

In addition, Skerlić reviewed the development of Serbian literature starting from the 1860s when patriotic poetry was at its peak.

That was when Djura Jakšić wrote his unforgettable verses. After the Berlin Congress of 1878, Svetozar Marković emerged as a representative of positivism with a new realistic attitude. There was a feeling of saturation from "the orgies of feeling," and many writers expressed disagreement with statements of emphatic nationalism. Laza Lazarević even cited the ideas shared by the members of the youth movement as "follies" when he wrote:

And as is unavoidable in public life, we have gone from one extreme to another. Instead of an obsession with the nationalism of 40 years ago, there appears to be a cold, formal futility in present day pessimism in our poetry, which is artistically not exciting, anti–human, and anti–nationalistic, and there is no connection to life. There appears to be a certain hatred for life, an indifference to all that is not subtle in feelings or distinguished in expression.[52]

Dučić started to write poetry in this spirit as revealed in the opening verses of his poem Moja poezija (My Poetry):

Mirna kao mramor, hladna kao sena,
Ti si bledo, tiho devojče što sneva.
Pusti pesma drugih neka bude žena
Što po nečistijem ulicama peva.
Ja ne mećem na te djindjuve sa trakom,
Nego žute ruže u te kose duge:
Budi odveć lepa da se svidjaš svakom,
Odveć gorda da bi živela za druge.

Immobile as marble, cool as a shadow
You are a pale, placid girl that dreams.
Let the song of others be a woman
That sings in littered streets.
I do not lay on you glass pearls and ribbons,
But yellow roses in your long hair:
Remain too beautiful to please everyone,
Too proud to live for others.

Furthermore, Skerlić noted that Sima Pandurović, as one of the "better younger poets," represented his generation as tired, disappointed, and without faith. This was a surprising assessment since Pandurović was president of the National Youth, a party that was the continuation of the Youth Movement and patriotic liberalism of the 1860s. Skerlić noted that, until recently, this party showed the tendency to return to old ideals. Skerlić concluded that in Pandurović's case his literary identity was stronger than his nationalistic orientation since his poems were not patriotic in spirit but depicted sombre feelings and a pessimistic outlook. The following verses that Pandurović published in *Srpski Književni Glasnik* in 1907 could serve as an example:[53]

> Siti smo svega, života i sveta
> Sumnja nam sad je oslonac jedini
> A mudrost glupa i prostačka šega
> Ljudima drugim i samima sobom.
> Sa tužnim prahom starih ideala.

> We are satiated with all of it, life and people
> Suspicion is the only support
> And foolish wisdom and boorish jest
> With others and ourselves
> With melancholy dust our old ideals.

Pandurović published his collected songs under the title *Posmrtne počasti (Posthumous Honors)* in Mostar in the *Mala biblioteka* edition. Skerlić's review of the collection which appeared in a seemingly derogatory title, " A Literary Epidemic," corroborated his opinion about Pandurović as a talented writer—"one of our better and more original young poets." However, the critics said that his collection of verses was characteristic for the literary credo of the younger generation. Skerlić expressed his concern about the exaggerated pessimism contained in these songs that suggested a possible literary illness:

> In Serbian literature lately we are accustomed to finding titles of poems which appear as if copied from tombstones . . . but such black pessimism as it is found in *Posthumous Honors* and other places in this book can make Dr. Laza Kostić look like a normal man and a reasonable Philistine, perhaps not a small insult for our disheveled poet of wild romanticism.[54]

Skerlić concluded that Pandurović was a hopeless pessimist. Indeed the titles of his poems were similar to funeral psalms—Na grobu velikih strasti (On the Tomb of Great Passions), Posle tame (After Darkness), Pada cveće (The Flowers are Falling Down), Mrtvi plamenovi (The Dead Flames), and Sumoran dan (A Sombre Day). This pessimism, due to its lost hope, was different from that described by Alfred de Vigny or Charles Leconte de Lisle.[55]

The beginning of a renaissance of patriotic poetry was associated with the poetic work of Aleksa Šantič (1868–1924). According to Skerlić, this return to the roots of the people started in Šantić's own homeland of Hercegovina. At a time when Serbian poetry was filled with empty words, Šantić created a poem that became famous, Ostajte ovdje (Remain Here). Šantić expressed ideas of beauty and truth in his verses that could stand comparison with the best of the poems by Jakšić and Zmaj. Skerlić concluded that Ostajte ovdje was more than a poem, it presented a good dead.[56]

Skerlić stressed that Šantić distinguished himself from older patriotic poets since his patriotism was realistic in essence. He did not depict the people as an exalted nation, but as everyday people, living men and women with simple existence. In this respect, Šantić's poetry is close to the social and national poetry of Djura Jakšić from the 1870s, particularly Jakšić's poems Ratari (Farmers) and Zemlja (Earth). This great affection towards the suffering peasant as a foundation of society was bordering on a cult similar to the one shared by Russian populists towards the mushik in the 1850s. In his poem, Pred kolibama (In Front of the Huts), Šantić devoted an entire hymn to the "impoverished friend of groves and wells."[57]

Another poet who distinguished himself as a writer of patriotic poetry was Veljko Petrović. Petrović and Mileta Jakšić continued the tradition of poets from Vojvodina whose poetry followed the tradition of Serbian poetry from 40 years ago. According to Skerlić, Petrović and Jakšić were the best poets of old Vojvodina. Petrović had some of the faults of his generation, but his decadence and literary snobbery was only a fashionable mask. His soul contained purity and fresh innocence, and most importantly, a deep feeling of devotion to his native land as an expression of a newer understanding of patriotism. The feeling of security and agitation, which was shared at the time by many, motivated Petrović in writing his poems that later appeared in a collection entitled *Rodoljubive pesme (Patriotic Poems)*. His poems described difficult moments of political and moral crises, and they were a unique testimony of historical events leading to World War I.

In a review written in 1912, Skerlić praised Petrović's poetic ability and the expressivness of his verses. He noted that Petrović's collection had the character of a document of its days and "whoever wanted to find out what the Serbs thought in the difficult year of 1908 . . . should read the *Patriotic Poems* by Veljko Petrović." These poems also pointed to the progress that Serbian poetry had achieved starting from the patriotic hymn of Vladislav Kaćanski and the bellicose poems of Mita Popović. In addition, he stressed that Petrović's poems showed that the poets in Vojvodina have continued to write poetry. The poets of Vojvodina had been writing poetry for more than 150 years addressing the whole Serbian nation. It would suffice to remember the literary legacy of Dositej Obradović, Sterija Popović, Jovan Jovanović-Zmaj, and Djura Jakšić.[58] Skerlić thought that Petrović's collection could not please everybody, especially those who acted like "conceited dandies and snobs." In particular, he praised the following poems: Sprska zemlja (Serbian Land), Povratak (Return), Kenigrec, Srbiji (For Serbia), and Vojvodino stara (The Old Vojvodina). In evaluating the entire collection, Skerlić praised the poet for writing a good book that excited and delighted the readers. Furthermore, the book proved that Skerlić's prophecy about the revival of patriotic poetry was not proclaimed in vain. Petrović showed that patriotism could serve as poetic inspiration as well as a profound and personal experience. As a poetic motive, it could serve equally well as "the fans of a marquise and little shoes of white silk.[59] This line made an allusion to the poetry of Dučić as well as to his frivolous sources of inspiration, according to Skerlić's interpretation. Dučić often depicted themes associated with the life of the nobility of Dubrovnik which had long since vanished.

Petrović also described the shortcomings and lack of fairness in the social fabric of his native land. But even then he confirmed his devotion to his native soil in his poem, Sa mojih ravnica (From My Plains). Petrović extolled the "lofty gestures" in Ratar (Farmer), which, due to its intense tone, resembled the poem by Victor Hugo about sowing.

During that same year, in 1908, Milorad M. Petrović published a slim volume of patriotic poems under the title *Vaskresenje (Resurrection)*. The poems presented a poetic response to the annexation of Bosnia and Hercegovina. Skerlić noted the appearance of this volume and commented that the poet wrote the poems "under a profound impression of the latest happenings." The collection consisted of eight poems dedicated to renowned personalities from different regions of Serbia.[60]

Skerlić described Milorad M. Petrović as one of "our better poets." However, some seven years earlier, at the time of the publication of the first collection of poems, *Seljančice (Young Peasant Girls)* by Petrović, Skerlić had expressed a different opinion. At that time it seemed to Skerlić that Petrović's collection was far from real poetry, although it had a certain value of its own.[61] The reason for this evaluation might have been due to Skerlić's thinking that most poets were narrow minded since their poetic themes lacked a wider human context and dealt mostly with the immediate parochial environment and simple pleasures of life. Petrović's songs were inspired by folk lyric poetry of the so-called ženske pesme (female songs). Often these poems described bucolic and idyllic romances in the villages, moonlight, and life in the country:

> The view of these poems is very narrow, too narrow. They
> do not extend further than the steeple of the village church
> . . . . The collection is cheerful and fresh, sometimes
> presenting the image of a very pretty peasant girl. But it
> is as monotonous as village life. Our young poetry as a
> whole is marred by the want of inspiration and narrowness
> of horizon.[62]

In his review for the second collection of  Petrović's  poems,
*Vaskrsenje*, Skerlić did not criticize the themes used. These poems
reflected the spirit of the times and they depicted by their contents
those emotions that were known and understandable to many.

Branko Lazarević, in his review of *Jauci sa Zmijanja (The Cries
from Zmijanje)* by Petar Kočić, published in Zagreb in 1910, discussed
Kočić's literary contribution. Lazarević stated that Kočić started
writing stories some ten years earlier when his first book of collected
stories, *Ispod planine (Under the Mountain)*, appeared in 1902. His
other books appeared in 1904 and 1905. It was apparent that every
new book by Koicć showed progress by abandoning stereotypes in his
writing and slowly gaining his individuality. There was the characteristic struggle between art and patriotism in his writings. Lazarević
thought that in Kočić's first works the artist was prevailing while in
later writings, the patriot was predominant. In his last book, *The
Cries from Zmjanje*, Kočić was walking a precarious balance between
art and patriotism. When Kočić's feelings for his homeland took over,
his narration approached the character of lamentations, sometimes
even slipping into lengthy tirades, as in his stories *Molitva (Prayer)*
and *Zmijanje*. Lazarević had the impression that Kočić's writings increasingly reflected a pessimistic attitude. His early stories were filled
with serenity, close in their cheerful expression to the stories of Janko
Veselinović. But, already in his third book, a pessimistic note was
present. Lazarević concluded that Kočić was endowed with a great
deal of talent and that his story, *Rakijo majko (Brandy Mother)*, could
be included among the 15 best Serbian stories.

Besides his commentary on the literary work of Kočić, as a literary critic of erudition, Lazarević offered important criteria about
literary works in general. He stressed that as soon as a literary genre
began to serve another goal than its own, by this very token this particular genre ceased to exist.[63] The essence of this remark referred
to the autonomy of the literary work since he felt that works of art
subjugated to any particular category outside the literary scope was
weakened and declined.

During 1912, the young poet, Miloš Vidaković, wrote an article which appeared in *Bosanska vila*, elucidating the spiritual atmosphere and the forebodings, while contemplating the possibility of terrors of an expanded war. Vidaković discerned that the national spirit was clearly contained in a number of art works. Ivan Meštrović, the sculptor, was the most powerful proponent of national consciousness. He not only created a Yugoslav artistic spirit but his work presented the "first call, the first summons to fight, the first blow." The most important supporters of the national spirit were found in the patriotic poems of Veljko Petrović and in the optimistic sermons of Nikolaj Velimirović, as well as in the activities of a number of Serbian scientists. Vidaković noted that at the moment many prominent personalities had collaborated in the great idea of unification. In addition, the publications sponsored by diverse youth organizations were supportive of the unification and promoted this idea "in a most enthusiastic manner."[64]

Vidaković felt that with the beginning of the second decade of the twentieth century the fear of approaching war made it necessary to raise one's head high in order to stay alive and victorious. The obligation of the youth was to participate in the righteous fight, if necessary:

> We would be . . . terribly miserable . . . if we allowed our nationalism to remain only verbal in some minor futile war . . . . The activities of the present are dedicated to the happiness of those who shall come and towards whom one must have . . . the selfless feelings of good fathers and protectors.[65]

## Awakening of National Consciousness

Towards the end of the first decade, Jovan Skerlić noticed a change in the attitude of the younger generation who were entering the various ranks of society. The new generation had faith in life and in progress as well as a feeling of national consciousness. Skerlić felt this change as an observer and as a sensitive literary critic who was well informed and tuned into the spiritual aspirations of the historic moment. However, Skerlić stressed, this change among the youth was not confined to Serbia alone but also appeared in other countries in Europe.[66] In France, an interesting book appeared describing the profile of the new generation. Its young writer, Gaston Riou, was French and he wrote about the youth of his country. However, his conclusions about the character of this generation could easily describe the young people in any of the countries in Europe at that time. In his book, *Aux Ecoutes de la France qui Vient (Trying to Hear the Arriv-*

*ing France)*, Riou showed how pessimism, skepticism, and boredom, which were observed as the social behavior and distinctions of the previous generation, started to fade away. The present generation was not indecisive and had a healthy love for life, a fighting energy, and a readiness for action. Most of all, the new generation had a deep feeling of national heritage and union.[67]

About the same time, similar findings resulted from a poll identified as, "A quoi revient les jeunes gens?" (What are the dreams of young people?), conducted by Emile Henriot. The results of the poll established that youth had an expressed feeling of national consciousness and an invigorating outlook toward the future, charged with confidence and energy.[68]

It is noteworthy that Skerlić was aware of these two French publications and that he discerned that a similar consciousness existed among Serbian youth. He stated that he noticed these changes as early as 1908 when the annexation of Bosnia and Hercegovina presented a "national disturbance that awakened even those Serbians that had fallen into a deep slumber."[69]

However, the situation in the country started to change and improve slowly. It was no longer a Serbia presented as a dark, wretched, and hopeless country as in *Stradija* by Radoje Domanović at the beginning of the century. This desperate time was also reflected in Božidar Knežević's collection, *Misli (Thoughts)*, published in 1901. Previous poetry of cinders, poems of death and nirvana, as well as the poetry of the fair maiden and the pale moon of the old romantic poetry went, according to Skerlić, into the "museum of literary antiquity:"

> The wind of change had obviously blown over our land, foreheads have been lifted and backs straightened. Instead of 'statics' of our anemic and exhausted presence, as Mr. Mitrinović would put it, the 'dynamics' of today are a new spirit of faith and life, love for work, and creation of national energy.

Skerlić thought that this new spirit inspired the sculptor, Ivan Meštrović, to create the Kosovo epics in his stone figures. Meštrović also portrayed the stamina of the Yugoslav people in the figure of Prince Marko. Many other artists, as eloquent speakers of their respective generation, recreated the same spirit in their new works. The poems of Milan Rakić, which were collected in *Kosovo*, the patriotic poetry of Aleksa Šantić, Veljko Petrović, and Mirko Korolija,—all these poetic works—spoke with a new and nationalistic language.

After the historic year 1912, a true national renewal started and the entire country was permeated with faith in progress. Skerlić thought that this new spirit guided the young people in the autumn of 1912 on the battlefields of Pčinja and on the Lab, Ibar, and Vardar rivers. The hard won victories brought the Serbian people a contentment that they had not experienced since the time of the Turkish occupation.[70]

However, Skerlić noticed that there appeared to emerge the gruesome "right of the fist," when human ideals, lawfulness, and righteousness were endangered. The chancellors of great powers, when dealing with weaker and smaller nations "talked in a language from the time of Teutonic warriors when the dagger and fire were used to annihilate the Slavic people from the Baltic." Skerlić expressed a fear that mankind was approaching one of the senseless perturbations when the borders and the future of nations were changed while accompanied by heavy losses of human life. Skerlić noted that during the past ten years four large wars had taken place:

> Everybody senses the terrible tempest in the air. The empires that lasted for 500 years are broken as worm–eaten tree trunks, and nobody is sure of the future. And who could even think in these sad times, together with the noble idealists of the first half of the nineteenth century, that mankind had matured and that a time for peace had arrived, for international justice and brotherhood. Who could vouch, together with Heine, that democracy is the great fatherland . . . and who could repeat the words of the magnificent 'Marseillaise of the Peace' by Lamartine, "I am a cohabitant of every soul that thinks. Truth is my Fatherland."[71]

Skerlić noted that the nationalism of the new generation should not be understood in the narrow sense of a political movement, nor in the sense of the romantic and pathetic, or even as anti–Western nationalism of the 1860s. The new nationalism was in its essence an instinct for life that united all generations, born in a wish for self defense of a people that wished to live their own life and become master of their own destiny. This is not the old, traditional nationalism that lived in the dreams of the past. The new nationalism meant faith in one's own strength and denial of all that offered servitude in the immediate surroundings or even in one's own personality. Therefore, the young generation strove to develop strong bodies and paid great attention to physical fitness, will power, and abstinence from alcoholic beverages. Embodying all these characteristics, the new nationalism adopted for its motto the words of Lukijan Mušicki—"Teško meni bez mene" (Woe to me without me). Trust in diplomatic missions and conferences of emperors was lost. The new nationalism was rational, realistic, and democratic.

Skerlić saw the source of new nationalism in the legacy of Dositej Obradović, a personality whose life and works he intimately understood. In his study of Serbian literature of the eighteenth century, Skerlić gave Obradović a leading place. Skerlić was also the principal initiator of the centennial commemoration of the death of Dositej Obradović in 1911. At that time, Skerlić was the editor–in–chief of *Srpski Književni Glasnik*, and in this capacity he initiated the centennial preparations. Furthermore, as a special homage, he dedicated the March 1911 issue of this journal to Obradović with a collection of studies and articles about his works and life. This issue also contained a review of the centennial events and speeches of prominent personalities who represented higher institutions.[72]

In the last part of the centennial celebration in 1914 an unveiling of a statue of Dositej Obradović was shown commemorating his death. At this occasion, Stojan Novaković delivered a speech, representing the Serbian Royal Academy. Ljubomir Jovanović, the minister of education, also addressed the group at this ceremony. Pavle Popović spoke on behalf of the University of Belgrade. The National Theater joined the celebration with a presentation of the play, *Mladost Dositeja Obradovića (The Youth of Dositej Obradović)*. The Metropolitan participated in a mass in the cathedral, and he also performed the benediction at the site of the newly erected Dositej monument. In summing up the review, it was stated that the centennial had the character of a successful Yugoslav Manifestation.[73]

In his evaluation, Skerlić accepted the established opinion about Obradović as "the originator of our consciousness." The new nationalism was a matter of conscience and reason and not a matter of imagination. It did not deal in lamentations over the past or wishes about future dreams. Skerlić thought that the new nationalism was concerned with feasible and useful matters that could be realized. His evaluation recalled the postulates formulated by Dositej Obradović about the need for all work to be useful to people—"Na polzu naroda."

> The new nationalism should be democratic and socially justifiable in its realistic attitudes, not for the sake of lofty words and beautiful language but because it is addressed to the people in general who are the source of national strength . . . . The new generation has shown a serene attitude, a healthier soul, and a stronger faith. They have been firmer and more masculine for they are a willful people and a people of action. They did not stand crying by the river of life

but threw themselves into the mainstream of life.[74]

One of the most important characteristics of the new generation was the profound and straightforward acceptance of the unification of Serbs and Croats, an attitude that was of primary interest, according to Skerlić. This ideology, entertained by philogists and historians, had become a platform for the political parties. The new generation accepted unification as a starting point. Many new journals published in Serbian centers throughout the country and abroad testified to this concern for national unity and for prosperity.[75]

Skerlić concluded, with a measure of resignation, that not all young people involved in these efforts were going to fulfill their aspirations. The enthusiastic youth would soon feel like their older predecessors who once walked the same path, for with the passing of time their enthusiasm would simmer and life would look more complex. The task would no longer look easy:

> The movement has been formed, for it embraces the strongest part of Serbian and Croatian youth and it already has produced not only apostles but martyrs as well. Inasmuch as no single generation has managed to accomplish all that was attempted, no effort remains without fruit. The duty of man is to attend to his work, not taking into account that he might not see the fruits of his efforts.[76]

With these words, Skerlić did predict the fate of many members of the younger generation. Inspired by a nationalism that was sincerely felt, many young men and women entered the fighting ranks as volunteers. Many of them lost their lives during World War I, and some became handicapped and scarred physically and mentally by the experience of war atrocities. Skerlić himself felt close to this young generation of patriots in his own way, although he died on the eve of World War I. His article about the young generation and about patriotism was one of his last writings. Skerlić supported the aspirations of the younger generation since it fulfilled his expectations about the rational and useful work of individuals within the framework of Serbian society during the first and at the beginning of the second decade of the twentieth century. In his role as critic, educator, and people's tribune, Skerlić's life was filled with a multitude of useful activities, but it ended too soon in 1914. He did not live long enough to see the results of his noble efforts.

Milan Kašanin wrote in retrospect, some ten years after the end of World War I, about the young fighters of national unification.[77] According to Kašanin, the representatives of this generation entered public life ten years before the outbreak of World War I. They were in agreement concerning the idea of national unification and the necessity of the creation of an indigenous cultural and artistic contribution.

In the majority of cases, Kašanin discovered that these young people were not the children of the urban upper class. Instead, they grew up in regions and provinces that were under five different jurisdictions and they were predominantly of peasant stock. Already as high school students and university students, before completing their education, they had entered the social scene, had founded youth organizations, prepared Yugoslav art exhibits as manifestations of national unity, edited journals and dailies, and took part in political actions and uprisings. Although their schooling was in general sporadic and insufficient, if they chose literature or art for their occupation, they engaged in the exploration of new means of expression. Their poetry spoke about deeper and more direct personal feelings, as opposed to the carefully crafted poetry of the leading poets of the previous generation. In the field of visual arts, instead of an academic approach that was previously used, the members of this generation depicted fresh impressions or deeply felt delineations of national characteristics. Their art critiques, which were published in periodicals and dailies, pointed to an adherence to the activistic aesthetics of Croce and the philosophy of intuition of Bergson. Kašanin recalled that around the turn of the century spiritual and cultural life was being slowly developed, and immediately before World War I it reached the high point of its unfoldment.[78]

Kašanin further explained that the young generation developed its enthusiasm and joint collaboration mainly because it was united and unanimous in its actions, led by a mutual desire for liberation. Although the members of this generation came from different regions there was no animosity or fighting for leadership:

> With the same . . . unselfishness and readiness for sacrifice, the national youth entered the wars . . . . A high number perished or were thrown out of its ranks becoming useless for their work, crushed and disappointed . . . . Many of those remaining acquired the mentality of survivors and became exhausted old men, identifying themselves with the previous generation. Could it have been otherwise? The ashes of experience covered the flame of naive enthusiasm . . . and life leveled out the spirits of the living as well as the graves of the dead.[79]

The national youth movement in Serbia was most often observed as a specific occurrence caused by historical development. But similar youth movements were widespread in Europe. The French youth movement, for example, was the subject of several polls, discussions, and examinations in various publications. Skerlić wrote about the French youth movement and compared it with the nationalistic activities of Serbian youth. The fact that Skerlić was informed about the French youth movement indicated his quest for information and his breadth of observation. Similar youth movements permeated with national enthusiasm existed in Austria, Great Britain, and Italy as well.[80]

In his capacity as a highly reputable literary critic and as an active participant in the political life of his country, Skerlić supported the newly awakened patriotic feelings among the youth. When the growth of the United Nationalistic Yugoslav Youth became particularly pronounced in 1909, Skerlić was acknowledged by this movement as their ideological leader.[81]

Skerlić considered the nationalist orientation as the leading and most valuable ideological credo of the time, and he was, therefore, not able to give similar support to poetic and prose works with subjective, expressionistic content. This was the reason for Skerlić's outspoken criticism of the poetry of Sima Pandurović and Vladislav Petković Dis, as well as the early prose works by Isidora Sekulić. He declared these works to be a tribute to fashionable literary decadence, falsehood, and thoughtless and empty words. These viewpoints were presented in his writings, " Lažni modernizam u srpskoj književnosti (False Modernism in Serbian Literature" and "Jedna književna zaraza (A Literary Disease."[82] Skerlić did not realize that the feelings of patriotism and nationalism also included writers who expressed their national aspirations indirectly and with less clarity.

Isidora Sekulić wrote about these disagreements and misunderstandings that Skerlić demonstrated in his judgments in a short essay under the title, "The Poets That Lie," which was published in 1911. The essay was published on the front page of *Bosanska vila* as an editorial. It was very likely that the editors of the journal felt that Sekulić's views presented a valuable contribution to clarifying the existing situation.

Sekulić quoted the spirited observation of Skerlić concerning the poetry of Aleksa Šantić. He stated that Šantić was a poet who did not lie. Sekulić commented on this statement by juxtaposing the contributions of poets with different attitudes:

> How nice that Mr. Šantić has a healthy heart artery and is
> not frightened by vampires or nirvana and convulsions. . . .
> However, today there is a return to backwardness . . . We
> have moved way from the sun and there are no gods without
> a dragging shadow, and it is not totally false when one sings

of admiration with a shadow of illness and fear, and amid love with a shadow of sin. Who knows, then, whether it is important for the entire poetry of a nation as well as for single poets to become "l'immensement perdu," and then only to achieve victory over life like Verhaaren and Šantić, to reach the conviction acknowledged by their nerves and blood and dreams, to achieve the courage to recapture love for the sake of love and work as well as love for the homeland and for faith.[83]

Skerlić remained consistent in his negative evaluation of the poetry of alienation and individualism; he condemned Sekulić's book *Saputnici (Fellow Travellers)* which he had started to read while on a train during the Balkan War:

I started reading this book on the train in an atmosphere of blood and death that was felt everywhere. The train reeked of disinfectants, and was filled with foreign physicians, nurses, and wives of officers dressed in black, going to the graves of those who had been killed . . . and before me this sight caused a horror that could never be forgotten. When one can see the abyss of human pain and misery, how can one look upon 17 pages of phrases about a headache? I never before felt in my life as at this very moment all the miserable emptiness of words and all the vanity contained in literature and in books.[84]

However, Sekulić's book, *Saputnici,* drew a number of favorable reviews. Veljko Milićević wrote a review, which appeared in *Bosanska vila,* praising the book and thought it should take its place in Serbian literature. The book was also interesting since it was written by a woman. Milićević stated that he did not, in particular, appreciate literature written by women, especially if it presented a feministic point of view, since very often these works were considered as "decoration, that concealed emptiness." The book by Sekulić, however, did not show such characteristics for there was no artificiality in it. Instead, *Saputnici* had a natural and sincere tone. Sekulić managed not to wander in a wasteland and with her work she made her own path. She worked like a man and remained personal, and she therefore gained the right to be equal.[85]

*Saputnici* was also reviewed by Luka Smodlaka in 1913. He noted that it was the literary work of an educated writer who wished to introduce new perspectives in literary creations. The value of the book was in presenting just this search for the new. The collected stories offered an analysis of personal happenings as well as philosophical theses or reminiscences from early childhood when all objects were colored by the help of imagination. Smodlaka noticed the ability of the author to project an inner life. All of these qualities distinguished the achievements of Sekulić from other writers.[86]

Jovan Dučić, a poet, wrote about Sekulić's book in the leading journal, *Srpski Književni Glasnik*. Dučić was at the time at the height of his poetic fame and the publication of his review apparently was a concession on the part of the editors since the book had already been reviewed in the journal by Skerlić. Dučić established that this was the first book by Sekulić and that it presented a fine achievement. The author had a true talent for writing, a poetic flow of words, and splendid metaphors. He concluded that *Saputnici* belonged to the group of ten best books of Serbian literature when he wrote:

> Everything here is in the realm of the spiritual and intellec-
> tual, of what one dreams and one thinks. There is a conflict
> between the illusion of life and the idea of life. . . . Like all
> poets, she is a thinker and a dreamer.[87]

In spite of the many reviews praising her first book, Isidora Sekulić could not overlook the rebuke by Skerlić, and she wrote about this dissension in retrospect many years later:

> Skerlić entered with a strong conviction and temperament
> into the mainstream of nationalism. He was a leader of the
> national youth in a truly magnificent manner. Especially
> during the period 1912–14 he became a popular and en-
> chanting figure. He was carried away by his mission into
> which he brought, as only he knew how, enormous energy
> . . . Skerlić became intolerant towards all that would con-
> tradict any tendencies to fight nationalism, such as a weak
> will, vagueness or skepticism. He could perhaps have been
> less zealous in his causes. We were all involved in national
> currents, more or less fanatic, and we all felt that the words
> of these extraordinary men were not the rhetoric for the
> occasion . . . His criticism, both literary and political,
> was against cosmopolitan ideas and styles, against the Eu-
> ropean spirit that at that time cultivated a pessimistic note
> in poems and novels. . . . Meanwhile, in the little, la-
> borious, simple Serbia at that time, who could have been
> a cosmopolitan, and with what? . . . We all could have
> had cosmopolitan elements, in a larger or smaller measure,
> only in our culture. And all the world had in its culture
> some cosmopolitan marks, including Skerlić, since culture is
> one in all mankind . . . and also the only uniting element,

since there was nothing else. Of course, on another level of
his life, Skerlić knew all this very well. The new, political
Skerlić, did not want to acknowledge that in Serbia a host
of national tasks had to be solved at the time.[88]

Sekulić noted correctly the diffusion of nationalism in the Serbian
milieu, and she therefore stated, "We have all been in the national
current." However, her evaluation of the European scene was less
accurate since she considered that writers throughout Europe "cultivated a pessimistic note in poems and novels." The same period
brought a renewal of patriotic poetry and a belief in the strength of
national entity based on tradition. Some poems written at that time
testified to a readiness to fight, even to rejoice at the possibility of a
battle.

In the course of 1913, Isidora Sekulić voiced her compassion for
all the victims of the Balkan War. Her thoughts about the personal
tragedies and the possibility of another war were depicted in the impressive narrative, *Pitanje (Question)*. In an imaginary point in time,
certain questions were coming to her mind which were stirred by recent military events. A disquieting vision, associated with this questioning, acquired a timeless quality and was therefore valid for the
past as well as for future happenings. Sekulić depicted the trans-
portation of the dead and wounded to an unknown hospital in the
dusk of a cold and windy day. She was a witness of this sad procession and she addressed the wounded with concern. The replies that
she received were utterances of stereotyped assurances of patriotism.
Sekulić felt that these verbal assurances were suggestions of the lofty
purpose of war. The repetition of these phrases by exhausted victims
seemed to extinguish fears and anxieties, although they sounded un-
real and false. Sekulić understood that love for the homeland was an
obstacle in a search for an all embracing human love:

> What is fatherland, and what is love for the fatherland?
> What cruel force was driving innocent people in the snow-
> storm and outburst of rage? What monster wanted you to
> attack . . . to be the finders that water their path with
> their own blood and brain and illuminate with fire? . . .
> The regiment is marching, and the flag is streaming in front
> . . . and after the burial, the sound of trumpets quickly
> take down the black cloth of mourning. The air is scented
> with champagne, and nobody is dreaming the dream of the
> fallen and dead.[89]

The war took many victims from different walks of life, the young
and the old, from towns and villages, including renowned personal-

ities, writers, and artists. Nadežda Petrović, an artist, joined as a volunteer in the Red Cross. She worked as a dedicated nurse and died from typhoid fever while on duty in 1915. She was dubbed by her fellow artists, "Jugoslovenska Nada" (Yugoslav Hope), due to her persistent efforts to uphold the idea of Yugoslav unity. An accomplished artist, she took an active part in cultural and political life. She organized public meetings, protests, and gave patriotic speeches in order to raise funds for the needy in occupied Macedonia. She strove, in particular, to encourage collaboration among fellow artists and promote the idea of Yugoslav unity by organizing The Yugoslav Colony. This organization united artists and sculptors of congenial artistic outlook. Petrović managed to continue her own artistic mission by painting even during the midst of war. She painted two variations of *Vezirov most (Vezir's Bridge)* and several variations of the monastery of Gračanica on the Kosovo field surrounded with red peonies. The picturesque township of Prizren attracted her attention as well, and she produced three paintings of Prizren. Among the last of her paintings should be mentioned *Valjevska Bolnica (The Hospital in Valjevo)*.

When Milutin Bojić, the poet, died in Thessalonica in 1917 at the age of 25, he left some remarkable poetic works in spite of his youth. His first published poems had already attracted the attention of Jovan Skerlić. Bojić found inspiration for his play, *Kraljeva jesen (The King's Autumn)* in the historic past reaffirming his affinity to past national glory.

Among the victims of the war were young writers and journalists holding great promise for the future—Vladislav Petković Dis, Milutin Usković, Milan Luković, Dragutin Mraz, Dimitrije Tucović, Petar Kočić, Vladimir Gaćinović, Miloš Vidaković, Nikola Antula, Jovan Varagić, Proka Jovkić, Velja Rajić, and Cvijeto Jov, among others. These young men distinguished themselves as active political and articulate civic leaders as well.

Milenko Paunović, a composer, joined the ranks of the Serbian army also. Paunović, who was of Serbian descent, was born in Šajkaši in the region of Bačka, which constituted at the time part of the Austro–Hungarian Empire. He was, therefore, considered an alien. Paunović retreated with the Serbian army through the snow covered mountains of Albania. Like many of them, he was undernourished and wore clothing and footwear that was soon worn out. Upon his arrival in Thessaloniki, he became sick with typhoid and was treated at the hospital by French physicians. While in hospital, Paunović was visited by his older colleague, Stanislav Binički, who urged the French physicians to take good care of him since he was a promising and talented young musician.[90] During his recuperation in the hospital, Paunović had a recurring musical theme in mind, and as soon as he could get up, he played the theme on the organ in the chapel. This musical theme served as the nucleus for the Yugoslav symphony. National aspiration of a unity of the South Slavs occupied Paunović even during the trying.moments of his illness.

After the end of the war, Paunović returned to his home in Jagodina where he had taught music in the Teachers' Middle School since 1913. He was greatly disappointed not to find any of the manuscripts of his compositions that he had left there before going to war.[91] Paunović himself returned from the war as a changed man, displaying an inability to cope with persistent difficulties. Alcoholism complicated his situation to a great extent.[92]

Another poet, Miloš Crnjanski, spent World War I in the uniform of an Austro–Hungarian officer on the battlefields of Galicia as well as some other combat duties. He also spent time recuperating in military hospitals. The suffering and devastation caused by war produced great anxieties for the poet. In order to find an inner peace, Crnjanski turned to writing poetry:

> Ja pevam tužnima
> da tuga od svega oslobodjava. (Prolog)

> I sing to the sad ones
> that sadness liberates from everything. (Prologue)

Crnjanski found the main inspiration for his poems in the historical past of the ancient cities of Troy and Mycenae. These poems were later collected under the title *Lirika Itake (The Lyrics from Ithaca).*

Many years later, during World War II, Crnjanski wrote a commentary for the poem, Prolog (Prologue). Repeating his conviction that the return from war presented the most sorrowful experience of a man, he upheld his belief that *The Odyssey* was the greatest poem of mankind. This ancient Greek epic poem remained for Crnjanski a profound source of inspiration and adulation. His poems written during World War I presented a response to the immense treasury of everlasting human experiences as recorded in *The Odyssey.*[93]

## The Renewal of Nationalism in Other European Countries

The feeling of an impending disastrous war awakened in many European countries a strong feeling of national consciousness. In Germany, nearly all poets, led by Hauptmann and Demel, believed their duty to be to revive an appreciation of the German tradition. They identified their roles with that held by ancient Germanic bards. Thus, Gerhard Hauptmann wrote in his poem published in 1914, The Poem for a Cavalryman, that the French are endangering German honor. The writing of Thomas Mann also contributed to German bellicose ideology. Mann felt that German culture with its moral conservatism and military morality stood opposed to Western civilization. German morality contained in its essence elements of the demonic and heroic at the same time.[94]

Instigated by the spirit of the time, many well known young artists volunteered for military duty. August Macke, overwhelmed by the thoughts of war, painted his well known canvass, *Parting*. The painting was executed in a dark hue that contributed to a pictorial projection of depression, anxiety, and fear. Macke joined others in the ranks of volunteers convinced about the inevitability of war. He became one of the first war victims in 1914.

Still other well known artists joined the rank of growing volunteers. They were Franz Marc, Otto Dix, Max Beckmann, George Grosz, Ernst Ludwig Kirchner, Max Ernst, and Oskar Kokoschka, among others. Writers and poets also voluntarily joined the military units. Among their ranks were Richard Demel, Fritz von Unruh, Walter Hasenklever, Erich Heckel, the painter, and Karl Sefler, the art historian. Sefler wrote about the "terrible beauty of war" in 1914. He also commented that the scenes of destruction and death gave way to "an arabesque of eternity."

Otto Dix shared similar views when, in 1915, he painted his *Self Portrait As Mars*. Dix portrayed his own likeness with splattered blood and a shiny helmet on his head, framed with scenes of destruction and dying. The painting gave an impression of the glorification of war. The painting, *Canon*, by the same artist expressed a similar connotation by presenting dilapidated dwellings with heavy artillery fire. Max Beckmann stressed that in the midst of destruction he could discern the giddy dance of expressionistic colors which were accompanied by the "magical and splendid noises of battle."[95]

The crude realities of war gradually brought a change in this outlook. The battles became more ferocious and there were many victims. Thus, Ernst Barlach, who entered the army as a volunteer and distinguished himself as a good soldier early in combat duty, produced in the midst of the war a woodcut, *Anno Domini 1916*. Barlach showed the dreary rows of tombstones in a military cemetery that spoke eloquently about the unnecessary sacrifices of men. Otto Dix, who at the beginning of the war glorified the Roman war god Mars in his own self image, saw soon enough that people in the midst of war were crawling around underground with mice and rats for protection. His *Self Portrait of a Sergeant* that Dix painted in 1917 presented a changed attitude towards war. Dix saw himself as a disheveled ruffian with a cigarette dangling from his deformed mouth. This humiliating appearance was in sharp contrast with the previous self-presentation emulating Mars. This change in attitude was due to an awareness of an ever increasing human sufferings and of general annihilation. Dix soon after wrote that he was hoping that peace would take place. However, when a peace treaty was signed, the memory of the destruction of war did not fade away easily. For some ten years Dix was haunted by scenes of devastation.

In a similar manner, when Max Beckmann ceased to search for aesthetic experiences in the visual images of battles, life during peacetime seemed to him a "paradise." Thus Beckmann created the painting, *Storm*, in 1916 that presented the horrors of war vividly, depleted of any symbolical connotations of justification.[96]

A former enthusiasm for military involvement, hailed by many as a possible path leading to a fulfillment of various aspects of radical changes, gradually proved to be inconceivable for the attainment of these goals. A previous glorification of war was once particularly promoted by Italian futurists. In the *Futuristic Manifesto* published by Tomazeo Marinetti in 1909, he explained a renewal of belligerancy:

> In the political arena there is no beauty without a fight. There is no great achievement without an aggressive character. . . . We want to celebrate war as a great hygiene of the world—militaristic, anarchistic, with a destructive gesture, killing ideas, and showing disdain for women!

Marinetti coined the slogan, "Marciare no mancire," meaning "To march and not to rot." He wanted to stress the necessity of a military movement, contrasting militant activism to a standstill, equating a standstill with rotting. Carlo Carra, an artist, used Marinetti's slogan on his collage, *The Composition with a Female Figure*, painted in 1915. The collage was dominated by a central female figure surrounded with cutouts from futuristic manifestoes, daily papers, and Marinetti's slogan.

The futurists often proclaimed their readiness for action and militancy on their pictorial compositions. Marinetti, Boccioni, Carra, Piatti, and Russolo created a pictorial presentation in 1914 entitled, *The Futuristic Synthesis of the War*. The future was presented in the form of a wedge denoting the nations of Italy, Serbia, Montenegro, and Belgium united in an entente. This wedge was directed towards a circular surface comprised of Germany and Austro–Hungary.

The members of the futuristic movement, next to their experimentations in the visual arts, participated in provocative political appearances, noisy speeches, meetings, marches, and various acts of disobedience.[97]

Many well known personalities of that time—writers, intellectuals, philosophers, painters, and artists—throughout Europe persistently supported the idea of national renewal, even, if necessity, with military intervention. Leading French writers belonging to the circle of Charles Pèguy, Maurice Barres, and Paul Claudel actively preached the necessity of French national renewal. They acknowledged the "discipline, heroism, and renaissance of the national spirit" as important requirements for the well being of a nation. In a similar fashion, Anatole France was ready to bear arms in spite of his advanced age. It was in this spirit that Henri Bergson started to write his book, *La Signification de la Guerre*, arguing the necessity of war for a moral regeneration of Europe.

In Germany in 1911, Thomas Mann maintained that only enemies of the national spirit could oppose war. War alone would allow for Germany to become stronger than ever, and be proud, free, and prosperous. Stefan Georg and Reiner Maria Rilke shared a similar conviction. Rilke felt the widespread extent of belligerency around him. He was aware that he shared a militant attitude himself. However, having the perception of a poet, Rilke soon understood that the true content of his future poems should not be heroism or fighting but suffering and pain.[98]

Stefan Zweig left a valuable testimony about the form and content of many poetic works of that time in his book, *Die Welt von Gestern*. As an interesting example, Zweig noted that during the month of August 1914 there were about 50,000 poems written every day.

> Almost all poets, with Hauptmann and Demel at the forefront, considered it their duty to include in their poems a message to instigate the fighters into a storm to die with enthusiasm, like the bards in ancient Germanic times. The proliferation of poems piled high with many naive rhymes. The writers swore that they should never agree to a cultural alliance with either France or England. And, in addition, they started to deny overnight that English or French culture ever existed. Those cultures were insignificant in comparison with German spirit, art, and stock.[99]

The list of names of well known avant-garde writers, philosophers, and artists who shared similar martial views was long enough to make it impossible to mention everyone. Among the writers, however, were such names as H. G. Wells, Henry James, Arnold Bennett, Georg Haym, Guillaume Apollinaire, and Maurice Maeterlinck;

among the philosophers were Henry Bergson, Rudolf Euken, Max Schelen, George Santayana, Ernest Haeckel, T. E. Hulme, and Frederic Harrison; also Aleksandar Skriabin, composer, Henri Gaudier-Brzeska, sculptor, and members of futuristic and vortistic movements. [100]

The martial and aggressive attitude that prevailed in the period leading to World War I seemed to be intentionally forgotten and not discussed until recently. The reason for overlooking this period of belligerent euphoria could be explained by the fact that these tendencies were soon enough understood by the survivors and coevals as being embarrassing at the beginning of the war. Interest in literature with militaristic overtones ceased to exist at the moment of confrontation with destruction and loss of human life. The public was not any longer inclined to read bellicose prose or poetry, and the writers ceased to celebrate annihilation in the name of high national goals.

# Chapter 7

## The War Years

### World War I Exodus — Reflections on Serbian and European Literature and Fine Arts

In the summer of 1914 after the outbreak of World War I in Serbia, a general evacuation was started by all important military and governmental institutions as well as most editorial offices of newspapers and professional publications. This evacuation was followed by the migration of some of the population from Belgrade and other Serbian regions to Niš, which became a populated cultural center. During 1914–15, around 20 different journals and newspapers were being published there.[1]

Niš was not without a literary and publishing tradition. Early in the 1900s, *Gradina (Garden)*, a journal, was started, which was edited and published by the high school teachers in Niš. The journal soon attracted outstanding contributors, such as Aleksa Šantić, Svetozar Ćorović, Jelena Dimitrijević, Božidar Nikolajević, Jelenko Mihailović, and Lujobomir Jovanović. Borisav Stanković published the first version of his novel, *Nečista krv (Tainted Blood)*, in *Gradina*, and Sima Matavulj published one of his best known literary works, *Kaludjerska posla (Monachal Deals)* in the same journal. After a double issue, which was numbered 36–37, appeared in November of 1901, the journal ceased to exist due to the strained political conditions in the country at that time.[2]

Shortly after the declaration of war, *Prosvetni glasnik (The Educational Herald)*, the official journal of the Ministry of Education and Ecclesiastic Affairs, was transferred to Niš. The editor of the journal was Miodrag Ibrovac, and the journal was published by the State Press of the Kingdom of Serbia, which had been partially relocated to Niš.[3]

The official daily newspaper of the Royal Kingdom of Serbia, *Srpske novine (Serbian Paper)* was also published in Niš. The editor of the paper was Professor Vlada T. Spasojević. An order issued by minister Ljuba Davidović about the dismissal of all schools in February of 1915 appeared in *Srpske novine*. Davidović addressed the teachers asking them to remain in the same location and "administer Samaritan's duties" if they were not already drafted by the military. Soon afterwards, as a form of service to the public, long lists of soldiers killed in action appeared in the newspaper.[4]

An obituary for Proka Jovkć, the poet, appeared in the May 1915 issue of *Radničke novine*.[5] Jovkić had the pseudonym of Nestor Žučni as his pen name. The obituary was written by his close friend, B. Graovac, who knew Jovkić from the days when they had both lived in Oakland, California. Graovac used the following verses of Jovkić as a motto:

> Hoću da sam čovek! Neću više torbu
> Prosjačku . . .
> Ja krećem u život, na rad i u borbu
> Gde se umom 'rve, obara i bije.

> I want to be a man! I do not want the bag
> Of a beggar . . .
> I am entering a life of work and struggle
> Where one's mind wrestles, attacks, and fights.

The *Delo* journal was among those published in Niš in 1915. *Delo* was described in the masthead as "the journal of science, literature, and social life." The editors were Dr. Dragoljub Pavlović and Dr. Marković, and the journal was published by the State Press of the Kingdom of Serbia which had been relocated from Belgrade to Niš. In May of 1915 a letter appeared in the journal written by M. Jorge, professor at the University of Bucharest, addressed to the editor, Lazar Marković. Jorge stated that he received two issues of the journal and that he was impressed by the appearance, content, and layout, and he acknowledged that it had been published under difficult circumstances:

> I received two issues of your beautiful journal. Its regular appearance, with carefully selected contents, is another indication of the quiet energy that you Serbs bring into all your acts of political life. You fight well and you publish good journals. In the meantime, you are facing new battles in which you are again going to fight well.[6]

*Delo*, which was a publication of the Radical Party, continued to be issued for six months during 1915. During this period, the editors strove to publish literary works and to safeguard the high quality of editorial principles. The following prose works were selected: *Zbeg,*

*Slika ratnih stradanja (The Refuge, The Picture of War Suffering)* by Ivo Ćipivo; *Dvoboj (Duel)* by Živojin Devečerski; *Hej Sloveni (Hail Slavs)* by Rista Odavić, and *Le Maitre* by Emile Verhaeren, translated into Serbo-Croatian from French. Among the newly written poetic works, the following lyrical poems were published: *Esamir* by Trifun Djukić, *Noć (Night)* by Proka Jovkić, *Jorgovan (Lilac)* by Milica Janković, *Tihe strofe (Silent Verses)* by Isidora Sekulić, *Proslava 1915 (Celebration 1915)* by Vladislav Petković Dis, and *Otadžbina (Fatherland)* by Rista Odavić. In the column, *Notes,* the reviews of foreign literature were presented. Thus, the appearance of *Aesthetics* by Arthur Schopenhauer was discussed. Attention was given to the poetry of Sir Rabindranath Tagore who received the Nobel prize for literature in 1913.[7]

The publication of a new journal, *Jugoslovenski Glasnik (The Yugoslav Herald),* was announced in the last issue of *Delo* in August of 1915. When it appeared in Niš on 1 August 1915, its ideological emphasis was already apparent in the title indicating the promotion of the Yugoslav idea. In the third issue, under the heading, *Beleške* (Notes), it was announced that thanks to the initiative of Nikola Velimirović a new bi-monthly journal, *Svejetlo (Light),* had started to appear in New York.[8]

Shortly after the retreat of the Serbian army and some of the population of Serbia over Albanian mountains, several new publishing centers were set up on Greek territory. In addition, there was another publishing center in Switzerland as well as one in Africa. Corfu Island became the seat of the State Press of the Kingdom of Serbia. In Thessalonika, the *Velika Srbija* and *Mlada Srbija* printing companies were set up. In addition, Vlad. R. Andjelković and M. Ristivojević opened their own companies. Ristivojević named his company *Srpska knjižara.* During the war years, a series entitled *Mala biblioteka* was published there. In Bizerte, Africa, the Štamparija srpskih invalida (Press of Serbian Invalids) started an edition of *Napred (Forward),* of which eventually 20 volumes were published.[9]

The Bosnian and Hercegovinian Society for Cultural Affairs, *Prosveta (Education),* which was started under the editorship of Pera Slepčević, was responsible for a series of lectures in Geneva. These lectures were published in a special edition of *Prosveta,* named after the Society. In addition, two journals, *Mali kurir (Little Courier)* and *Ujedinjenje (Unification),* were published in Geneva.[10]

One of the most important events of cultural life in exile was the renewal of the publication *Srpske novine (Serbian Newspaper).* After the first issue appeared on 7 April 1916, the paper introduced a weekly supplement, *Zabavnik (Magazine).* Branko Lazarević was named the editor of the supplement. It proved to be an excellent choice since he was at one time a student of Bogdan Popović and a contributer to *Srpski Književni Glasnik*. He brought his professional skills as well as a formal and ideological concept to the newly founded paper which was previously developed in *Glasnik*. Therefore, the retention of columns and headings as used in *Glasnik* worked to the same advantage in *Zabavnik* aiding in the conciseness and classification of the presented material. Lazarević introduced to this publication an editorial dedicated to the development of political events and situations at the war front.

In his remarkable introductory editorial, Lazarević reminded readers that in 1813, more than a century earlier, the daily newspaper *Novine serbske* was started in Vienna, a foreign city far away from Serbian borders. The editors, in a wish to expand the scope of the paper, introduced a magazine in 1815, *Zabavnik*. History was repeating itself, and in 1916 the renewed newspaper *Srpske novine*, appeared again on the island of Corfu, far away from Serbia. Lazarević added that the recent preparations for the renewal of the paper had been very thorough. The editorial office soon became the meeting place of writers and artists. Lazarević stressed that the editors strove to open the pages of the newspaper to all those wishing to contribute. Lazarević's editorial position reflected the editorial policies of *Srpski Književni Glasnik*, its founder and first editor, Popović. Popović stressed his wish to attract the contributions of writers and artists of varied artistic profiles.

Lazarević further noted in the same editorial that there was a relatively small number of writers in Corfu. The majority of the Serbian intelligentsia—educators at the college or high school level, journalists, politicians, and scientists—had found refuge in France and Sweden. However, as often was the case, the major national and propaganda related tasks were performed by a minority while the majority of the men of letters stood by idly. Among the active participants supporting national issues were famous personalities in their own areas of academic research as well as educators at the University of Belgrade: Jovan Cvijić, a geographer; Pavle Popović, an historian; Aleksandar Belić, a Slavic philologist; Tihomir Djordjević, an ethnographer; professor Svetozar Petrović; and Miodrag Ibrovac, a literary historian and Romanesque scholar.[11]

In spite of the difficult life in emigration, the writers and poets struggled to continue their literary and artistic endeavors. *Srpske novine* and *Zabavnik* carried some of their writings and served as a chronicle of political and social events as well. Lazarević commented on this situation in his review of a recently published collection of poems by Milutin Bojić called *Pesme bola i ponosa (The Poems of Pain and Pride)*, when he wrote:

Our art shows where we are at the present time. We lost our territories, but we did not lose our souls . . . . We were tossed out in a manner that nobody ever has been, and now, like tigers, we are standing on our feet. We are dispersed throughout Europe, America, and Africa, yet we are able to express our artistic thoughts boldly.12

A growing interest in Serbian culture was reflected not only in the publications of Serbian writers and politicians, but also by foreign statesmen, historians, writers, and artists who started to write about Serbia. Sometimes these writings observed, on a broader scale, Yugoslav national and cultural entity.

One such writer was Todor Manojlović, a poet, who reported in *Zabavnik* that the well known art historian, Gabriel Millet, had published an excellent study of old Serbian art. This study appeared in a French art magazine, *L'Art et les Artistes*, under the title "La Serbie Glorieuse." Manojlović commented that the study was written with admiration for the history of Serbian pictorial art and architecture. The study encompassed the period from the first rulers of the Nemanjić dynasty and their architectural legacy through the depiction of monuments erected by the last descendants of the Hrebeljanović royal family.[13]

R. W. Seton-Watson, a professor of history at the University of London, conducted research on Austro-Hungarian and Balkan history. Following the annexation of Bosnia and Hercegovina by the Austro-Hungarian Empire, Seton-Watson wrote *The Southern Slav Question* in 1911. In 1916, he published a comprehensive volume describing the plight of the Serbian people. This publication was distributed to 12,000 schools in England. Its impact was that the English youth felt compelled to help the needy in devasted Serbia, and led by Seton-Watson, the Serbian Relief Fund was started. In 1917, Seton-Watson also published *The Rise of Nationality in the Balkans*.[14]

A review of the book by Dr. Bogumil Vosnjak, *A Dying Empire*, which was published in London, appeared in the February 1918 issue of *Zabavnik*. Vosnjak, who was of Slovenian descent, was a docent at the University of Zagreb. The preface was written by Thomas Power O'Connor, a member of Parliament and founder of several newspapers in London. In an effort to inform the English public about the Yugoslav question, Vosnjak discussed the disintegration of the Austro-Hungarian Empire into the national states of Yugoslavia,

Hungary, and Bohemia. This writer had previously published another book in English explaining the Slavic position.[15] Even musical art was not neglected. It should be noted that choral groups were formed on the island of Corfu. In 1916, Miloje Milojević composed, *Opus 18, Na Vidov dan 1916 (On Saint Vitus' Day 1916), Poruka (Message),* and *Molitva izgnanika (The Prayer of Expatriates).* During his stay in Thessalonika, Milojević composed *Prva liturgija (First Liturgy) Opus 16.* He also made sketches for the play, *Kraljeva jesen (King's Autumn),* and he finished the orchestral score for the symphonic prologue, *Danilo and Simonida,* pertaining to the same work by Bojić. However, both manuscripts seem to have been lost.[16]

In addition, while in Thessalonika, Milojević composed *Srpska rapsodija (Serbian Rhapsody)* for stringed instruments as well as a number of piano transcriptions. The piano compositions were inspired by the Serbian folk song and dances: *Bojerka, More, izvir voda (The Babbling Spring), Ala imaš oči (What Lovely Eyes), Cigančica (Gypsy Girl), Razbole se belo Done (Fair Done is Ill,* and *Lepojko devojko (Beautiful Girl).* Milojević revived the pleasant memories of his native land in these musical vignettes. These piano pieces were later collected and published in Paris under the title, *Dans mon Pays (In My Homeland).* The second collection for piano and voice was later published in Paris under the title *Melodies Populaires Serbes pour Piano et Chant,* with a French translation of the songs.[17]

During this same period, Milojević composed Prva liturgija (The First Liturgy) that attracted the attention of singers as well as authorities in the field of church music. Thus, Damaskin Grdanički wrote a review of this work under the heading "Arts Review," published in *Zabavnik* in 1918. Grdanički noted that the liturgy was published in 1916, in a modest, lithographic form with only 20 copies. Probably due to these circumstances the review of Milojević's work was delayed. Grdanički thought that the Liturgy was of great importance for the musical literature of the church since it was composed in a new style. Milojević introduced secular folk motives in his work which were transformed to serve liturgical purposes. Grdanički noted that a similar approach was cultivated in Russian church music by A. G. Grechaninov and S. B. Panchenko:

> The Liturgy of Mr. Milojević . . . (is) the first serious effort to introduce our secular motives into church use . . .
> . The Psalms, Skaži mi Gospodi (Tell me, Lord) for tenor solo and choir as well as Tebe pojem (I Sing unto You) were written with an abundance of melodic and harmonic color. Both songs, and especially the first one with the fugue in the

second half, serve as an effort to create music for our church, corresponding to the needs of the church, and at the same time are modelled in accordance with the musical culture of the West.[18]

During that same year, another musical work was composed for the church. Kosta P. Manojlović finished his Liturgy for male choir while he was in the military hospital in Fier, Albania, convalescing after an illness caused by typhoid fever. Manojlović started composing the Liturgy after the outbreak of World War I in Kragujevac where he was assigned to nursing duty. Soon afterwards, while in the hospital in Kragujevac, Manojlović organized a choir made of of his fellow nurses. The members of the choir performed at funerals during the autumn months in 1914, singing next to the freshly dug graves of young solders killed in action. In Kragujevac, Manolović composed the greater part of his Liturgy during the difficult war years. A polyphonic principle was often used throughout his composition and the individual voices are distinguished by an expressive melodic line. Manojlović introduced the reading of the scriptures by a priest between movements of the Liturgy as a new feature.[19]

Manojlović's Liturgy was declared as one of the most remarkable works of spiritual music due to the strength and expressiveness of its artistic content. This opinion was corroborated, about 20 years later, by Miloje Milojević who stated that it would be hard to find in Serbian church music similar examples of well written polyphonic movements: "The voices have individuality, their own motion, melodic inflection. The voices merge into a whole richly interwoven and powerful sound."[20]

While on the island of Corfu, Manojlović formed a military choir. Since there was little musical material available there, he was forced to reconstruct some musical scores from memory. Under his guiding hand, the choral recitals excelled with time until the choir, together with Mnojlović, was transferred to Thessalonika to continue further with performances of popular choral pieces. In April of 1917, Manojlović was finally relieved of his military duties and he was sent to England to finish his musical education. He enrolled at the University of Oxford but even then continued directing musical groups. He organized a choir consisting of Yugoslav students who were pursuing studies in England. The young Yugoslav students felt compelled to present Yugoslav music to the English public in order to show their appreciation for the generous help extended to the Serbian people as well as to show their gratitude for an opportunity to continue their education. Manojlović appeared with his choir in Oxford, London, Reading, and Birmingham.

In order to satisfy the demand for choral works of Yugoslav composers, Manojlović prepared a collection of choral compositions entitled *Jugoslovenske narodne pesme (Yugoslav Folk Songs)*. Rosa Newmarch, an English musicologist, collaborated in the preparation of these compositions and supplied the English translation of the collection containing 43 songs. It is of special interest to mention that the eminent Yugoslav sculptor, Ivan Meštrović, participated as well in this project by providing the design for the cover. Meštrović was an avid supporter of the Yugoslav idea of unification of the South Slavs.

During his studies at Oxford, Manojlović composed his well known composition for violin and piano, Igra udovica (The Widow's Dance). He supplied the following motto referring to folk customs that originally explained this dance: "The dance is performed by persons dressed in black with a black scarf on their heads during the late night when the dead lead the dance. The dance is accompanied with music of sorrow and the dead beat of a drummer."

Manojlović devoted most of his time and thought to the preparation of his composition, *Psalm 137, Pokraj voda vavilonskih (Psalm 137, By the Water of Babylon)*. While at Oxford, Manojlović studied under Hugh Percy Allen, who was a well known musical scholar and professor of music at Oxford, and in 1918 became director of the Royal College of Music in London. *Psalm 137* was accepted as part of the requirements necessary for Manojlović's graduation from Oxford in 1919. He composed *Psalm 137* in the form of a cantata for two mixed choirs, solo baritone, and orchestra. The main musical theme was derived from a church folk melody, Na rijekah vavilonskih (By the River of Babylon).[21]

It is noteworthy that Manojlović provided a motto for Psalm 137 which was written by Živojin Devečerski. Devečerski's poem, written in prose, first attracted Manojlović's attention when it was published in *Zabavnik*. It referred to the painful experiences that accompanied the retreat of the Serbian Army:

> Na vodama albanskim, na vodama Smrti, ustavismo umorne
> čete. Na rekama albanskim Škumbi, Semeni i Vojtuši us-
> tavismo se da odmorimo kosti. Samo nam kosti još ostadoše,
> kosti, smrt i čast na zastavama slave. (By the Albanian wa-
> ters, by the waters of death, we stopped our tired companies.
> By the Albanian rivers of Škumba, Semena, and Vojtuša we
> stopped to rest our bones. Only the bones remained, bones,
> death, and honor on the flags of glory.[22]

During the war years a number of elementary and high school students were evacuated to France. In order to continue with their education, they attended various schools in Bordeaux, Nice, and Bolieux. Vladimir R. Djordjević, a composer and folklorist who also emigrated to France, was assigned to conduct the choirs and provide musical instruction. While in France, Djordjević managed to compose a number of musical pieces which were primarily intended as a supplement for concerts of pupils under his care. These compositions, which were published in France, must have found popular appeal since several editions of some of his works appeared. The compositions were entitled, *Trente-cinq Chansons Populaires Serbes pour piano avec Chant ad Libitum; Deux Marches Serbes pour Piano;* and *Trente Dances Serbes pour Piano.* As their titles indicated, these compositions were based on folk music idiom. The French public apparently appreciated the unusual beauty of these songs and dances.[23]

The publication of the comprehensive *Anthology* in two volumes, published in Nice in 1917, was a unique achievement. These collections contained selected poems as well as prose works of Serbian poets and writers. Both *Anthologies* were compiled by Milivoje Pavlović who taught Serbian students in France. These students had emigrated from Serbia following the evacuation of military forces. Pavlović was faced with the necessity of supplying the students with textbooks and reading materials for their course work in Serbian literature. This presented a challenge due to the scarcity of such books abroad. Under the circumstances, Pavlović compiled the necessary material and he even wrote down some of the poems from memory with few or no omissions. In the introduction to the second edition some ten years later, Jaša Prodanović reminded readers that:

> Both anthologies would have deserved praise even if they were compiled in our country during peacetime. And how much more is their value and usefulness since they were compiled at a time of severe national catastrophe in a foreign land with little means . . . . The work at a time of dreadful uncertainty and foreboding demanded a suppression of fear, restraint of sorrow and sad thoughts . . . For such work one needs moral courage without which it could not have been accomplished.[24]

In 1918, the French Academy published *Gorski vijenac (Mountain Wreath)* by Petar Petrović–Njegoš, in translation. The translator was Divna Veković and the preface was written by the poet and novelist, Henri de Regnier. A review by Dragomir Kostić, published in *Zabavnik*, presented a very detailed comparison of the French translation with the original Serbian text and provided commentaries of some of the more difficult passages in the translation. Kostić mentioned that an English translation of this outstanding work by Njegoš was in preparation.[25]

Pavle Stevanović, a writer, wrote a review of a book by Pavle Popović entitled *Jugoslovenska književnost (Yugoslav Literature)*, published in 1918 by the Cambridge University Press. Stevanović mentioned that there were even earlier books that presented the literary development in a Yugoslav context. One should only remember, he said, the history of literature by Vatroslav Jagić and the history of Yugoslav literature by Matija Murko. Popović managed to show the historical periods in the development of Yugoslav literature in mutual dependency as a critical review of one literary development. Stevanović paid special attention to Popović's explanations of the reforms by Vuk Karadžić as well as the introduction of folk language. Popović presented as a parallel development the role of Ljudevit Gaj and the foundation of the Illyrian movement. Stevanović expressed his pleasure that the first Yugoslav history of literature was written by Pavle Popović, professor of Yugoslav literature at the university and writer of many other literary articles and studies in the same field.

Furthermore, Stevanović recalled that the University of Belgrade was founded in 1905, concurrent with the manifestations of the literary and spiritual union of the South Slavs. He was obviously alluding to the First Yugoslav Artistic Exhibit and the First Conference of Writers and Artists in 1904. Stevanović noted that the last pages of Popović's book, containing the names of writers that perished in the war, testified to "the wish to be one, to enter from this terrible period into a better one where everything will be leading to a union of the people and not to their dispersion into small factions."[26]

Popović's book, *Jugoslovenska književnost*, was written under difficult circumstances in emigration in a foreign land, very much like the *Anthologies* of Pavlović. The ideological concept was based on the thesis of the spiritual unity of Serbs, Croats, and Slovenes. In his preface, Popović noted that he strove to present the literature of the Serbs, Croats, and Slovenes in its entirety, as one distinctive whole. Popović stressed, in particular, the presence of Yugoslav ideology in the literary development of the twentieth century. He singled out the centennial celebration of the Serbian uprising as an event of great importance which left its mark on the cultural profile of this period. This event gave an opportunity to Croatian and Slovenian writers to establish a meaningful contact with their Serbian colleagues during the First Congress of Yugoslav Writers.[27]

From that time on, several similar meetings took place, and various literary anniversaries gave opportunities for additional meetings. Among important literary events of this nature, mention should be made of the commemoration of Slovene writers, Trubar, Vraz, and Prešern in Ljubljana, Zagreg, and Belgrade, as well as the commemoration of Njegoš in Zagreb and Prague and Dositej's memorial festivities in Belgrade and Dalmatia.[28]

Yugoslav unity was further strengthened by publications of the Srpska Književna Zadruga (Serbian Literary Association) that included one Croatian book annually. Also, Matica Hrvatska (The Croatian Queen Bee) published one Serbian and one Slovenian literary work annually. The Serbian Royal Academy in Belgrade and the Yugoslav Academy in Zagreb, as well as Matica Slovenska in Ljubljana, enjoyed steady collaboration. All three institutions started a joint effort in producing the *Jugoslovenska Enciklopedija (The Yugoslav Encyclopedia.)* In addition, the Unviersity of Zagreb introduced a course on Serbian literature, whereas the University of Belgrade had long ago introduced lectures on Croatian literature followed later by a series on Slovene literature.[29]

The literary journals also supported Yugoslav unity. *Srpski Književni Glasnik (The Serbian Literary Herald)* counted among its collaborators almost all the Croatian poets, narrators, dramatists, and critics, including also a number of Slovene writers. The Croatian literary journal, *Savremenik (Contemporary),* as well as the Slovene journal, *Veda,* published works of Serbian writers. Milan Ćurčin, a poet, edited the Serbo–Croatian *Almanac.* Popović thought that almost every important literary activity was recorded and commented on in these journals. The *Antologija novije srske lirike (The Anthology of the Newer Serbian Lyrics)* by Bogdan Popović was published by the reputable literary association, Matica hrvatska, in Zagreb and presented another fine example of Yugoslav collaboration. Pavle Popović noted that this *Anthology* was circulated among the soldiers during World War I. It was acclaimed a most popular book.[30]

All of these thriving literary activities were abruptly stopped with the outbreak of the war. Next to the irreplaceable losses of human lives, the general turmoil caused the displacement and even destruction of a number of literary manuscripts, paintings, and musical scores. The greatest concern, above all, was the death of promising young men. Such was deemed the death of Nikola Antula, a young writer and contributor to *Srpski Književni Glasnik,* among many others, as was written, " Nikola Antula was a great hope among the young intellectuals of Serbia, and after him fell many other youths, the ones that were coming of age . . . with developing literary ambitions."[31]

Popović expressed his hope that after this terrible period a much better one would follow. The Serbs, Croats, and Slovenes should share a joint literature with a broader base. The writers should have a wider range of topics and, as a consequence, the public would show a greater interest in their works. Popović concluded that everything should be better since it would strengthen the unity of the people without the previous fragmentations, and it would thereby enhance the entity of the nation.[32]

## Literary and Artistic Activities as Recorded in Zabavnik

As the war dragged on and the days and months became years, the Serbian literary minds turned with spontaneity to recording recollections of the changed world or creating a new one by seeking shelter in the past. Some of the poets who were living in foreign lands at the time now turned to the ethos of antique poetry in order to reaffirm the continuity of human life by connecting the past with the present. They were searching for a lost affirmation of the dignity of human existence and for peace within themselves as well as around them which appeared to be lost.

The poet and art critic, Todor Manojlović, described in his poem, Apoliniski odbles (Apollonian Reflection), the reasons for directing his attention to the past. The poem was published in the second issue of *Zabavnik* in 1917.

Apoliniski odbles

U trenutnom zatišju
Divljeg urnebesa
Slušaj, uhvati
Mudrim i oštrim
Sluhom daleki tanki glas
Minule čarobno—slatke radosti
Što ljupko i sumorno
Kao zulutala
Ptica selica
Starome gnezdu hoće da se vrati
Srcu tvom
Slušaj zanosno–nežni
Milujući ćurlik frule
Vaskrsli zlatni zvuk
Dražesne stare harfe
Usled mahnite rike
Svirepih truba
Slušaj — i sećaj se.
I sećaj se da nekad pevasmo

Te zanose, ta prividjenja
U snažnim, zvonkim, svetlim ritmovima
Da obnoviš taj sjaj:
Da nasilno presečeš
Današnju mutnu žalopojku
Da glomazni crni oblak jada
Munjevito prorešetaš
Zasleplivo sjajnim
Sunčanim zracima
Jedne drevne i nove
Neslućene pesme.

Apollonian Reflection

In the momentary calm
Of the wild uproar
Listen, and capture
Within the wise and keen
Hearing the distant little voice
Of the enchanting past — sweet joy
That gracefully and melancholy
As a lost
Migrating bird
Wants to return to the old nest
Your heart
Listen enthralling — tender
Caress of the flute's trill
The return of the golden sound
Of the charming old harp
In the midst of the roar
Of the merciless trumpets
Listen — and remember.
Remember that we sang
These raptures, these visions
In strong and bright rhythms
To renew this radiance
And forcefully to cut off
The present day's gloomy lament
To riddle like lightning
The heavy black cloud of sorrow
With the dazzling bright
Sun rays
Of an ancient and new

Never heard song.

The poet tried to forget the existing chaos and the merciless call of the trumpets. He believed that the new and never heard song would disperse gloom and unite with its radiance the ancient with the new. The tranquility of the envisioned moment was associated with the dignity and serenity of the Apollonian cult of ancient Greece.

Ivo Andrić noted a similar resurgence of literary activity among Yugoslav writers living in regions under Austro–Hungarian domination. After years of stringent and taciturn attitudes after the outbreak of the war, the writers started slowly to publish again.[33]

Ancient Greece reappeared as a source of inspiration to the poet Miloš Crnjanski, who fought as an officer in the invading Austrian army. In the turmoil of war, Crnjanski felt inspired to write poems which were seen as comments of the *Odyssey*. Crnjanski published his poems in the *Savremenik (The Contemporary)* journal under his full name, thereby displaying a resolute and fearless disposition. According to his testimony, the intention that guided the writing and publication of these poems was patriotic, political, and anarchic.

Crnjanski considered the *Odyssey* the greatest poem of mankind, an opinion which he retained throughout his life. Equally interesting was the fact that these poems were read not only during World War I, but they continued to be read afterwards. Crnjanski thought that in an inexplicable way these poems became meaningful again during World War II, when the following commentary was made:

> The Trojan and Mycenaean allusions in these verses were intentional. The poet considered the *Odyssey* the greatest poem written by man, even to this day, and the return from war as the saddest experience of man. Though his own songs fall behind these monumental creations in verse, the feeling was their main content. During the war, with the limited number of readers around *Savremenik*, these poems remained a literary episode. In Belgrade, they resounded as a bomb after the war. However, these poems became dreadfully up–to–date after the last war, without any merit of the poet. There lies their mysterious fate.[34]

The "mysterious fate" of the everlasting appeal of the verses by Crnjanski was most definitely the merit of the poet. The public felt his keen ability to understand and project human emotions with great truthfulness. His poetic legacy remained timely and opportune.

In retrospect, some eight years after the end of World War I, in a conversation with Branimir Ćosić, Crnjanski mentioned that his maturing as a poet occurred shortly before the war and during the war:

> I matured during the last year of the war and during the war. In prison and on the battlefield, as a simple Austrian soldier, I suffered, became sick, ran away, and attacked. . . . Thus, I cannot and do not want to forget the war. During those five years I wrote *The Mask, The Diary about Čarnojević*, and my poems . . . . In the great chaos of World War I, I became firm in my sorrows, pensiveness, and gloomy feelings of solitude. Not even any joy after the war could change me.[35]

The long war years slowly summoned forth deliberations about unresolved questions. Amidst destruction and annihilation there was a desire for a peaceful and serene human existence and a need for rebuilding of lives. A veritable thirst for reading developed and the publishing companies mushroomed trying to fulfill these needs. Lectures, art exhibits, and concerts were arranged frequently, and the writers and poets rediscovered their craft and their aspirations.

Veselin Čajkanović wrote about the cultural and literary activities that developed in Africa after the exodus from Serbia, where a part of the evacuated Serbian army was stationed. Čajkanović traced the founding of the newspaper, *Napred (Forward)*, which appeared in February 1916. *Napred* was one of the first journalistic efforts started during the war. It was successful, and by September 1917, 500 issues had been published. In order to mark this occasion, the printing house of the association of Srpski invalidi (Serbian Invalides) published a keepsake edition called *Srpstvo u Africi (The Serbs in Africa)*.

Čajkanović noted that literary life in Africa was closely associated with *Napred* and the printing house of Serbian Invalides. The prose and poetic works written by Serbian writers and poets living in exile were published in *Napred*. War stories, such as *S puškom u ruci (With the Gun in Hand)* by Milorad B. Nedić and the patriotic poems of Milosav Jelić, *Živojin Devešerčki, and Mijušković* appeared in this newspaper. In camp Lasuaz, in the vicinity of Bizerte, the Srpsko vojničko logorsko pozorište (Serbian Military Camp Theater) was established. It was an open air theater, modeled after the ancient structures, with a seating capacity of 3,000 people. Čajkanović praised the stage curtain as a masterpiece. The curtain, the work of Josif Car, a painter, was fashioned as a triptych, the middle panel representing King Petar in Albanian snow, the left panel depicting a feeble soldier, and the right panel portraying a recuperating and proud soldier with a flag. Čajkanović declared that this was one of the best military theaters.[36]

During the war the refugees in Paris formed a Cultural Council directed toward promoting artistic achievements of the South Slavs in a systematic manner. The Council arranged a number of concerts in Paris, Versailles, Nice, Lyons, Cannes, and Monte Carlo.[37]

A group of young Serb, Croat and Slovene students, who had been evacuated to Paris during World War I, kept close contact with one another. During their meetings these young men decided to write a manifesto jointly in order to make their position clear about Yugoslav unification. This project was completed in 1915 when a slim volume was published under the characteristic title, *L'Unité Yugoslave Manifeste de la Jeunesse Serbe, Croate et Slovene Reunie (The Manifest of Yugoslav Unity by Reunited Serbian, Croatian, and Slovene Youth)*. Following the title on the front page was a statement that the publication contained a preface written by Tomaš Masaryk.[38]

This well known Czech cultural and political leader had shown great interest in the idea of Pan-Slavic collaboration among Slavic students even before the outbreak of World War I. Miloš Crnjanski, a writer, gave valuable testimony about Masaryk's influence on the actions of the Zora Association of Students in Vienna. This popular Association was frequented by students, and according to Crnjanski, these students from the territory of the present state of Yugoslavia conducted their political activities in compliance with the directives offered from Prague, not from Belgrade or Zagreb. Furthermore, Crnjanski stressed that the students usually emulated the ideas of Masaryk. Crnjanski remembered the request for participation of students at a specific demonstration that demanded the opening of a new university in Vienna for students of Slavic origin. This request was originally formulated by Masaryk.[39]

Masaryk's interest in furthering a Pan-Slavic collaboration during the war years was confirmed by his association with young South-Slavic students during their emigration to Paris. In Masaryk's preface to their "Manifesto" he explored the Yugoslav idea in a wider Pan-Slavic context:

> This pamphlet brought to light the nature of our struggle against German imperialism. The Slavs from the north, the Czechs and Poles, the Slavs from the South (and I do not doubt that the Bulgarians will comprehend this), all comprise a wall against the Drang nach Osten. That is why such great importance is paid to the general politics concerning the Slavic question, in particular the Czech, Polish, and Yugoslav . . . . Yugoslav land, weakened and rav-

aged by war, will require a wise and prudent government, good agriculture, commerce, financial planning, industry, and entrepreneurship. Prepare yourselves, my young Yugoslav friends, for this extraordinary work.[40] In Geneva, during World War I, the Prosveta Cultural Society started a series of books with the same title under the editorship of Pero Slepčević. The Society also published its *Almanah (Almanac)* and arranged ten conferences dedicated to the Yugoslav question. For a number of years before the war, Slepčević also worked with the Prosveta Cultural Society to establish ties with emigrants in America. He was instrumental in the founding of an endowment for support of emigrants from Bosnia and Hercegovina.[41]

The bibliography of publications that was published in *Zabavnik* during the war years is very valuable. It was recorded there that the *Napred* series in Bizert published a collection of articles by the distinguished ethnographer Tihomir Djordjević entitled *Jugoslovensko jedinstvo (The Yugoslav Unity.)* These articles had been published before in different languages and in several foreign countries in order to bring information about the Yugoslav question to the public abroad. The articles were authoritative and presented many facts of interest. Djordjević's titles furnished general information on the topics under discussed which were of wide importance, such as: the South Slavs, the Yugoslavs as objects of scientific investigation, the Yugoslav press and Yugoslav unity, and religious tolerance among South Slavs.[42]

The publication of another book by Tihomir Djordjević, entitled *Iz srpskog folklora (From Serbian Folklore)* was noted in the same journal. The book was published in English. The review was written by Veselin Čajkanović.[43]

The founding of a new journal in Paris, *Učitelj (Teacher)*, was also reported in *Zabavnik*, which first appeared in November 1917. This journal, a publication of the newly founded Teachers' Association of Serbs, Croats, and Slovenes, united "the best teachers that were located in France." The editor of the journal was Milan St. Nedeljković, a former supervisor of public schools in Serbia.[44]

In the same issue of *Zabavnik* an announcement appeared regarding newly received bibliographical data about current Serbian periodicals in the United States. These periodicals were: *Bulletin Yugoslav*, Washington, D.C.; *Serb Sentinel*, New York, New York; *Slovenski Svet*, Cleveland, Ohio; *Jugoslovenski Sokolski Glasnik*, Cleveland, Ohio; and *Jadran*, San Francisco, California.

An announcement of a monumental work on Serbian architecture and pictorial art also appeared in *Zabavnik*. This representative work, entitled *South Slav Monuments, Serbian Orthodox Church,* was due to the efforts of Mihailo I. Pupin, a distinguished scientist and professor at Columbia University, who served as editor. The introduction was written by Thomas Graham Jackson. The editor was obviously guided by a wish to present to the English speaking public the splendor of the architectural masterpieces erected before the Turkish invasion of the Balkan peninsula. The book included 54 well chosen photographs of Serbian monasteries and fresco paintings. A commentary was supplied by Kosta Jovanović, an architect. A map was included in the appendix as well as a chronological table of the Serbian dynasty produced by Dr. N. Županić.[45]

An imposing erudition of the collaborators' assessment of domestic and foreign literary works were often shown in *Zabavnik.* They also evaluated works in music and the fine arts of Yugoslav and foreign writers and artists. The literary critic, Pero Slepčević, wrote about the pictorial art of Mirko Rački, who emigrated from his native land and lived in Geneva during World War I. Slepčević himself was an émigré in charge of many functions associated with the Prosveta Society and its *Almanac* located in Geneva.

Slepčević paid a visit to Rački in his atelier in the mansard of a building close to Lake Geneva. Rački complained that it was hard to paint far away from his native landscapes and that he could hardly remember the "warm colors and the atmosphere . . . and it was so hard to work from memory." Rački longed to paint landscapes of the area where he grew up and lived before the outbreak of the war. In Geneva, he was engaged in recreating historical scenes for his monumental paintings depicting heroes of national history, as in Smail–Aga Čengić, or in the Stradanja (Sufferings), which referred to the turmoil of World War I. However, Slepčević noticed a duality in the creative aspirations of Rački:

> Rački . . . had a feeling for national art, and by rejecting
> Western European art, he aimed at understanding the soul
> of our race . . . . That is the course of his diligence in paint-
> ing our past sufferings in *Smail–Aga Čengić,* and the cycle
> *Stradanje* from our present day. This is the source of his love
> for folk poetry. However, against any conscious inclination
> that is drawing him into reality, there is one opposing and
> therefore stonger inclination towards a free play of imagina-
> tion and dreams, towards the unending melody of pictorial
> hues that are elevated above every national reality. . . .
> The artist is centered in this conflict of sky and earth, joy
> and pain . . . changing his paintings incessantly.[46]

Todor Manojlović's poetry was published in *Zabavnik*. As a well versed art critic, he also reviewed exhibits in the fine arts. However, a well written study about Claude Debussy revealed that Manojlović was a connoisseur of the musical arts as well. This is even more remarkable having in mind that Debussy opened a new page in the development of French and, consequently, European music.[47]

It was upon the death of Claude Debussy that Manojlović wrote thus study. Within a few weeks, the Swiss artist, Ferdinand Holder, died, too. Manojlović recorded the passing away of these two artists as a loss for all of mankind. Manojlović quoted the following words of Arthur Rimbaud in his summary of the essence of Debussy's music: "Je notais l'inexprimable, je fixais des vertiges." (I recorded the inexpressive, defined the vertigo.) As a man of his times, Debussy appreciated the novel beauty of the verses of Charles Baudelaire, Paul Verlaine, and Stephane Mallarmé. Debussy confronted the authority of German and Italian music and found his own stronghold in the seemingly forgotten music of Rameau, one of the representatives of French musical tradition. His sojourn to Moscow was also very important where he became acquainted with the music of Musorgsky. Manojlović noted that Debussy started composing at a very young age and his compositions astonished and even overwhelmed his teachers. That is why he soon became known as a "revolutionary" and as a "destroyer of the most basic rules of music." Occasionally, Debussy's music found approval but there were more critics with negative comments, as indicated by the following: "The conservatives attacked him with fanatic vehemence and bitterness calling him a barbarian and decadent. These were the usual titles that . . . the intelligent public bestowed upon future idols."[48]

Manojlović observed accurately that Debussy often found inspiration in French poetry. He set into composition Verlaine's Ariettes Oubliées and Fêtes Galantes, as well as Five Poems by Baudelaire. The musical expressions of these songs were described by Manojlović in a poetic manner, yet truthfully, as much as it was possible to describe the music verbally. Manojlović explicated Debussy's music as if it consisted of a succession of tones "translucent like mother of pearl, seemingly very lightly sketched . . . and sounding as if conceived in a dream." Furthermore, Manojlović quoted Debussy's piano pieces of *Préludes, Images, Estampes, Arabesques,* and *Dance* as examples of inspired lyrical music. In Debussy's orchestral compositions, Manojlović pointed out the delicacy in the orchestration and the clever use of distinctive instrumental timbre. All of these qualities were present in Debussy's Prélude à l'Après-Midi d'une Faune.

Debussy had a great deal of difficulty finding an appropriate libretto since he wanted to avoid pompous theatrical effects. He finally chose the drama, *Pelléas et Mélisande* by Maurice Maeterlinck for the libretto of his opera, which was completed in 1902. Manojlović rightly discerned that the musical language of this opera greatly differed from German or Italian style. There was no trace of declamation or bel canto:

> *Pelléas et Mélisande* (1902) is the first French opera that differs from German or Italian style. . . . The dramatization is reduced to a simple, naive expression, to portraying the finest spiritual emotions with a means of almost whispering sonorities that tenderly and softly—like a silken veil—follow the action and words of the singers.[49]

Among Debussy's last work Manojlović mentioned the symphony, *La Mer.* This work once again showed the freshness of his invention and richness of orchestration. *Sonata en Trio* contained classical clarity of expression and was the last larger work of this distinguished French master, his swan song.[50]

In existing musiciological literature about Debussy it would be hard to find an equally well written study, both precise and with a great command of knowledge of Debussy's contributions. Manojlović presented Debussy within the tradition of French music while pointing to the newer qualities of his musical language and expression that left a mark on the general development of contemporary music. Among other remarkable studies pointing to the erudition and talent of the collaborators of *Zabavnik,* a study by an editor of this journal, Branko Lazarević, should be singled out. Lazarević wrote about the influence of Serbian folk poetry on literature. It was Lazarević's opinion that Serbian folk poetry transcended the limitations of its national boundaries. Although his poetry was associated in time and space with local names, places, and events, in its essence it remained all embracing and uniting in human experience, similar to the poetry of Homer:

> Our folk poetry escapes an inner circle. It is, generally speaking, universally human . . . and succeeded in producing a universal and true religion, a universal and true love, a universal and true hero . . . [51]

These are the reasons why Serbian folk poetry was translated into many foreign languages. Serbian folk poetry was translated by the English writers Walter Scott and Robert Browning. The French writers, Charles Nodier and Prosper Mérimée, also translated Serbian folk poetry. Mérimée even tried to imitate some of the poems. Adam Mickiewicz, a Polish writer, taught a course on Serbian poetry at the College de France in Paris. In Germany, Therese von Jakob and Johann Wolfgang Goethe translated some of the Serbian folk epics. Folk poetry attracted many of the South Slavic writers and artists. It would suffice to recall the poetic works starting with Petar Petrović–Njegoš and Branko Radičević, followed by the efforts of Jovan Jovanović–Zmaj, Jovan Dučić, Milan Rakić, Ivan Meštrović, and Rački.[52] Lazarević thought that Dučić and Rakić succeeded in producing splendid sonnets that were permeated with a new feeling of refinement and anxiety that were part of the spirit of the times. Their poetry is therefore removed from the aura of folk epics. The Kosovo Field in Rakić's poem, Na Gazi Mestanu (At Gazi Mestan), was not the same field as described in the folk epics, in metaphors, as both earthy and celestial.

On the other hand, Radičević, and especially Njegoš, came close to the universal qualities as expressed in the folk epics. Similarly, Meštrović succeeded in reviving a similar spirituality in his sculptures. He expressed the sorrow of Jugović's mother and also the overpowering stamina of Prince Marko. Mirko Rački managed to preserve in his pictorial work the essential qualities pertaining to the time and the people. Ivo Vojnović understood, to a certain degree, the mysticism of Jugović's mother. However, many other writers and poets thought that it would be enough to quote the verses, proverbs, and metaphors in order for their work to achieve a recognizable national flavor. At the time of great popularity of folk poetry, numerous writers tried to imitate it in a superficial manner. Skerlić criticized the new works that were trying only to emulate folk poetry, and he even assumed a negative attitude about folk poetry in general. In time, however, Skerlić changed his negative opinion about folk poetry and realized its true value.[53]

The exhibits of various painters and sculptors during the war years were reported on the pages of *Zabavnik* by Todor Manojlović. These exhibits, arranged in various European metropolitan communities, served to inform the public about the new artists and about the general artistic development among the South Slavs. Thus, in Geneva, the Exhibit of Yugoslav Artists opened in June of 1918 under the sponsorship of L'École de Beaux Arts and a group of prominent writers. Manojlović wrote about this exhibit stating that similar exhibits were previously held in London, Rome, and Lyons.[54]

Manojlović named the artists who participated at the exhibit in Geneva. They were Nikola Bešević, Joza Kljaković, Milan Milovanović, Branimir Petrović, Petar Poček, and Mirko Rački. Manojlović singled out the paintings by Rački since he believed that Rački's paintings depicted "the fight for stylistic simplicity and harmony, and the suppression of decorative qualities for a stronger and more truthful expression of feelings and spirituality." Rački exhibited *Sejači (Men Sowing,), Majka Jugovića (The Jugović's Mother)*, and *Devojčica (Little Girl)*. From his monumental compositions Rački presented *Kneževa večera (The Prince's Supper)*. The paintings of Jozo Kljaković left on Manojlivić an uneven and disturbing impression. Kljaković presented his paintings, *Vila Ravijojla (The Fairy Ravijojla)*, a portrait of Karadjordje, some illustrations, and a few drawings for the *Almanac* published by the Prosveta Society in Geneva. The paintings by Nikola Bešević were marked by clarity and freshness, while Branimir Petrović presented himself as a poetic impressionist with his painting of *Pastirče (The Little Shepherd)*.[55]

The well known poet, Jovan Dučić, was among the frequent contributors to *Zabavnik*. During the war years, Dučić continued to write poems for *Carski soneti (Tsar's Sonnets)* and *Plave legende (The Blue Legends)*. Dučić felt compelled to evoke the once glorious past, and thus also to reaffirm the continuity of an established and cultivated society on native ground. Svetislav Stefanović often wrote poems that were published in *Zabavnik*. His poetic output showed a great similarity to the style introduced by Dučić. Dragoljub Filipović and Milosav Jelić continued to write peoms that presented the reaffirmation of patriotic poetry. Sources of their inspiration were lyric and epic folk poems. Croatian and Slovene poets, who were living outside their countries, steadily made contributions to *Zabavnik*. Josip Kosor wrote a hymn in prose dedicated to Serbia and the exodus caused by the war, linking the enormous sufferings to the biblical Golgotha. Vladimir Čerina and Josip Miličić also published their contributions in *Zabavnik*.

The last issue of *Zabavnik* appeared on 18 October 1918. Branko Lazarević, the editor, and his collaborators left a unique testimony of human dignity and perserverance during the upheaval caused by World War I. On foreign grounds, in the midst of exile, the pages of *Zabavnik* vividly preserved the days of uncertainty and suffering, and most importantly, the efforts to resist spiritual annihilation. These years, described by the young poet Milutin Bojić in his poems as the years of "suffering and pride," left a record of the indistinguishable human desire for preservation of tradition, national unity, and a strong belief in a better tomorrow.

## The Wartime Legacy of Writers and Artists

Immediately following World War I, while the cataclysmic experiences were still vividly imprinted on the minds of the survivors, Ivo Andrić evaluated with remarkable insight the current literary situation. Andrić, as a young and knowledgeable writer, knew about the whereabouts of his fellow writers and their recently published works or the ones still in progress. Therefore, his short yet comprehensive study, published in *Slovenski Jug* in 1918, vividly portrayed the aspirations and goals of the Serbo-Croatian writers. In his introductory statement, Andrić claimed that his findings were applicable only to Serbo-Croatian literature under Austro-Hungarian rule. However, the acuity of his judgment had a wider scope and embraced Serbo-Croatian literature as a whole.

In a motto in his study, Andrić chose the inspired words of Henri Nathansen declaring the end of World War I as the beginning of a new era. Nathansen truly believed that a new life would develop in accordance with new laws and a new structure. Solidarity and altruism would prevail instead of individualism and separatism. The writers, as always, would be in the forefront of an eternal search for eternal goals.[56] Andrić obviously was in agreement with Nathansen's views.

As the war continued for four long years, a spiritual resurgence slowly took place and various literary activities were resumed. The atrocities of war did not seem to be in vain since those experiences enabled a new comprehension of life at all levels. It seemed that the evacuation and an austere military life had enhanced a lively literary interest. Every new publication was joyfully acclaimed. There was a veritable thirst for reading material resulting in an ever increasing translation of works. Newly published works were printed in unusually high numbers. Thus, a war that had initially silenced literary activities served to encourage growth in that area.[57]

Andrić thought that the writers were in a particularly difficult moral and material position after the war ended in 1918. Everybody was aware of the great changes that took place during the years of suffering, yet, due to strained circumstances, it was not possible to express all that had happened with ease:

> I want only to draw attention to the difficult moral circulus vitiosus of our present writers. One the one hand, we all know very well how much has changed during these years of suffering for mankind and for everyone among us, and, on the other hand, the conditions of the time prevent us from expressing all . . . however, all this cannot hinder us from seeing the shallowness and misery of the so-called literature written before the war and the triviality of its motives. We can all appreciate literature, and that indicates at least one advantage of the war, how much some of the peacetime truth turned into a lie, and how another life and different literature

are in in the works.[58]

Due to all of these circumstances, new goals were set for Serbo–Croatian literature. The public, who testified to the horrible consequences of war, could perceive much of the present literature as false and impotent, lacking the forcefullness of past events. However, Andrić thought it unjust to expect a well rounded artistic chronology from the writers so soon, since the writers felt the tragedy of this period as deeply as anybody else. It was too early to give an assessment, and time was needed to recuperate and capture lost strength. Therefore, Serbo–Croatian literature had a transitory quality, presenting only an obscure doorway leading to a bright future. A long shadow of expectation was cast on the whole of life and on literary creations.[59]

Andrić further stated that the war had shifted the accent from the individual to the group, and this notion appeared in the main literary direction as well. Writers had, therefore, a serious and consuming pledge to honor, according to Andrić:

> The main task of contemporary literature is to maintain a continuity of the former spiritual life, to preserve the ideals of one's youth which became the ideals of a whole people, and to carry them through the deluge of suffering and evil into better days.[60]

Andrić further stressed that if the writers persevered in upholding the intensity of their spiritual life, as they did in the pre–war period, then they would accomplish an important task. Thus, a free and honorable road would be maintained for the more fortunate and better artists as may be seen in the approaching peaceful years.[61]

The war years were obviously understood as an historic breaking point that enabled a more truthful understanding of past achievements as well as of future goals. The moral and ethical equilibrium of human existence was established once again and there was in sight a period of prosperous growth in all areas of human endeavor. The writers attempted to preserve the purity of their visions in accordance with their responsible role in the new chapter of national history. Aware of these self–imposed high principles and in an everlasting search for uniqueness of their vision, it seemed as if the writers were hesitating and re–examining their tasks. There was an understandable feeling of physical exhaustion as a consequence of wartime events. The writers felt it necessary to re–examine their possible goals and evaluate their strengths. This situation led Andrić to believe that literature was in a transient state. The gate that led to the new seemed closed.

In retrospect, the literary and artistic development which took place during the war, as well as the brief period immediately following any military involvement, presented a continuation of the direction that had been established in the years preceding the catastrophic events. Literary, musical, and artistic works were permeated at that time with patriotic messages, ideas of national identity, and Yugoslav unity. The historical apotheosis of freedom and national unity and a re-evaluation of tradition and of future direction was vividly portrayed in literary and artistic creations. These works constituted the strongest confirmation of the existence of people and of all of mankind as well.

# Footnotes

All the translations from Serbian into English of literary quotations and selected poems are my own.

## Chapter 1

[1] Radovan Samardžić, "Ipolit Ten kod Srba," *Filološki pregled,* **1–2,** Belgrade, 1976, p. 4.

[2] Wayne S. Vucinich, *Serbia between East and West,* Stanford: Stanford University Press, 1954, p. 232.

[3] Jovan Skerlić, *Istorija nove srpske književnosti,* Belgrade, 1914, reprinted: Belgrade, Prosveta, 1967, p. 435.

[4] Jovan Skerlić, "Omladinski kongres," *Srpski Književni Glasnik (SKG),* Vol. 13, No. 2, p. 123.

[5] Skerlić, "Omladinski kongres," p. 141.

[6] Sekulić, "Vrsta uvodne reči," *Pisma iz Norveške,* Belgrade: Matica Srpska, 1961, pp. 145–147.

[7] Predrag Protić, "Dominantni i usputni tokovi u srpskoj književnosti," *Razvojne etape u srpskoj književnosti XX veka i njihove osnovne odlike,* Belgrade: SANU, 1981, pp. 60–61. Compare also: Predrag Palavestra, "Kritička tradicija Jovana Skerlića," *Kritika i Avangarda u modernoj srpskoj književnosti.* Belgrade: Prosveta, 1979, pp. 30-32; Sveltana Velmar–Janković, "O nekim shvatanjima pojma moderan u spskoj književnosti," *Razvojne etape,* p. 86.

[8] Dejan Medaković, *Srpska umetnost u XIX veku,* Belgrade: Srpska književna zadruga, 1981, pp. 197–203.

[9] Nadežda Petrović, "Prva jugoslovenska umetnička izložba," *Delo,* **33,** 1904. Reprinted in L. Todorović: *Srpska likovna kritika,* Belgrade: Srpska Književna Zadruga, 1967, p. 214; Compare also: Bogdan Popović: "Prva jugoslovenska umetnička izložba," *SKG,* **13,,** No. 6, 1904.

[10] Katarina Ambrozić, *Nadežda Petrović,* Belgrade: Srpska književna zadruga, 1978, pp. 262–263.

[11] Ambrozić, *Nadežda Petrović,* p. 145.

[12] Dimitrije Djordjević and Stephen Fischer–Galati, *The Balkan Revolutionary Tradition,* New York: Columbia University Press, 1981, pp. 184–185.

13 Ibid., p. 189.
14 Ambrozić, Nadežeda Petrović, p. 248.
15 Ibid., pp. 248–259.
16 Ibid., p. 260.
17 Predrag Palavesta, *Avangardne težnje u srpskoj književnosti XX veka, Razvojne etape u srpskoj književnosti XX veka i njihove osnovne odlike*, Belgrade: SANU, 1981, pp. 75–76.
18 Predrag Palavestra, *Književnost Mlade Bosne*, Sarajevo: Svijetlost, 1965, pp. 14–15.
19 Skerlić, *Istorija*, p. 442.
20 Popović, *Antologija novije srpske lirike*. Belgrade: Državna Štamparija, 1936, pp. 236–237.
21 Milan L. Popović, "Poezija M. Ćurčina," *Delo*, No. 31, pp. 174–182.
22 Bogdan Popović: *Antologija*, pp. 235–236.
23 Skerlić, *Istorija*, p. 444.
24 Miodrag Ibrovac, "Lazarevo Vaskrsenje," *SKG*, 1913, No. 11, p. 863.
25 Predrag Palavestra, "Kritička tradicija Jovana Skerlića," *Kritika avangarda*, Belgrade: Proveta, 1979, p. 29.
26 Stana Djurić–Klajn, *Serbian Music through the Ages*, Belgrade: Association of Composers, 1972, pp. 90–92; Compare also Milenko Živković, *Rukoveti Stevana Mokranjca*, Belgrade: SANU, 1957; Vojislav Vučković, *Muzički realizam Stevana Mokranjca, Izbor eseja*, Belgrade, 1955; Kosta Manojlović, *Spomenica St. St. Mokranjcu*, Belgrade, Državna štamparija, 1923, p. 4.
27 Manojlović, *Spomenica*, pp. 112–113.
28 Manojlović, *Spomenica*, p. 114.
29 Skerlić, *Istorija*, p. 449.
30 Dragiša Vitošević, *Srpsko pesništvo*, Beograd: Vuk Karadžić, 1975, p. 280.
31 Quoted after Roland Stromberg, "The Intellectuals and the Coming of War," *Journal of European Studies*, No. 3, 1973, p. 113.
32 Vladimir Jovičić, *Srpsko rodoljubivo pesništvo*, Belgrade: Nolit, 1976, p. 439.
33 Pavle Popović, *Jugoslovenska književnost*, Cambridge, 1918, p. 30.
34 Slobodan Rakitić, "Od Itake do pividjenja," *Miloš Crnjanski*, Belgrade: Institut za književnost i umetnost, 1972, p. 124.

## Chapter 2

[1] Katarina Ambrozić, *Nadežda Petrović*, Belgrade, Srpska književna zadruga, 1978, pp. 76–77.

[2] Božidar S. Nikolajević, "Srpska umetnost na Pariskoj izložbi," *Brankovo kolo*, Vol. VI, No. 1, 1900. Reprinted in *Srpska likovna kritika*, Lazar Trifunović, Editor, Beograde: Srpska književna zadruga, 1967, pp. 161–173.

[3] Ibid.

[4] Dejan Medaković, *Srpska umetnost u XXIX veku*. Belgrade: Srpska književna zadruga, 1981, p. 198.

[5] Radmila Antić, *Paja Jovanović*. Belgrade: Muzej grada Beograda, 1970, pp. 15–19.

[6] Ibid., p. 16.

[7] Ibid., p. 17.

[8] Ibid., p. 18.

[9] Ibid., p. 19.

[10] Medaković, *Srpska umetnost*, p. 200.

[11] Medaković, *Srpska umetnost*, p. 200.

[12] Bogdan Popović: "Krunisanje cara Dušana u Skoplju," *Srpski Književni Glasnik*, Vol. II, 1901, p. 224. Bogdan Popović, "Prva jugoslovenska umetnička izložba, *SKG*, Vol. XII, 1904, p. 537. Nadežda Petrović, "Prva jugoslovenska umetnička izložba," *Delo*, No. 35, 1904, pp. 214–215.

[13] Antić, *Paja Jovanović*, p. 18.

[14] Antić, *Paja Jovanović*, p. 38.

[15] Antić, *Paja Jovanović*, p. 18.

[16] Bogdan Popović, "Pad Stalaća," *SKG*, Vol. I, No. 4, 1901, p. 307.

[17] Bogdan Popović, "Umetnički pregled," *SKG*, Vol. II, No. 3, p. 223.

[18] Ibid., p. 223.

[19] Katarina Ambrozić, *Nadežda Petrović*, Beograd: Srpska književna zadruga, 1978, pp. 122–123.

[20] Ibid., 122–123.

[21] V. Carićević, "Srpski i južnoslovenski omladinski zbor u Beogradu," *Brankovo kolo*, No. 34, p. 127. Quoted after Ambrozić, *Nadežda Petrović*, p. 122.

[22] Ibid., p. 122.

[23] Ambrozić, *Nadežda Petrović*, p. 122.

[24] Jovan Skerlić, "Omladinski kongres," *SKG*, Vol. XIII, No. 2, 1905, p. 123.

[25] Ambrozić, *Nadežda Petrović*, p. 123.

[26] Ambrozić, *Nadežda Petrović*, p. 123.

[27] Ambrozić, *Nadežda Petrović*, p. 124.

[28] Bogdan Popović, "Prva jugoslovenska umetnička izložba," *SKG*, Vol. XIII, No. 7, 1904, p. 535.

[29] Ibid., 535.

[30] Ibid., 535.

[31] Nadežda Petrović, "Prva jugoslovenska umetnička izložba," *Delo*, No. 33, 1904. Quoted after Lazar Trifunović, Editor, *Srpska likovna kritika*, Beograd: Srpska književna zadruga, 1967, p. 219.

[32] Ibid., 219.

[33] Jovan Skerlić, "Omladinski kongres," *SKG*, Vol. XIII, No. 2, 1904, p. 123.

[34] Ibid., 141.

[35] Ambrozić, *Nadežda Petrović*, p. 147.

[36] Ambrozić, *Nadežda Petrović*, p. 147.

[37] "Jugoslovenski sastanak," *SKG*, Vol. XV, No. 9, 1905, pp. 714–718.

[38] Ambrozić, *Nadežda Petrović*, p. 148.

[39] Bogdan Popović, "Izložba srpske Lade," *SKG*, Vol XVI, No. 8, 1906, pp. 626–628.

[40] Jaša M. Prodanović, *Naši i strani*, Belgrade, 1924, p. 60. Quoted from Ambrozić, *Nadežda Petrović*, Belgrade: Srpska književna zadruga, 1978, p. 107.

[41] Ambrozić, *Nadežda Petrović*, p. 107.

[42] Nadežda Petrović, manuscript. Quoted after Ambrozić, *Nadežda Petrović*, p. 107.

[43] Delfa Ivanić, "After Twenty Years," Vardar Calendar, 1924. Quoted after Ambrozić, *Nadežda Petrović*, p. 108.

[44] Documents of Nadežda Petrović, manuscript. National Museum, Belgrade.

[45] Ivanić, Calendar, p. 14.

[46] Nadežda Petrović, "Izveštaj Upravi Kola srpskih sestara," manuscript. Quoted after Ambrozić, *Nadežda Petrović*, pp. 117–118.

[47] Ibid., p. 118.

[48] Ibid., p. 118.

[49] Ibid., p. 120.

[50] Ibid., p. 120.

[51] Branko Popović, "Nadežda Petrović," *Umetnički pregled*, 1938. Quoted after Ambrozić, *Nadežda Petrović*, p. 159.

[52] Ambrozić, *Nadežda Petrović*, pp. 145–146.

[53] Quoted from Ambrozić, *Nadežda Petrović*, pp. 159–160.

[54] Quoted after Ambrozić, *Nadežda Petrović*, pp. 183–184.

[55] Ambrozić, *Nadežda Petrović*, p. 169.

[56] Ambrozić, *Nadežda Petrović*, p. 190.
[57] Ambrozić, *Nadežda Petrović*, p. 190.
[58] Božidar S. Nikolajević, "Izložba jugoslovenske umetničke kolonije, *SKG*, Vol. XVIII, No. 1, pp. 208–212.
[59] Anton Gustav Matoš, "Izložba umjetničke kolonije u Beogradu," *Hrvatska smotra*, 1907. Quoted after Ambrozić, *Nadežda Petrović*, pp. 201–204.
[60] Ambrozić, *Nadežda Petrović*, p. 205.
[61] Ambrozić, *Nadežda Petrović*, pp. 184–189.
[62] Ambrozić, *Nadežda Petrović*, pp. 184–189.
[63] Ambrozić, *Nadežda Petrović*, pp. 27–28.
[64] Miodrag B. Protić, *Srpsko slikarstvo XX veka*. Beograd: Nolit, 1974, p. 43.
[65] Ibid., p. 43.
[66] B. L., "Izložba Umetničko–Zanatske Škole," *SKG*, 1910, Vol. XXV, No. 1, pp. 54–55.
[67] Ibid., p. 55.
[68] B.L., "Izložba Zanatsko–Umetničke Škole," *SKG*, 1911, Vol. XXVII, No. 2, p. 213.

## Chapter 3

[1] Pavle Popović, "Konferencija jugoslovenskih književnika i umetnika," *Srpski Književni Glasnik (SKG)*, Vol. 13, No. 2, 1904, p. 128.
[2] Bogdan Popović, "Prva Jugoslovenska umetnička izložba," *SKG*, Vol. XIII, No. 2, pp. 145–156.
[3] Bogdan Popović, "Prva Jugoslovenska umetnička izložba," *SKG*, Vol. XV, No. 1, 1905, p. 65.
[4] *Srpski Književni Glasnik*, Vol. XIII, No. 3, p. 236.
[5] J. N. Tomić, "Ocene i prikazi," Vol. XI, No. 2, 1904, pp. 153–155.
[6] Beleška, *SKG*, Vol. X, No. 15, 1905, p. 772.
[7] Beleška, *SKG*, Vol. X, No. 15, 1905, p. 789.
[8] Pavle Popović, "Stanje današnje književnosti," *SKG*, Vol. XV, No. 12, pp. 918–928.
[9] Popović, "Stanje," p. 921.
[10] Popović, "Stanje," p. 922.
[11] Beleška, *SKG*, 1909, pp. 869–872.
[12] Beleška, *SKG*, p. 871.
[13] "Desetogodišnjica Srpskog književnog glasnika," *SKG*, Vol. XXVI, No. 1, p. 248.
[14] Jovan Skerlić, *Istorija nove srpske književosti*, Belgrade, 1914. Reprinted in Belgrade: Prosveta, 1967, p. 436.

15 Bogdan Popović, *Antologija novije srpske lirike*, Belgrade: Državna štamparija, 1936, 7th edition, p. xi.

16 Branko Ćosić, *Deset picaca deset razgovora*, Belgrade: Gecakon, 1931, p. 133.

17 Jovan Skerlić, *Istorija nove srpske književnosti*, Belgrade: Prosveta, 1967, p. 406.

18 D. M. Janković, "Vojislavljevo veče," *Srpski književni glasnik*, Vol. 2, No. 5, p. 383.

19 Skerlić, *Istorija*, p. 447.

20 Skerlić, *Istorija*, p. 449.

21 Petar Krstić, "Komadi s pevanjem u Kraljevskom Narodnom Pozorištu," *SKG*, No. XI, 1905, p. 865.

22 Stevan Hristić, "Dvadesetpetogodišnjica G. Stevana Mokranjca," *SKG*, Vol. XXII, No. 1, 1909, p. 65.

23 Stevan Hristić, "Čajkovskovo veče u Narodonom pozorištu," *SKG*, Vol. XXII, No. 1, 1909, p. 65.

24 Miloje Milojević, "Vaskrsenje," *SKG*, No. 11, 1912, p. 862.

25 Miloje Milojević, "Iz naših krajeva," *SKG*, No. 21, 1908, p. 300.

26 Marko Car, "Pia Desideria," *SKG*, Vol. XXVI, No. 10, pp. 760–764.

27 Car, "Pia Desideria," p. 764.

28 Marko Car, "Nacionalna umetnost," *SKG*, Vol. XXXII, No. 7, pp. 505–513.

29 "Nacionalna umetnost," *SKG*, p. 509.

30 "Nacionalna umetnost," *SKG*, p. 510.

31 "Nacionalna umetnost," *SKG*, p. 510.

32 "Nacionalna umetnost," *SKG*, p. 515.

33 *Bosanska vila*, No. 23, 1911, p. 360.

34 Vladimir Ćorović, "Govor o proslavi," *Bosanska vila*, Vol. XXVII, No. 1, p. 3.

35 Ćorović, "Govor o proslavi," p. 15.

36 Ćorović, "Govor o proslavi," p. 15.

37 Sima Pandurović, "Bez programa," *Bosanska vila*, Vol. XXVI, No. 19, Sarajevo, 1911, p. 289.

38 Pandurović, "Bez programa," p. 290.

39 Pandurović, "Bez programa," p. 290.

40 Milutin Uskoković, "Osrpskom romanu." *Bosanska vila*, Vol. 28, No. 21, p. 289.

41 Uskoković, *Bosanska vila*, p. 289.

42 M. M., "Došljaci," *SKG*, Vol. XXVI, No. 1, 1911, p. 53.

43 M. M., "Došljaci," p. 53.

44 Skerlić, *Istorija*, p. 461.

[45] Jovan Dučić, "Petar Kočić," *Bosanska vila*, Vol. XXVI, Nos. 7–8, 1911, p. 97.

[46] Dučić, "Petar Kočić," p. 98.

[47] Dučić, "Petar Kočić," p. 99.

[48] Jovan Skerlić, "Lažni modernizam u srpskoj književnosti," *SKG*, Vol. XXVII, No. 5, 1911, pp. 348–363.

[49] M. Dimitrijević, "Dis, Utopljene duše," *Bosanska vila*, No. 13–14, p. 213..

[50] Branko Lazarević, "Pesnik stiha i nervoze," *Bosanska vila*, No. 20, 1911, p. 305.

[51] Lazarević, "Pesnik stiha," p. 305.

[52] Lazarević, "Pesnik stiha," p. 307.

[53] "Književnost srpska i hrvatska," *Bosanska vila*, Vol. XXVI, No. 18, p. 288.

[54] Dimitrije Mitrinović, "Za naš književni rad," *Bosanska vila*, 1908. Quoted after Predrag Palavestra, *Književnost Mlade Bosne*, *Hrestomatija*, Sarajevo: Svjetlost, 1908, p. 39.

[55] Palavestra, *Hrestomatija*, pp. 38–40.

[56] Palavestra, *Hrestomatija*, p. 42.

[57] Dimitrije Mitrinović, "Lirika Vladimira Nazora," *Bosanska vila*, No. 7–8, 1911, p. 117.

[58] Ibid., p. 118.

[59] Ibid., p. 119.

[60] Pera Slepčević, "Narodna drama," *Bosanska vila*, No. 7–8, 1911, p. 114.

[61] Ibid., 116.

[62] Sima Pandurović, "Dosadna književnost," Vol. XXVI, 1911, p. 1.

[63] Ibid., p. 3.

[64] Svetislav Stefanović, "Pismo kritičaru," *Bosanska vila*, Vol. XXVIII, Nos. 13 and 14, p. 185.

[65] Sima Pandurović, "Modernizam u književnosti," *Bosanska vila*, No. 17–18, 1912, p. 234.

[66] Pandurović, *Bosanska vila*, No. 9, XXIX, 1914, p. 9.

[67] Sima Pandurović, "Književna hronika," *Bosanska vila*, No. 23, 1913, p. 332.

[68] Introduction, *Sto godina Filozofskog fakulteta*, 1863–1963, Radovan Samardžić, Editor, Belgrade: Narodna knjiga, 1963, p. 5.

[69] Svet. Radovanović, *Treba li nam Univerzitet?* Belgrade: Dositej Obradović, 1901, p. 14.

[70] M. Jovanović–Batut, *Je li za Srbiju Univerzitet preka potreba?* Beograd: Državna štamparija Kraljevine Srbije, 1902, p. 30.

71 Petar M. Vukićević, "Beleška o Univerzitetu," *SKG*, Vol. XIII, No. 8, 1904, pp. 599–601.

72 Ibid., 600.

73 Ibid., 601.

74 Ibid., 595.

75 Ž. Čeković, "Prirodno–matematički fakultet," *Trideset godina Priorodno–matematičkog fakulteta Univerziteta u Beogradu 1947–1977*, Belgrade: Prirodno–matematički fakultet, pp. 14–15.

76 Samardžić, Ed., *Sto godina filozofskog fakulteta*, p. 54.

77 Ibid., p. 54.

78 Vojislav J. Djurić, "Sto godina filozofskog fakulteta," *Proslave stogodišnjice filozofskog fakulteta u Beogradu 1863–1963*, Belgrade, 1964, p. 30.

79 "Naša univerzitetska omladina," *SKG*, Vol. XXIV, No. 2, 1910, p. 189.

80 Bogdan Gavrilović, "Socijalni zadatak univerziteta," *SKG*, Vol. 28, No. 4–5, 1912, p. 346–349.

81 Ibid., 346–349.

82 Ibid., 346–349.

83 Tihomir R. Djordjević, "O srpskim ženama," *SKG*, Vol. XXVIII, No. 3, 1912, pp. 188–189.

84 Ibid., 188–189.

85 Ibid., 188–189.

86 Slobodan Jovanović, "Univerzitetsko pitanje," *SKG*, 1914, Vol. XXXII, No. 3, pp. 192–195.

87 Ibid., 192–195.

88 Ibid., 192–195.

89 Ibid., p. 195.

## Chapter Four

1 Jovan Skerlić, "Omladinski kongres," *Srpski Književni Glasnik (SKG)*, Vol. 13, No. 2, pp. 123–125.

2 Ibid., pp. 123–125.

3 Bogdan Popović, "Prva Jugoslovenska umetnička izložba," *SKG*, Vol. XIII, No. 7, 1904, p. 535.

4 Bogdan Popović, "Književni listovi," *SKG*, Vol. I, no. 1, 1901, pp. 27–36.

5 Kosta P. Manojlović, *Spomenica St. St. Mokranjcu*, Beograd: Državna Štamparija, 1923, p. 97.

6 Wayne S. Vucinich, *Serbia between East and West*, Stanford and London: Oxford University Press, 1954, p. 54.

7 Manojlović, *Spomenica*, p. 97.

[8] Manojlović, *Spomenica*, pp. 99–100.

[9] Manojlović, *Spomenica*, pp. 102–105.

[10] Manojlović, *Spomenica*, p. 102.

[11] Manojlović, *Spomenica*, pp. 104–105.

[12] "Umetnički pregled: Jugoslovensko veče," *SKG*, Vol. XXXIII, No. 2, 1094, pp. 139–140.

[13] Veroslava Petrović, *Scenska muzika na repertoaru Narodnog pozorišta u Beogradu 1868–1914*, Beograd: Muzej pozorišne umetnosti, 1976, p. 25.

[14] Dragomir M. Janković, "Vojislavljevo veče," *SKG*, Vol. 2, No. 5, 1900, p. 383.

[15] Den., *Kolo*, No. 8, 16 May 1901, pp. 516–517. Quoted after Petrović, *Scenska muzika*, p. 44.

[16] Commentator, "Književnost–pozorište," *Zvezda*, 1901, pp. 478–484. Quoted after Petrović, *Scenska muzika*, p. 26.

[17] Vlastimir Peričić, *Muzički stvaraoci u Srbiji*, Belgrade, 1967, pp. 59–60.

[18] Peričić, *Muzički stvaraoci*, p. 174.

[19] Stana Djurić–Klajn, *Serbian Music through the Ages*, Belgrade, 1972, pp. 105–106.

[20] Ibid., 105–106.

[21] Milan Grol, "Pitanje operete u Narodnom pozorištu," *SKG*, Vol. II, No. 4, 1904, p. 302.

[22] Ibid., p. 305.

[23] Ibid., p. 305.

[24] Petar Krstić, "Muzika i opereta u Narodnom pozorištu," *SKG*, Vol. 15, No. 4, 1905, p. 273.

[25] Dušan Janković, "Opereta u Narodnom pozorištu," *Delo*, Vol. 35, No. 2, 1905. Quoted after Vlastimir Peričić, *Josif Marinković, Život i delo*. Belgrade: SANU, Special Editions, Vol. CDXIV, 1967, pp. 51-52.

[26] Petar Krstić, "Muzika i opereta u Narodnom pozorištu," *SKG*, Vol. XV, No. 4, 1905, p. 275.

[27] Ibid., p. 278.

[28] Ibid., p. 281.

[29] Ibid., p. 284.

[30] Ibid., p. 285.

[31] Ibid., p. 286.

[32] Ibid., p. 290.

[33] Petar Kristić, "Komadi s pevanjem u Kraljevskom Srpskom Narodnom Pozorištu," *SKG*, No. XI, 1905, p. 865.

[34] Ibid., p. 865.

[35] Ibid., pp. 866–867.

[36] Peričić, *Muzički stvaraoci*, pp. 214–215.

[37] Milan Grol, "Čučuk–Stana," *SKG*, Vol. XIX, No. 7, 1907, p. 543.

[38] Ibid., 544.

[39] Ibid., p. 544.

[40] Petar Konjović, *Stevan Mokranjac*, Belgrade: Nolit, 1958, pp. 222-223.

[41] Ibid., pp. 222–223.

[42] Milan Grol, "Opera u Narodnom pozorištu," *SKG*, Vol. XVII, No. 11, pp. 257–261.

[43] Anonim, "Lutka," *Politika*, No. 443, 5.IV, 1905, p. 3. Quoted after Petrović, *Scenska muzika*, p. 27.

[44] Stevan Hristić, "Dvadesetpetogodišnjica G. Stevana Mokranjca." *SKG*, Vol. XXII, No. 10, 1909, p. 779.

[45] Ibid., 780.

[46] Ibid., 780.

[47] Miloje Milojević, "Muški horovi Antona Ferstera," *SKG*, 1911, Vol. XXVII, No. 4, p. 302.

[48] Stevan Hristić, "Čajkovskovo veče u Narodnom pozorištu," *SKG*, Vol. XXII, No. 1, p. 65.

[49] Miloje Milojević, "Vaskrsenje," *SKG*, No. 11, p. 862.

[50] Ibid., pp. 867–868.

[51] Stevan Hristić, "Koncert u Narodnom pozorištu," *SKG*, Vol. XXII, No. 8, p. 621.

[52] Ibid., p. 621.

[53] Ibid., p. 624.

[54] Miloje Milojević, "Gostovanje Operske trupe Kraljevsko Zemaljskog kazališta u Zagrebu," *SKG*, 1911, Vol. XXVII, Nos. 1 and 2, p. 62.

[55] Ibid., p. 140.

[56] Miloje Milojević, "Povodom jednog gostovanja," *SKG*, 1911, Vol. XXVII, No. 7, p. 542.

[57] Ibid., p. 545.

[58] Ibid., p. 546.

[59] Ibid., p. 547.

[60] Ibid., p. 547.

[61] Miloje Milojević, "Bastijen i Bastijena," *SKG*, 1912, Vol. 28, p. 69.

[62] Milojević, "Jedna srpska premijera u Narodnom Pozorištu," *SKG*, 1913, Vol. 31, No. 5, p. 69.

[63] Miloje Milojević, "Naš muzičko–umetnički program," *SKG*, 1913, Vol. 31, No. 5, p. 394.

[64] Ibid., p. 394.

65 G. I. B., "Srpska muzička škola i njen ovogodišnji koncert," *SKG*, 1908, No. 2, p. 158.

66 Ibid., pp. 159–160.

67 Stanislav Binički, "Koncert učenika Srpske muzičke škole," *SKG*, 1909, Vol. XXII No. 7.

68 Jovan Zorko, "Ispitni koncert Srpske muzičke škole," *SKG*, Vol. XXV, No. 1, 1910, p. 57.

69 Miloje Milojević, "Koncert Srpske muzičke škole u Narodnom pozorištu 4 mart 1911," *SKG*, Vol. XXVI, No. 7, 1911, p. 555.

70 Jedan muzičar, "Udruženje za kamernu muziku nastavnika Srpske muzičke škole," Vol. XXVII, No. 9, 1911, p. 703.

71 "Srpska muzička škola," *SKG*, Vol. XXIX, No. 1, pp. 62–64.

72 Ibid., pp. 62–64.

73 Miloje Milojević, "The Symphonic Orchestra of the Royal Guard," *SKG*, No. 5, 1912, p. 389.

74 Ibid., p. 390.

75 Petar J. Krstić, "Otvaranje doma Pevačke družine Stanković," *SKG*, Vol. XXXII, No. 4, p. 390.

76 *Prvi godišnji izveštaj 1898–1899*, quoted after Vladimir R. Djordjević, *Prilozi biografskom rečniku srpskih muzičara*, Belgrade SAN, Posebna izdanja CLXIX, p. 11.

77 Ibid., p. 11.

78 Ibid., p. 12.

79 Ibid., p. 12.

80 Vladimir R. Djordjević, *Srpske narodne melodije (Južna Srbija)*, Skoplje: Skopsko naučno društvo, 1928, 154 pp.

81 Vladimir R. Djordjević, *Srpske narodne melodije (predratna Srbija)*, Belgrade: Geca Kon, 1931, 150 pp.

82 Miloje Milojević, *Koncert muškog hora Bogoslovije Svetog Save u Narodnom pozorištu. Umetnost u našim srednjim školama*, *SKG*, 1911, Vol. XXVII, No. 12, p. 947.

83 Ibid., p. 947.

84 Miloje Milojević, "Koncert g–djice Jelice Subotić," *SKG*, Vol. XXXII, No. 1, p. 54.

85 Ibid., p. 54.

86 Ibid., p. 54.

87 Milojević, "Koncert G. Pere Stojanovića u Narodnom pozorištu," *SKG*, Vol XXXII, No. 11, 1914, p. 773.

88 Miloje Milojević, "Povodom koncerta pevačke družine Car Uroš iz Uroševca," *SKG*, Vol. XXXII, No. 11, p. 860.

89 Jela Miljoković–Djurić, "The Role of the Choral Societies in the 19th Century among the Slavs," Acta Universitatis Stockholmiensis, Studia Baltica Stockholmiensa, 1985, pp. 475–482.

90  Ibid., pp. 475–482.

## Chapter Five

1  Milan Grol, "Opera u Narodnom pozorištu, *SKG*, Vol. XVII, No. 9, 1906, pp. 857–860.

2  Ibid., pp. 857–860.

3  Milan Grol "Pozorišna beleška," *SKG*, Vol XVI, No. 5 1906, p. 397.

4  Dragomir M. Janković, "Penzioni fond Narodnog Pozorišta," *SKG*, 1906, Vol. XVI, No. 6, p. 464.

5  Ibid., pp. 464–465.

6  Ibid., p. 469.

7  Pitanje režije u Narodnom pozorištu," *SKG*, No. 7, 1906, p. 540.

8  Dragomir M. Janković, "Pozorišni pregled, Povećanje subvencija," *SKG*, No. 5, 1907, p. 358.

9  Milan Grol, "Narodno pozorište," *SKG*, No. 11, 1908, p. 839.

10  Grol, "Narodno", No. 12, p. 912.

11  Milan Grol, "Pokret, O našem pozorištu," *SKG*, Vol. XXV, No. 8, 1910, p. 612.

12  Quoted after: Grol, *Pokret*, p. 612.

13  Grol, *Pokret*, pp. 612–613.

14  Dragomir M. Janković, "Naša putnička pozorišna društva," *SKG*, Vol. XV, No. 12, 1905, pp. 946–947.

15  Ibid., p. 944.

16  Petar Krstić, "Pozorišni orkestar i muzika izmedju činova," *SKG*, Vol. XVI, No. 3, 1905, p. 227.

17  X, "Beogradsko pozorište u Skoplju," *SKG*, Vol. XXIII, p. 781.

18  Ibid., p. 781.

19  Ibid., p. 782.

20  Ibid., p. 783.

21  Ibid., p. 783.

22  Provizorni, "Proslava četrdesetogošnjice doma Narodnog Pozorišta," *SKG*, No. 10, 1909, pp. 778–780.

23  Ibid., pp. 778–780.

24  Milan Grol, "Glumačka škola," *SKG*, Vol. XXIII, No. 10, p. 944.

25  Ibid., p. 948.

26  Ibid., p. 948.

27  Milan Grol, "Glumačka škola, Ispitne Predstave," *SKG*, Vol. 25, No. 2, p. 143.

28  Ibid., p. 143.

30  Lazarević, "Marginalije," p. 218.

31  Lazarević, "Marginalije," p. 218.

[32] Branko Lazarević, "Pozorišni pregled," *SKG*, Vol. XXVI, No. 7, p. 550.

[33] Milan Begović, "O našem modernom pozorištu," *SKG*, Vol. XXVI, No. 12, 1911, pp. 917–932.

[34] Ibid., pp. 917–932.

[35] Ibid., pp. 917–932.

[36] Ibid., pp. 917–932.

[37] Ibid., pp. 917–932.

[38] Quoted after Provizorni, "Pozorišni godišnjak za 1911–1912," *SKG*, Vol. XXX, No. 2, 1913, p. 148.

[39] Ibid., p. 156.

[40] Milan Grol, "Pozorišni godišnjak," p. 156.

[41] Ibid., pp. 350–356.

[42] Ibid., pp. 350–356.

[43] Ibid., pp. 350–356.

[44] Olga Milovanović, *Beogradska scenografija i kostimografija 1868–1948*, Belgrade: Muzej pozorišne umetnosti SR Srbije, Univerzitet umetnosti, Belgrade 1983, pp. 97–99.

[45] Ibid., p. 101.

[46] Ibid., p. 126.

[47] B. Stojković, "Narodno pozorište u Beogradu," *Enciklopedija Jugoslavije*, Zagreb, 1968, p. 569.

### Chapter Six

[1] Kosta Strajnić, "Za našu umetničku kulturu," *Srpski Književni Glasnik (SKG)*, Vol. 31, No. 11/12, 1913, pp. 902–904.

[2] Katarina Ambrozić, *Nadežda Petrović*, Belgrade: Srpska književna zadruga, 1978, p. 376.

[3] Ibid., p. 376.

[4] Strajnić, "Za našu,". 904.

[5] Strajnić, "Za našu," p. 905.

[6] Strajnić, "Za našu," p. 906.

[7] Strajnić, "Za našu," p. 906.

[8] Strajnić, "Za našu," p. 907.

[9] Strajnić, "Za našu," pp. 909–910.

[10] Strajinć, "Za našu," pp. 910–911.

[11] Jovan Skerlić, *Istorija nove srpske književnosti*, Beograd: Prsveta, 1967, reprinted on the occasion of the 50th anniversary of his death, pp. 436–437.

[12] Ibid., pp. 436–437.

[13] Ibid., p. 437.

[14] Ibid., p. 437.

[15] Ibid., p. 437.

[16] Albert Galeb, *Bulletin mensuel de la Société de Legislation comparee*, review in *SKG*, Vol. XXV, No. 1, p. 75.

[17] Viator, "Sveslovenski kongres u Sofiji," *SKG*, Vol. XXV, No. 2, 1910, p. 131.

[18] Ibid., p. 131.

[19] Ibid., p. 136.

[20] Ibid., p. 136.

[21] Miodrag Ibrovac, "Kratke priče Ivana Vazova," *SKG*, Vol. XIII, No. 6, p. 467.

[22] Jovan Skerlić, *SKG*, Vol. XXIII, No. 10, 1909, p. 793.

[23] *SKG*, 1911, Vol. XXVI, No. 4, p. 335.

[24] *Bosanska vila*, No. 13–14, 1912, p. 207.

[25] "Jugoslavenska Akademija 1909 godine," *SKG*, Vol. XXV, No. 8, pp. 629–630.

[26] *SKG*, Vol. XXVI, No. 12, p. 863.

[27] *SKG*, Vol. XXVII, No. 2, p. 157.

[28] Milorad Pavlović, "Deseti kongres slovenskih novinara u Beogradu," *Bosanska vila*, Vol. XXVI, Nos. 15 and 16, 1911, p. 225.

[29] Jovan Erdeljanović, "Slovenstvo u prošlosti i sadašnjosti," *SKG*, Vol. XXIX, Nos. 1, 2, and 3, pp. 66-67.

[30] Ibid., p. 68.

[31] Ibid., (No. 3), p. 218.

[32] Ibid., p. 221.

[33] Ibid., p. 221.

[34] Ibid., p. 221.

[35] Ružena Svobodova, "Ivo Vojnović: Smrt Majke Jugovića," *Pijemont*, 10 januar 1913, Vol. III, No. 10, p. 1.

[36] Quoted after Olga Milovanović, *Beogradska scenografijai kostimografija 1868–1941* Univerzitet umetnosti u Beogradu, Beograd, 1983, p. 133.

[37] Milan Grol, *Iz pozorišta predratne Srbije*, Belgrade, Srpska Kniževna Zadruga, 1952, XLVI, Vol. 318, p. 28.

[38] "Srpska umetnička izložba u Somboru," *SKG*, Vol. XXIII, No. 9, p. 789-790.

[39] Ibid., pp. 791-793.

[40] Ibid., pp. 791-793.

[41] Tihomir Ostojić, *SKG*, Vol. XXVI, No. 12, p. 959.

[42] *SKG*, 1910, Vol. XXIII, No. 9, p. 715.

[43] *SKG*, 1910, Vol. XXIII, No. 9, p. 715.

[44] *SKG*, 1910, Vol. XXIII, No. 9, p. 715.

[45] *SKG*, 1911, Vol. XXVI, No. 6, p. 417.

[46] *SKG*, 1911, Vol. XXVI, No. 6, p. 417.

[47] *SKG*, 1912, Vol. XXVI, No. 7, pp. 571–573.

[48] L., "Srpska knjiga u Americi," *SKG*, Vol. XXVII, No. 4, p. 318.

[49] Ibid., p. 318.

[50] Ibid., p. 318.

[51] Jovan Skerlić, "Obnova naše rodoljubive poezije," *Srpski Književni Glasnik (SKG)*, Vol. XXI, No. 11, pp. 826–838.

[52] Ibid., p. 826.

[53] Ibid., p. 828.

[54] Ibid., p. 828.

[55] Ibid., p. 828.

[56] Ibid., p. 829.

[57] Ibid., p. 831.

[58] Jovan Skerlić, "Veljko Petrović–Rodoljubive pesme," *SKG*, No. 5, 1912, pp. 394–395.

[59] Ibid., p. 396.

[60] Jovan Skerlić, "Milorad M. Petrović: Vaskrsenje," *SKG*, Vol. XXII, No. 2, 1909, p. 145.

[61] Jovan Skerlić, "Milorad M. Petrović, Seljančice," *SKG*, Vol. V, No. 5, pp. 386–389.

[62] Ibid., pp. 386–389.

[63] Branko Lazarević, "Povodom Jauka sa Zmijanja," *SKG*, Vol. XXIV, No. 7, 1910, pp. 613–614.

[64] Miloš Vidaković, "Na početku dela, Srpska omladina 1912," reprinted in Predrag Palavestra, *Književnost Mlade Bosne*, Sarajevo, 1965, Vol. II, p. 10.

[65] Ibid., p. 11.

[66] Jovan Skerlić, "Novi omladinski listovi i naš novi naraštaj," *SKG*, Vol. XXX, No. 3, 1913, pp. 219–220.

[67] Ibid., pp. 219–220.

[68] Ibid., pp. 219–220.

[69] Jovan Skerlić, "Novi omladinski listovi i naš novi naraštaj." *SKG*, Vol. XXX, No. 3, p. 213.

[70] Ibid., pp. 220–221.

[71] Ibid., pp. 220–221.

[72] *SKG*, Vol. XXVI, No. 6, 1911, p. 417.

[73] *SKG*, Vol. XXXII, No. 11, p. 872.

[74] Skerlić, "Novi omladinski," p. 222.

[75] Skerlić, "Novi omladinski," p. 223.

[76] Skerlić, "Novi omladinski," p. 244.

[77] Milan Kašanin, "Tri književna naraštaja," *Letopis Matice Srpske*, Vol. 321, No. 2, 1929, pp. 84–89.

[78] Ibid., pp. 84–89.

[79] Ibid., pp. 84–89.

80 'Agathon.' *Les jeunes gens d'aujourd'hui*, Paris: Plon–Nourrit, 1913. Quoted after R. N. Stromberg, "The Intellectuals and the Coming of War in 1914," *Journal of European Studies*, No. 3, 1973, p. 110.

81 Velibor Gligorić, "Jovan Skerlić," *Srpska književnoj u književenoj kritici*, Editor Predrag Palavestra, Belgrade: Nolit, 1972, p. 228.

82 Jovan Skerlić, *SKG*, Vol. XXII, No. 8, 1909, pp. 589–598, and *SKG*, Vol. XXVII, No. 5, 1911, pp. 348–363.

83 Isidora Sekulić, "Pesnici koji lažu," *Bosanska vila*, Vol. XXVI, No. 24, pp. 361–362.

84 Jovan Skerlić, "Dve ženske knjige," *SKG*, Vol. XXXI, No. 5, pp. 379–391.

85 Ibid., pp. 379–391.

86 Luka Smodlaka, "Književna hronika," *Bosanska vila*, No. 21, 1913, p. 299.

87 Jovan Dučić, "Isidora Sekulić," *SKG*, 1914. Quoted after P. Palavestra: *Kritika i avangarda*, Belgrade: Provesta, 1979, p. 271.

88 Isidora Sekulić, "Vrsta uvodne reči," *Pisma iz Norveške*, Sabrana dela, Vol. I, Novi Sad: Matica Srpska, 1961, pp. 145–147.

89 Isidora Sekulić, "Pitanje," *Karlovac*, No. 78, 1913, p. 2. Published again in *Saputnici, Pisma iz Norveška*, Collected Works, Beograd: Matica srpska, M. Leskovac, Editor, 1961, p. 130.

90 Jelena Paunović–Subotić: Collected material for biography, manuscript, Belgrade: Muzikološki institut.

91 Paunović–Subotić: Collected.

92 Jelena Milojković–Djurić: Conversation with composer Stanojlo Rajičić, former student of Paunović, manuscript, 1982.

93 Miloš Crnjanski, *Itaka i komentari*, Belgrade: Prosveta, 1959, pp. 9–10.

94 Andreja Mitrović, *Angažovano i lepo, Umetnost u razdoblju svetskih ratova*, Belgrade: Narodna knjiga, 1983, p. 47.

95 Ibid., p. 50.

96 Ibid., pp. 53–54.

97 Ibid., p. 45.

98 Ibid., p. 53

99 Ibid., p. 47.

100 R. N. Stromberg, "The Intellectuals and the Coming of War in 1914," *Journal of European Studies*, 1973, No. 3, pp. 109–111.

## Chapter Seven

1 Vera Cenić, *Časopisi u Južnoj Srbiji na raskrsnici XIX i XX stoleća*, Vranje: Narodni Muzej, Posebna izdanja, No. 7, 1982, p. 213.

2  Ibid., p. 101.
3  Ibid., p. 216.
4  Ibid., p. 219.
5  Ibid., p. 250.
6  Ibid., p. 257.
7  Ibid., p. 257.
8  Ibid., p. 278.
9  Dragiša Vitošević, "Krfski Zabavnik" Branko        Lazarevića, *Književna istorija*, Vol. X, 38, Belgrade, 1978, pp. 285–286.
10  *Zabavnik*, Vol. II, No. 12, Corfu, 1918, p. 23.
11  Vitošević, "Krfski Zabavnik," p. 288.
12  Branko Lavarević, "M. Bojić, Pesme bola i ponosa," *Zabavnik*, No. 4, 1917, p. 12.
13  Todor Manolović, "Naša stara i nova umetnost," *Zabavnik*, 15 August 1917, p. 13.
14  Stanoje Stanojević, *Narodna Enciklopedija*, Belgrade, 1937.
15  Beleška, *Zabavnik*, Corfu 17, February 1918, No. 19, p. 15.
16  Petar Konjović, *Miloje Milojević*, Belgrade: SAN, No. CCXX, 1954, pp. 52–53.
17  Ibid., pp. 52–53.
18  Damaskin Grdanički, "Miloje Milojević, Liturgija Sv. Jovana Zlatoustog," *Zabavnik*, No. 9, 15 January 1918.
19  Jelena Milojković–Djurić, *Kosta P. Manojlović u medjuratnom razvoju muzičke kulture*, manuscript, 1985, pp. 24–26.
20  Miloje Milojević, "Muzika i pravoslavna crkva," Belgrade and Sremski Karlovci: Srpska manastirska štamparija, 1938, p. 130.
21  Milojković–Djurić, *Kosta P. Manojlović*, pp. 26–27.
22  Živojin Devečerski, *Na vodama albanskim*, *Zabavnik*, Corfu, 1.1, 1917, pp. 11-12.
23  Vladimir R. Djordjević, *Prilozi biografskom rečniku srpskih muzičara*, Beograd: SAN, Vol. CLXIX, 1950, pp. 11-12.
24  Jaša Prodanović, "Predgovor," *Antologija*, 2nd edition, Belgrade: Geca Kon, 1927, p. vii.
25  *Zabavnik*, No. 13–14, May–June, 1918, pp. 17–18.
26  Pavle Stevanović, "Pavle Popović: *Jugoslovenska književnost*," *Zabavnik*, No. 13–14, May–June 1918, pp. 21 and 14.
27  Popović, *Jugoslovenska književnost*, p. 129.
28  Popović, *Jugoslovenska književnost*, p. 129.
29  Popović, *Jugoslovenska književnost*, p. 30.
30  Popović, *Jugoslovenska književnost*, p. 30.
31  Popović, *Jugoslovenska književnost*, p. 151.
32  Popović, *Jugoslovenska književnost*, p. 151.

[33] Ivo Andrić, *Istorije i legende, Eseji*, "Naša književnost i rat," Belgrade, 1977, p. 169.

[34] Miloš Crnjanski, *Itaka i komentari*, Belgrade: Prosveta, 1959, pp. 9–10.

[35] Branko Ćosić, *Deset pisaca deset razagovora*, Beograd: Geca Kon, 1931, p. 87.

[36] Veselin Čajkanović, "Iz Bizerte," *Zabavnik*, Vol. II, No. 15, 1918, p. 3.

[37] Miloje Milojević, "Koncert g–djice M. Mihailović, *Muzika*, Beograd, No. 2, February 1928, p. 52.

[38] *L'Unité Yugoslave Manifeste de la Jeunesse Serbe, Croate et Slovene Reunie*, Paris: Plan–Nourit, 1915.

[39] Crnjanski, *Itaka*, p. 56.

[40] *L'Unité Yugoslave*, Paris, 1915, pp. viii-ix.

[41] "Književni pregled," *Zabavnik*, br. 15, 15, July 1918, p. 22.

[42] Tihomir Djordjević, *Jugoslovensko jedinstvo*, Biblioteka Napred, Vol. 12, Bizerte, 1918. Review in *Zabavnik*, Vol. II, No. 15, April 1918, p. 23.

[43] Veselin Čajkanović, Beleške, *Zabavnik*, Vol. II, No. 15, pp. 19–20.

[44] Beleška, *Zabavnik*, Vol. II, No. 9, January 1918, p. 23.

[45] London: John Murray, 1918, p. 9.

[46] Pero Slepčević, "Mirko Rački," *Zabavnik*, April 1918, p. 9.

[47] Todor Manojlović, "Klod Debisi, 1862–1918;" "Ferdinand Hodler 1853–1918," *Zabavnik*, No. 14, 1918, pp. 19–21.

[48] Ibid., p. 20.

[49] Ibid., p. 21.

[50] Ibid., p. 21.

[51] Branko Lazarević, "O nacionalnom tlu u umetnosti," *Zabavnik*, No. 10, 17 February 1918, p. 14.

[52] Ibid., p. 14.

[53] Ibid., p. 15.

[54] Todor Manojlović, "Izložba Jugoslovenskih umetnika u Ženevi," *Zabavnik*, No. 14, 1918, p. 23.

[55] Ibid., p. 23.

[56] Ivo Andrić, "Naša književnost i rat." *Istorije i legende, Eseji*, Vol. 1, *Sabrana dela*, No. 12, Belgrade, 1977, p. 169.

[57] Ibid., p. 171.

[58] Ibid., p. 172.

[59] Ibid., pp. 172–173.

[60] Ibid., p. 173.

[61] Ibid., p. 173.

# Index

## List of Illustrations

1. Bogdan Popović. Sculpture by Ivan Meštrović. National Museum, Belgrade.

2. Nadežda Petrović: Self–Portrait. National Museum, Belgrade.

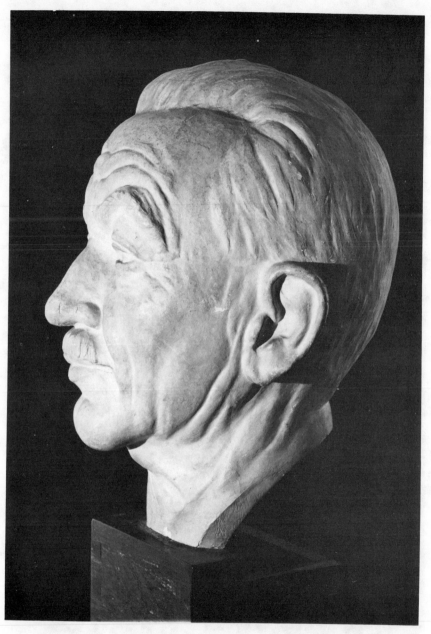

3. Milan Rakić. Sculpture by Ivan Meštrović. National Museum, Belgrade.

4. Paja Jovanović: Self-Portrait. National Museum, Belgrade.

5. Paja Jovanović: Proclamation of Dušan's Law Codex. Matica Srpska, Novi Sad.

6. Paja Jovanović: Migration of Serbs. National Museum, Belgrade.

7. Certificate of membership of the First Singers Society designed
   by Paja Jovanović. Prvo beogradsko pevačko društvo, Belgrade.

8. Composer Miloje Milojević in a Serbian military uniform during World War I.

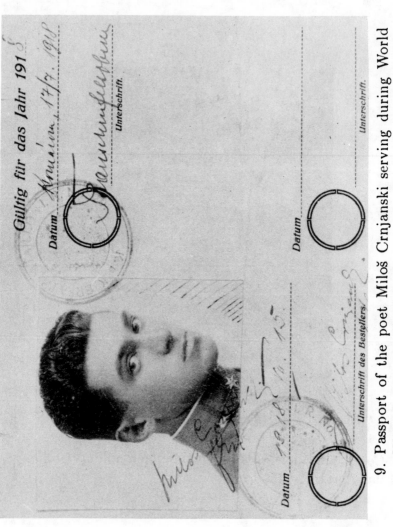

9. Passport of the poet Miloš Crnjanski serving during World
   War I in the Austrian Army.

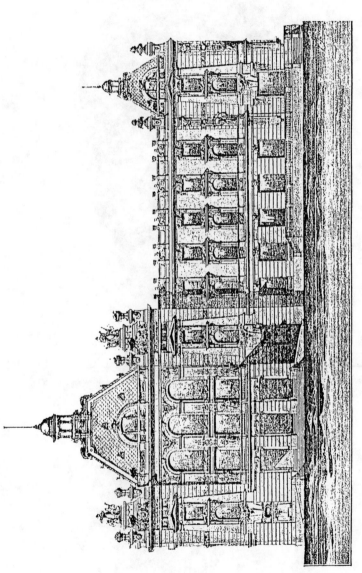

10. Fine Arts Home "Mokranjac." Plan for the Façade possibly drawn by the architect Nikola Nestorović in 1903. Prvo beogradsko pevačko društvo, Belgrade.

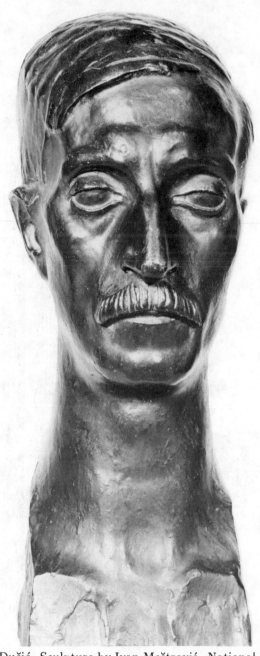

11. Jovan Dučić. Sculpture by Ivan Meštrović. National Museum, Belgrade.

12. Group of leading artists shortly after the end of World War 1. From left to right: political cartoonist Pjer Križanić with wife, sculptor Toma Rosandić, poet Jovan Dučić, Palavicini's wife, composer Miloje Milojević, sculptor Petar Palavicini.

## CHAPTER 17

# REVOLUTION AND REPUBLIC
## 1952–79

Disaffection among army officers centred upon the relationship of their corps to the King. The latter had always tried to control the army through his senior military appointees, and the matter of army commissions had been a source of conflict between the monarch and the Wafd ever since independence in 1923. The Wafd at least for a while after 1936–7 had gained a measure of popularity with younger army officers when it liberalized entry into the Military Academy.

What really kept sedition out of the army was British control over it from 1882 until 1948. In 1882, the old Egyptian Army at the time of the Orabi Rebellion had been disbanded. Various military schools, founded by Muhammad Ali, expanded and improved by Khedive Ismail, were closed down. Many of the Egyptian Army units had been sent to the Sudan during the Mahdia war. Among these, some had perished in the ill-fated Hicks expedition against the Mahdi in 1883. A smaller force (about fifteen thousand) was then organized under the command of a British Sirdar. Conscription, since the introduction of the *badaliyya*[1] system, had been at a minimum. Yet both nationalists and the ambitious young Khedive Abbas Hilmi had constantly tried to expand and strengthen this army with a view to eroding British control over it. Khedive Abbas even urged some of the Egyptian Army personnel to commit acts of mutiny.

With independence in 1923, the Egyptian government wished to strengthen the army. This eventually led to the crisis of 1927 when Britain reasserted its control over the Egyptian Army by invoking the defence provisions of the 1922 Declaration. The 1936 Treaty abolished the office of Sirdar, but it provided for a British Military Mission to train the Egyptian Army. Moreover, it submitted this army to indirect British control in so far as both its training and equipment were to be exclusively provided by Britain. This state of affairs continued until 1948.